FINNISH FOR FOREIGNERS 1

FINNISH FOR FOREIGNERS

Maija-Hellikki Aaltio

HELSINGISSÄ KUSTANNUSOSAKEYHTIÖ OTAVA

Seventeenth edition

Drawings: Jorma Nousiainen
Layout: Merja Askola
Editor: Kaija Niskakoski, Pauliina Luoto

Binding: OTABIND

Otava Book Printing Ltd
Keuruu 2007

ISBN-13: 978-0-88432-541-3

TO THE READER

The present textbook is a continuation of the author's *Finnish for Foreigners 1* which, first published in 1963 and revised in 1973, has in thirteen editions served students of the Finnish language all over the world. The book, which now appears in two parts, a Textbook including the grammar, and a separate Exercise book, has undergone a thorough revision. A few old chapters have been replaced by new ones; a number of less frequent words have been left out; the order of the structural features presented has frequently been changed. On the basis of the author's experience and the students' wishes, special attention and considerably more space than before have been devoted to two points of central importance in learning Finnish: the use of the different noun and verb types, and the partitive case.

The purpose of *Finnish for Foreigners 1* is, above all, to teach the learner spoken Finnish. Most topics have been selected with special regard to practical situations facing every foreigner in Finland; the basic structure and vocabulary are taught in gradual installments; and throughout there are also hints about colloquial usage in the Helsinki area. (These hints, useful to foreigners already in Finland, can easily be skipped by students learning Finnish in their own countries.) At the same time, of course, students will learn to master the fundamentals of written Finnish; structural points typical of written language alone will be introduced in *Finnish for Foreigners 2.*

The chapters of this book are divided into three parts:
1) dialogue or narrative, 2) structural notes, and 3) vocabulary.

1) Due to the spoken-language approach of this book, most lessons are based on a *dialogue,* which is by far the most important part of the lesson. As it contains vocabulary and phrases typical of the situation and includes useful structural patterns, memorizing as many of the dialogues as possible is strongly recommended, especially in the beginning stages. To save time and to forestall errors for those studying Finnish without a teacher, all lessons include an idiomatic English

translation. The English is also a useful help in checking how well the Finnish has been memorized and in looking ahead for phrases and words eventually needed;

2) The presentation of the *structure* of Finnish proceeds from the frequent and/or easier to the rare and/or more difficult. The use of grammatical terminology characteristic of Finnish alone has been reduced to a minimum. This book is not meant to be a complete grammar. It is concerned with the essentials rather than with all the details;

3) The vocabulary section shows the inflection of the Finnish words and their English equivalents. It may also include other information, for instance examples illustrating the use of the new words.

All the dialogues and other texts, as well as the pronunciation exercises following the first few lessons, are available on two cassettes which also include the listening comprehension exercises in the Exercise book for each chapter.

I am grateful to my colleagues Hannele Jönsson-Korhola and Eila Hämäläinen for reading the manuscript and offering valuable suggestions. My thanks are due to Mark Shackleton, Lecturer in English at Helsinki University, for correcting my English; for any remaining errors I am solely responsible. I would also like to thank Tiina Saaristo and Tapani Aaltio, two representatives of the present student generation, for their comments on the dialogues, particularly those with a colloquial flavor. And finally, I am very much indebted to many of my students at Helsinki University who through their criticism and suggestions have greatly helped me in my work.

I hope that the new version of *Finnish for Foreigners 1* will prove a useful basic textbook to many English-speaking students of Finnish throughout the world.

Kauniainen, Finland, September 1984.

Maija-Hellikki Aaltio

CONTENTS

PRONUNCIATION

The Finnish language has eight vowel sounds and thirteen consonant sounds. Each (with the exception of one consonant) has its own symbol in writing.

Most sounds in Finnish may be short or long. The long sound has the same quality as the short one, being just prolonged. It is extremely important to distinguish clearly between long and short sounds, as difference in length also reflects difference in meaning.

The descriptions of sounds given below must necessarily be considered rough approximations, and learning the pronunciation of Finnish by imitating a native speaker of the language, for instance by listening to cassettes or tapes, is strongly recommended.

VOWELS

Finnish vowels are, in general, more sharply and vigorously pronounced than their English counterparts. They retain the same quality in all positions within a word: they must never be slurred or swallowed, not even in unstressed syllables.

		Short sound	Long sound
i	like in *sit* (but raising the tongue higher towards the roof of the mouth)	*nimi* name *lasi* glass	*niin* so *lasiin* into a glass
e	like in *set* (but raising the tongue higher)	*meri* sea *kolme* three	*Meeri* (girl's name) *kolmeen* until three
ä	like a in *hat* (but opening the mouth wider in all directions)	*sä* you, thou (colloq.) *älä* don't (sing.)	*sää* weather *älkää* don't (pl.)
y	like German ü, French u (that is, like i but with rounded lips)	*kylä* village *syksy* fall	*kyy* viper *syksyyn* till fall, autumn
ö	like German ö, French eu (that is, like e but with rounded lips)	*hölmö* fool	*Töölö* (district in Helsinki) *Töölöön* to Töölö
u	like u in *loose* (but with tightly pursed lips)	*uni* sleep *suku* family, relatives	*uuni* oven *sukuun* into the family
o	like o in *hot* (British pronunciation; but with more rounded lips)	*jo* already *sano!* say!	*joo* yes (colloq.) *sanoo* he says
a	like a in *father*	*ja* and	*Jaana* (girl's name) *Vantaa* (city near Helsinki)

Diphthongs

The Finnish language has a large number of diphthongs (combinations of two vowels which belong to the same syllable). Each vowel in a Finnish diphthong is pronounced in the same way it is as a single vowel.

Diphthongs ending in **i** may occur in any syllable of a word.

Examples:
ai *aika* time, *punainen* red, *kirjain* letter (in alphabet)
ei *seinä* wall, *melkein* almost
oi *oikea* right, *sanoi* he said
ui *uinti* swimming, *kaduilla* in the streets, *puhui* he spoke
yi *hyi* fie, shame on you, *kysyi* he asked
äi *äiti* mother, *jäinen* icy, *eläin* animal
öi *söi* he ate, *ympäröi* surrounds

Diphthongs ending in **u** and **y** occur only rarely after the first syllable.

Examples:
au *sauna* Finnish bath, *rauha* peace, *vapautua* to be set free
eu *neula* needle, *seura* company, *vaikeutua* to become more difficult
iu *viulu* violin, *kiuas* sauna oven, *kotiutua* to (begin to) feel at home
ou *Oulu* (city in Finland), *nousta* to rise, *rentoutua* to relax
ey *peseytyy* he washes (himself)
äy *täynnä* full, *kieltäytyä* to refuse
öy *pöytä* table, *löydän* I find

Diphthongs occurring in the first syllable only:
ie *mies* man, *viedä* to take (away)
uo *Suomi* Finland, *tuoli* chair
yö *yö* night, *syödä* to eat

Vowel combinations other than diphthongs

Finnish has a large variety of combinations of two vowels belonging to two different syllables.

Examples:
sok**ea** blind, p**ia**n soon, put**oa**n I fall, ap**ua**! help!
h**ae**n I fetch, poik**ie**n the boys', k**oe**ttaa to try, l**ue**mme we read, lähest**ye**n approaching, n**äe**t you see
kaak**ao** cocoa, mus**eo** museum, kolm**io** triangle
rakk**au**s love, kork**eu**s height, valm**iu**s readiness, heikk**ou**s weakness
vihr**ey**s greenness, äit**iy**s motherhood, hyökk**äy**s attack, hölm**öy**s stupidity
lev**eä** broad, ets**iä** to look for, näk**yä** to be seen
ilm**iö** phenomenon

Combinations of more than two vowels (*kauan* for a long time, *aiot* you intend etc.) are always divided into two syllables (→Syllable division, p. 15); Finnish has no triphthongs.

CONSONANTS

The pronunciation of Finnish consonants is rather lax compared to English. This is particularly true of the so-called stops **p, t,** and **k,** which are always unaspirated, as in French. This means that the slight puff of breath that follows the English sound is lacking in Finnish. A practical way of checking your pronunciation is to keep your hand in front of your mouth when pronouncing **p, t, k**: the less breath you feel on your hand, the better the stop sound is.

		Short sound	Long sound
p	like p in *spin* (the long sound as in *top‿part*)	*papu* bean	*pappi* clergyman
t	like t in *stop (at‿table)*; the Finnish sound is made by touching the upper teeth lightly with the tip of a flat tongue, **not** by pushing the tip of a hollowed tongue vigorously against the gum ridge	*tee!* do! *teet* you do *otan* I take	 *ottaa* he takes
k	like k in *skin (sick‿king)*	*kuka* who	*kukka* flower
d	like d in *do*	*sade* rain	
m	like m in *mix (room-mate)*	*aamen* amen	*amme* tub
n	like n in *net (pen-nib)*	*sana* word	*Sanna* (girl's name)
n (k)	like n in *think*	*kenkä* shoe [keŋkä]	
ng	like ng in *singing* (**not** as in *finger*)		*kengät* the shoes [keŋŋät]
l	like the "clear" l pronounced initially in standard British English and in *William, million* by most Americans	*eli* he lived *ali* under *oli* was *tuli* fire *askel* step	*Elli* (girl's name) *Alli* (girl's name) *Olli* (boy's name) *tulli* customs
r	(somewhat) like r in *brr* (as said when one is cold); it is slightly rolled. N.B. **Do not** let your r blur the sharp quality of the neighboring vowels.	*ruoka* food *suru* sorrow *ranskatar* Frenchwoman	 *surra* to grieve
s	like s in *sit (this‿city)* N.B. The Finnish s may sometimes sound to you like sh. There is, however, no sh sound in Finnish. Note also that there is no voiced s — like s in *rose* — in Finnish.	*sota* war *lasi* glass *viisi* five *vapaus* freedom	 *Lassi* (boy's name)

h	like h in *hen* but somewhat stronger at the end of a syllable (that is, before another consonant)	*he* they *vähän* a little *ihme* wonder *tehdä* to do *Lahti* (city in F.) *kohta* soon
v	like v in *veal*	*vain* only *sivu* page
j	like y in *yes*	*jos* if *ajaa* to drive

b, g, and **f** may occur in recent loan-words: *banaani* banana, *geologia* geology, *filmi* film

STRESS

The main stress is always on the first syllable.
Note. Do not place the stress on the second syllable even if it is long and the first syllable short:

ánteeksi excuse me, *húomenta* good morning, *kádulla* on the street, *púhutte* you speak, *bánaani* banana.

In compound words, which are very numerous, the first syllable of the second component carries a secondary stress.

káhvi coffee *kúppi* cup *káhvi/kùppi* coffee-cup

ORTHOGRAPHY

Finnish is spelled very nearly as it is pronounced. Each letter always stands for one and the same sound. An exception is **n**, which may also have the sound value of **ng** [ŋ] (before **k** and **g**). No silent letters exist.

Short sounds are always written with one letter, long sounds with two letters.

x and **z**, which may occur in recent loan-words or names, are pronounced **ks** and **ts**, respectively.

Another exception to the "phonetic" spelling of Finnish:

sade rain *sade/päivä* (pronounced *sadep‿päivä*) rainy day
sano say! *sano se!* (pronounced *sanos‿se)* say it!
olla to be *olla/ko?* (pronounced *ollakko*) to be?

The doubling of consonant which in standard Finnish pronunciation occurs between certain words (and forms) and the next word is not indicated in writing.

Syllable division in Finnish

To be able to understand certain consonant changes which occur in the inflection of nouns and verbs, it is important to know how Finnish words are divided into syllables.

The dividing line between two syllables goes

— before one consonant:
ka-tu street, *Lii-sa, suo-ma-lai-nen* Finn;
— between two consonants:
kyl-lä yes, *A-me-rik-ka* America, *met-sä* forest, *haus-ka* nice;
— before the last of three consonants:
Rans-ka France, *kort-ti* card;
— between two vowels which do not form a diphthong (see p. 12):
lu-en I read, *mai-to-a* some milk, *ha-lu-ai-sin* I'd like to, *ra-di-o* radio.

A syllable ending in a vowel is called **open**.
A syllable ending in a consonant is called **closed**.

Mikä tämä on?

1. Se on Suomi.
2. Se on radio.
3. Se on televisio.
4. Se on auto.
5. Se on bussi.
6. Se on talo.
7. Se on huone.

Mikä tuo on?

8. Se on katu.
9. Se on kauppa.
10. Se on mies.
11. Se on nainen.
12. Se on poika.
13. Se on tyttö.

Kuka tämä on?

14. Se on Aleksis Kivi.

Kuka tuo on?

15. Se on Jean Sibelius.

What is this?

1. It is Finland.
2. It is a radio.
3. It is a television.
4. It is a car.
5. It is a bus.
6. It is a house.
7. It is a room.

What is that?

8. It is a street.
9. It is a shop.
10. It is a man.
11. It is a woman.
12. It is a boy.
13. It is a girl.

Who is this?

14. It is Aleksis Kivi.

Who is that?

15. It is Jean Sibelius.

Mikä tämä on? Radio, kuva, mies.
Kuka tämä on? Aleksis Kivi, Liisa Salo, Ville.

Mikä päivä tänään on?
Tänään on maanantai.

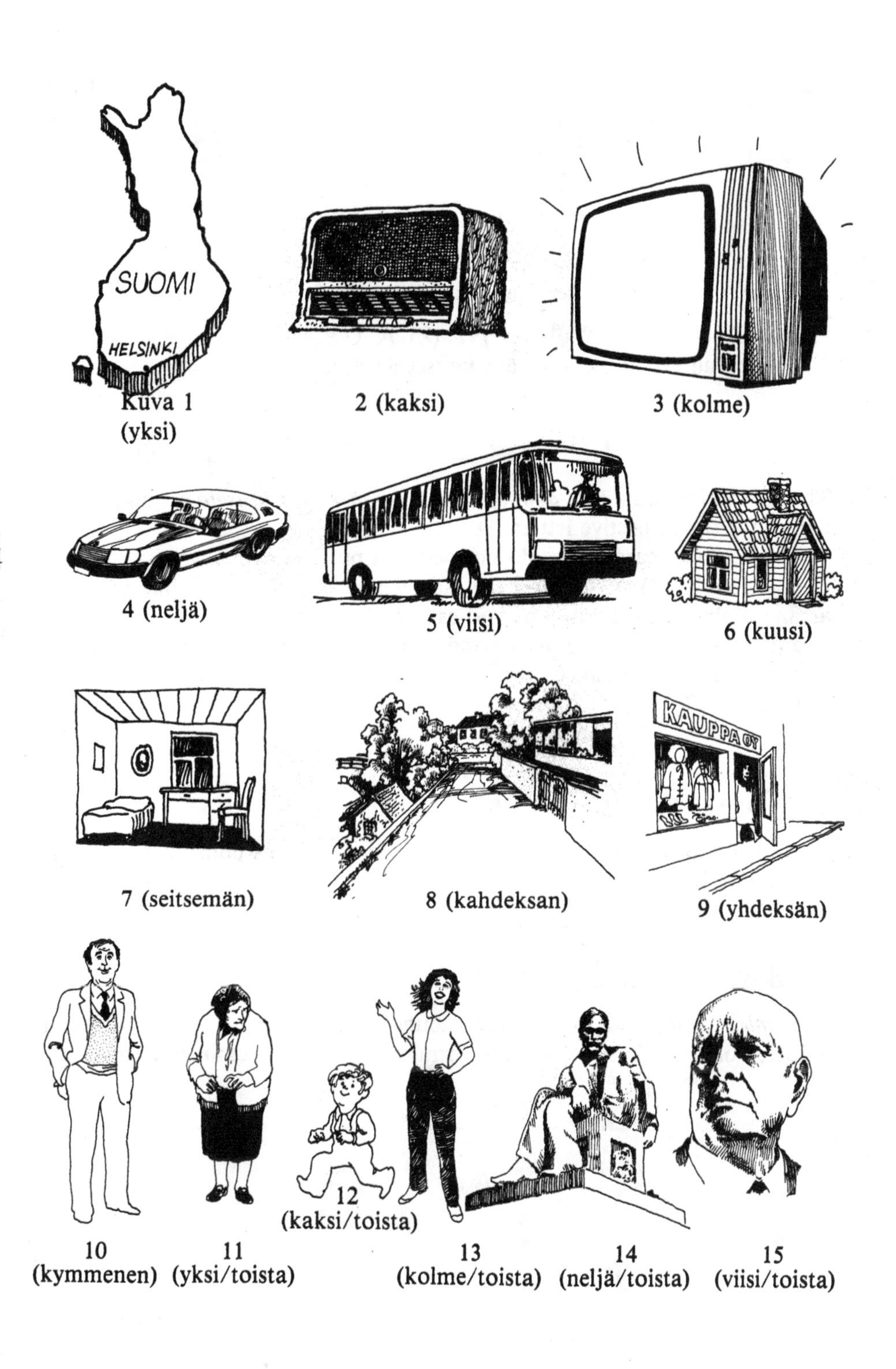

Kuva 1 (yksi) 2 (kaksi) 3 (kolme)

4 (neljä) 5 (viisi) 6 (kuusi)

7 (seitsemän) 8 (kahdeksan) 9 (yhdeksän)

10 (kymmenen) 11 (yksi/toista) 12 (kaksi/toista) 13 (kolme/toista) 14 (neljä/toista) 15 (viisi/toista)

Kielioppia — Structural notes

1. Finnish alphabet

A (B) (C) D E (F) G H I J K L M N O P (Q)
aa bee see dee ee äf gee hoo ii jii koo äl äm än oo pee kuu

R S T U V (W) (X) Y (Z) Ä Ö
är äs tee uu vee kaksois-vee äks yy tset ää öö

The alternative terms *ällä, ämmä, ännä, ärrä, ässä, äksä, tseta* are also used as names for the respective letters.

The letters in parentheses do not occur in purely Finnish words.

w (''double v'') occurs in a few names and is pronounced like v; in lists arranged alphabetically it is treated as a **v**.

å (the Swedish o) — between **z** and **ä** in the alphabet — occurs in a number of family and place names, e.g. *Ålander* (family name), *Åbo* Turku, *Borgå* Porvoo.

2. No article in Finnish

There is no article in Finnish. *talo,* for instance, means both ''a house'' and ''the house''.

3. Basic form of nouns

talo, mies, tyttö, and all the other nouns in this lesson appear in the non-inflected or basic form (dictionary form) of the noun (**nominative singular**).

Sanasto — Vocabulary

auto	car, automobile
bussi	bus
huone	room
kappale	piece, bit; paragraph; lesson, chapter
katu	street
kauppa	shop, store
kuka?	who?
kuva	picture
mies	man; husband
mikä?	what? which?
nainen	woman, lady
on (from *olla* to be)	is
poika	boy; son
radio	radio, wireless
se	it
se (mies)	(with nouns:) the, that (man)
Suomi	Finland
talo	house
televisio	television
tuo (colloq. *toi*)	that, that one
tyttö	girl
tämä (colloq. *tää*)	this, this one

☆ (new words in structural notes, reader, exercises etc.)

maanantai	Monday
numero	number, figure
päivä	day
sivu (abbr. *s.*)	page (*p.*)
tänään	today

Millainen tämä on?

1. Millainen poika on?
2. Hän on pieni.
Mies on iso.
3. Millainen tyttö on?
4. Hän on nuori ja kaunis.
Nainen on vanha ja sairas.
5. Millainen talo on?
6. Se on vanha.
Auto on uusi.
7. Onko se hyvä?
8. On.
9. Onko tämä hyvä radio?
10. Ei (ole). Se on huono.

What is this like?

1. What is the boy like?
2. He is small.
The man is big.
3. What is the girl like?
4. She is young and pretty.
The woman is old and ill.
5. What is the house like?
6. It is old.
The car is new.
7. Is it a good one?
8. Yes, it is.
9. Is this a good radio?
10. No, it is not. It is a bad one.

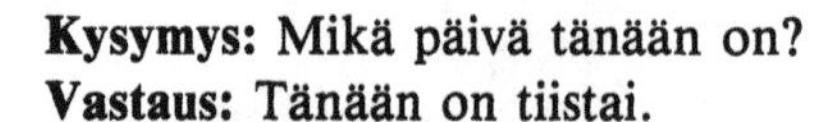

Kysymys: Mikä päivä tänään on?
Vastaus: Tänään on tiistai.

k p t **kaunis kuva, kaunis kauppa**
pieni poika, pieni kauppa
tämä talo, tuo televisio, tuo tyttö

s se on kaunis televisio, se on uusi bussi
Liisa ei ole sairas

Kielioppia — Structural notes

1. No grammatical gender in Finnish

There is no grammatical gender (masculine, feminine, or neuter) in Finnish. Even the pronoun *hän* means both ''he'' and ''she''. *hän* is used of people only, *se* is used to refer to animals and inanimate objects.

In careless every-day speech *se* is commonly used to refer to people as well.

2. How to form questions

a) *Mikä tämä on?* — What is this?

When a question begins with an interrogative word (e.g. *mikä*), the word-order is the same as in an ordinary statement, not reversed as in English.

b) *On/ko Helsinki kaunis?* — Is Helsinki beautiful?

When the question begins with a verb, the word-order is reversed, and the interrogative suffix **-ko** (or **-kö,** see 4:2) is added to the verb.

It should be noted that Finnish ''yes/no'' questions do not show the rising intonation typical of English. The pitch of the voice in Finnish sentences normally goes down, even in questions.

Short colloquial forms occur: *onk(o) se?* etc.

The suffix **-ko (-kö)** may also be added to words other than verbs:

Minä/kö?	Me?
Tämä poika/ko?	This boy?
Tänään/kö?	Today?

It can also be used to create a special emphasis; cp. these three questions:

On/ko hän sairas?	Is he ill?
Hän/kö on sairas?	Is **he** ill? **He** is ill?
Sairas/ko hän on?	Is he **ill**?

Sanasto — Vocabulary

ei	no
ei ole	(no,) it is not
huono	bad, poor
hyvä	good
hän	he, she
iso	big, large
ja	and
kaunis (≠ *ruma*)	pretty, beautiful
-ko (-kö)	interrogative suffix
millainen?	what ... like? what kind of?
nuori	young
pieni	small, little
sairas (≠ *terve*)	ill, sick
uusi	new
vanha	old, ancient

☆

kysymys	question
tiistai	Tuesday
vastaus	answer, reply

Kappale **3** Lesson

Hei, Meg!

1. Pekka Oksa. Hei! Minä olen Pekka Oksa. Minä olen suomalainen.
2. Meg Smith. Minä olen Meg Smith. Meg, tai Margaret.
3. P. Sinä olet ulkomaalainen. Oletko sinä amerikkalainen?
4. M. Olen. Puhutko sinä englantia?
5. P. Puhun. Puhutko sinä ranskaa?
6. M. En (puhu). Minä puhun vain englantia. Ja vähän suomea.
7. P. Sinä puhut hyvin suomea.
8. M. Kiitos!

Hello, Meg!

1. P.O. Hello! I'm Pekka Oksa. I'm Finnish.
2. M.S. I'm Meg Smith. Meg, or Margaret.
3. P. You are a foreigner. Are you American?
4. M. Yes, I am. Do you speak English?
5. P. Yes, I do. Do you speak French?
6. M. No, I don't. I only speak English. And a little Finnish.
7. P. You speak Finnish well.
8. M. Thank you!

Mikä päivä tänään on?
Tänään on keskiviikko. Eilen oli tiistai.

3

EUROOPPA

Maa	Kieli		
Englanti	englanti	but: Puhun	englanti**a**.
Suomi	suomi		suom**ea**.
Ranska	ranska		ransk**aa**.

Minkämaalainen sinä olet?
Minä olen ranskalainen.
Mitä kieltä sinä puhut?
Minä puhun ranskaa.

Kielioppia — Structural notes

1. Present tense of verb: 1st and 2nd person

(minä) ole/n	I am	*(sinä) ole/t*	you are
(minä) puhu/n	I speak, I am speaking	*(sinä) puhu/t*	you speak, you are speaking

minä, sinä are usually omitted in written Finnish, unless there is a special emphasis on the pronouns. In speech they are extensively used.

Short colloquial forms of *minä* and *sinä* are *mä* and *sä*: *mä puhun*; *mä oon* = *minä olen*; *sä puhut*; *sä oot* = *sinä olet*; *oot(ko) sä?* = *oletko sinä?*

The complete present tense will be discussed in lesson 10:2 (affirmative) and 12:2 (negative).

All inflected forms of Finnish verbs and nouns consist, like those above, of two parts,

stem + ending

ole-	-n -t

The stem is the unchanging part that carries the meaning, whereas each form has a different ending of its own.

2. How to answer "yes" and "no"

Oletko (sinä) japanilainen?	Are you Japanese?
Olen (kyllä).	Yes, I am.
Kyllä (olen).	
En (ole).	No, I am not.
Onko tämä hyvä auto?	Is this a good car?
On (kyllä).	Yes, it is.
Kyllä (on).	
Ei (ole).	No, it is not.

The most common way to give a short affirmative answer is to repeat the verb of the question. *kyllä* occurs less frequently alone; however, it often combines with the verb to add some emphasis to the answer.

The negation "no"is *en* for the 1st pers. and *ei* for the 3rd pers. sing. The verb often combines with the negation: *en ole, en puhu/ei ole, ei puhu.*

In casual every-day speech *joo* is commonly heard in affirmative answers: *Puhut(ko) sä englantia? — Joo.*

Sanasto — Vocabulary

amerikkalainen	American
en	no, I . . . not, I don't
Englanti	England (often used loosely to mean Britain)
englanti (englantia)	English (language)
englantilainen	English (British), Englishman, Englishwoman
hei!	hello, hi, cheerio
hyvin	well; very
kiitos	thank you, thanks
minä (colloq. *mä*)	I
mitä? (from *mikä?*)	what?
puhu/a (puhun, puhut)	to speak, talk
sinä (colloq. *sä*)	you (sing.)
suomalainen	Finn, Finnish
suomi (suomea)	Finnish (language)
tai	or
ulko/maalainen	foreigner
vain	only, just
vähän	(a) little

☆

eilen	yesterday
kartta	map
keski/viikko	Wednesday
kieli (kieltä)	language, tongue
kyllä	yes; also used as an emphasizing word
maa	country, land; earth; ground; soil
minkä/maalainen?	from what country?
oli	was
Ranska	France
ranska (ranskaa)	French (language)
ranskalainen	French, Frenchman, Frenchwoman

3

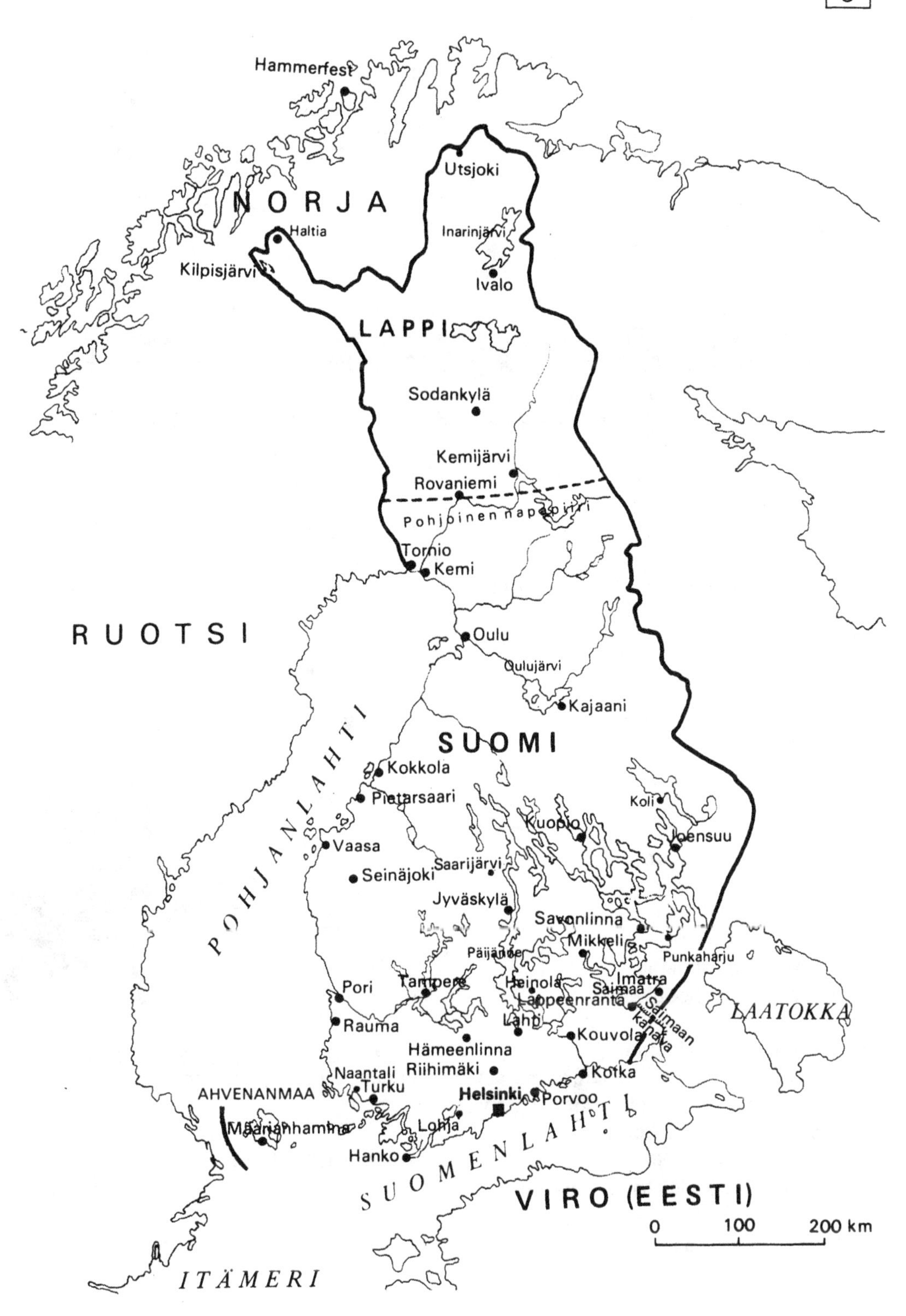

Hammerfest
NORJA
Utsjoki
Haltia
Inarinjärvi
Kilpisjärvi
Ivalo
LAPPI
Sodankylä
Kemijärvi
Rovaniemi
Pohjoinen napapiiri
Tornio
Kemi
RUOTSI
Oulu
Oulujärvi
Kajaani
SUOMI
POHJANLAHTI
Kokkola
Pietarsaari
Koli
Kuopio
Joensuu
Vaasa
Seinäjoki
Saarijärvi
Jyväskylä
Savonlinna
Mikkeli
Punkaharju
Päijänne
Pori
Tampere
Heinola
Imatra
Saimaa
Lappeenranta
Saimaan kanava
LAATOKKA
Rauma
Lahti
Kouvola
Hämeenlinna
Naantali
Riihimäki
Kotka
AHVENANMAA
Turku
Helsinki
Porvoo
Maarianhamina
Lohja
Hanko
SUOMENLAHTI
VIRO (EESTI)
0 100 200 km
ITÄMERI

Hyvää päivää

1. Pekka Mäki. Hyvää päivää. Minä olen Pekka Mäki.
2. Peter Hill. Hyvää päivää. Minä olen Peter Hill.
3. P.M. Mitä kuuluu?
4. P.H. Kiitos, hyvää. Entä teille?
5. P.M. Hyvää vain. Te olette ulkomaalainen. Oletteko te englantilainen?
6. P.H. En (ole). Minä olen kanadalainen.
7. P.M. Te puhutte oikein hyvin suomea.
8. P.H. Kiitos. Puhutteko te englantia?
9. P.M. Kyllä, minä puhun englantia, mutta huonosti.
10. P.H. Näkemiin.
11. P.M. Näkemiin.

How do you do

1. P.M. How do you do. I'm Pekka Mäki.
2. P.H. How do you do. I'm Peter Hill.
3. P.M. How are you?
4. P.H. Fine, thanks. And you?
5. P.M. Just fine. You're a foreigner. Are you English?
6. P.H. No, I'm not. I'm Canadian.
7. P.M. You speak Finnish very well.
8. P.H. Thank you. Do you speak English?
9. P.M. Yes, I speak English, but badly.
10. P.H. Goodbye.
11. P.M. Goodbye.

Televisio on **hyvä**, mutta radio on **huono**.
Puhun **hyvin** englantia, mutta **huonosti** suomea.

Englanti — englantilainen
Suomi — suom**a**lainen
Ruotsi — ruots**a**lainen
Venäjä — **venäläinen**
Helsinki — helsinkiläinen
Liverpool — liverpoo**l**ilainen

ä tämä päivä, näkemiin
ä-a vähän **vanha**, vain vähän, tämä **amerikkalainen**, tämä **afrikkalainen**, tämä **aasialainen**, tämä **kaunis** päivä
u puhun, puhutte, **kuuluu**, **uusi**
u-y puhun kyllä, kyllä puhun, puh**u**t hyvin, hyvä k**u**va, hyvin **uusi**, **kuuluu**ko hyvää? kyllä, hyvää **kuuluu**

Mikä päivä tänään on?
Tänään on torstai. Eilen oli keskiviikko.

Kielioppia — Structural notes

1. Formal and informal "you"

The pronoun *te* is always used when addressing many persons:

Ole/tte/ko te Mary ja John Smith?	Are you Mary and John Smith?
Te puhu/tte hyvin suomea.	You speak Finnish well.

One person is addressed with *sinä* in informal speech — with relatives and friends, children and young people, and within various kinds of closed groups — and with *te* in formal speech. If you use a person's title and family name, use *te*; if you call someone by his first name, use *sinä*. (*sinä* is far more common than "tu" in French or "du" in German.)

Kuka sinä ole/t? Minä olen Liisa (Salo).	Who are you? I'm Liisa (Salo).
Kuka te ole/tte? Minä olen professori Viisas.	Who are you? I'm Professor Viisas.
Puhu/t/ko sinä saksaa, Liisa?	Do you speak German, Liisa?
Puhu/tte/ko te saksaa, professori Viisas?	Do you speak German, Professor Viisas?

te is omitted in written Finnish like *minä* and *sinä*.

2. Vowel harmony

Due to a pattern of sounds called **vowel harmony**, Finnish words may have two parallel suffixes or endings.

If the stem part of the word contains a **back vowel (a, o, u)**, back vowels will also appear in the suffix or ending:

poika boy	*poika/ko?* a boy?
Englanti England	*englanti/lainen* English(man)

Otherwise the suffix or ending will have a **front vowel (ä, ö, y)**:

sinä you	*sinä/kö?* you?
Töölö (a district of Helsinki)	*töölö/läinen* resident of Töölö
Helsinki	*helsinki/läinen*
se it; the, that	*se/kö nainen?* that woman?

In compound words, the last component decides whether a back or front vowel must be used:

Kööpen/hamina Copenhagen	*kööpen/hamina/lainen*

Sanasto — Vocabulary

entä?	what about? how about? and?
entä (mitä kuuluu) sinulle/teille?	and how are you?
huonosti	badly, poorly
(hyvää) päivää	how do you do (lit. ''good day'')
kanadalainen	Canadian
kuuluu:	
mitä (sinulle/teille) kuuluu?	how are you (''what's the news?'')
-lainen (-läinen)	suffix denoting ''native or resident of an area''
mutta	but
näkemiin (from *nähdä* to see)	goodbye, so long, I'll see you
oikein	right, correctly; very
te	you (pl. and formal)

☆

herra	Mr.; gentleman
kaikki	everything, all; all people, everybody
rouva	Mrs., madam; (older) lady
ruotsalainen	Swede, Swedish
Ruotsi	Sweden
tohtori (abbr. *tri*)	doctor
torstai	Thursday
Venäjä	Russia
venäläinen	Russian

Kappale 5 Lesson

Mikä sinun nimesi on?

What's your name?

Uusi opiskelija tulee kurssille

1. Opiskelija. Päivää. Minä olen uusi opiskelija.
2. Opettaja. Päivää. Mikä sinun nimesi on?
3. A. Andy Powell.
4. O. Anteeksi, kuinka?
5. A. Minun etunimeni on Andy, A-n-d-y, ja minun sukunimeni on Powell, P-o-w-e-l-l.
6. O. Ole hyvä ja kirjoita se. Kiitos. Mikä sinun osoitteesi on?
7. A. Minun osoitteeni on Kalevankatu 10 A 17.
8. O. Ja sinun puhelinnumerosi?
9. A. Minun puhelinnumeroni on yksi-kaksi-kolme-neljä-viisi-nolla.
10. O. Ja mikä sinun kotimaasi on?
11. A. Minun kotimaani on Australia.
12. O. Tervetuloa kurssille. Ole hyvä ja istu.

A new student comes to the course

1. Student. How do you do. I'm a new student.
2. Teacher. How do you do. What's your name?
3. A. Andy Powell.
4. T. I beg your pardon?
5. A. My first name is Andy, A-n-d-y, and my family name is Powell, P-o-w-e-l-l.
6. T. Please write it down. Thank you. What's your address?
7. A. My address is Kalevankatu 10 A 17.
8. T. And your telephone number?
9. A My telephone number is one-two-three-four-five-zero.
10. T. And what's your home country?
11. A. My home country is Australia.
12. T. Welcome to the course. Please sit down.

5

Mikä teidän nimenne on?	What's your name?
Minun nimeni on Anna Virtanen.	My name is Anna Virtanen.
Mikä teidän osoitteenne on?	What's your address?
Entä teidän puhelinnumeronne?	And your telephone number?

Mikä päivä tänään on? Tänään on lauantai.
Eilen oli perjantai. Huomenna on sunnuntai.

2

Kielioppia — Structural notes

1. Possessive suffixes for ''my'', ''your''

(minun) talo/ni my house
(minun) nime/ni my name

(sinun) talo/si your house
(sinun) nime/si your name
(teidän) talo/nne your house
(teidän) nime/nne your name

To express the idea indicated in English by possessive pronouns, Finnish uses possessive suffixes: **-ni** my, **-si** and **-nne** your. The pronouns *minun* (gen. of *minä*), *sinun* (gen. of *sinä*) and *teidän* (gen. of *te*) are also often added in speech but omitted in written Finnish, unless they carry emphasis.

minun also means ''mine'', *sinun* ''yours'', *teidän* ''yours'':

Onko tuo auto sinun/teidän?	Is that car yours?
Se huone on minun.	That room is mine.

In casual every-day speech, particularly in the Helsinki area, possessive suffixes are often dropped. Note also the short colloquial forms of the pronouns:

mun auto = *(minun) autoni* *teidän nimi* = *(teidän) nimenne*
sun osoite = *(sinun) osoitteesi*

More about possessive suffixes in 29:1, 2 and 40:1.

2. Informal imperative (affirmative)

The **imperative** expresses an order or a request.

Puhu suomea, Bill!	Speak Finnish, Bill!
Ole hyvä ja istu, Liisa!	Please (lit. ''be good and'') sit down, Liisa!

The **informal imperative (imperative sing.)** is used when speaking to a child, young person, relative, friend etc. whom you call *sinä*. It is formed by dropping the ending **-n** of the 1st person present tense:

puhu/n	I speak	*puhu!*	speak!
kirjoita/n	I write	*kirjoita!*	write!

More about the imperative in 7:2, 30:1.

Sanasto — Vocabulary

anteeksi	excuse me, pardon me, I'm sorry
ei (se) mitään	never mind
etu/nimi	first name, Christian name
istu/a (istun istut istutte)	to sit (down)
kirjoitta/a (kirjoitan kirjoitat kirjoitatte)	to write
koti	home
kuinka?	how?
kurssi	course
nimi	name
nolla	0, nought, zero
ole hyvä!	please; here you are; help yourself (informally to one person)
opettaja	teacher, instructor
opiskelija	student
osoite	address
puhelin	telephone
suku	family, relatives
terve/tuloa!	welcome, glad to see you here
tul/la (tulen tulet tulette)	to come; to become

☆

huomenna	tomorrow
kahvi	coffee
lauantai	Saturday
musiikki	music
otta/a (otan otat otatte)	to take
perjantai	Friday
sano/a (sanon sanot sanotte)	to say
soitta/a (soitan soitat soitatte)	to play; to ring; to phone, call
sunnuntai	Sunday
tanssi/a (tanssin tanssit tanssitte)	to dance

Mikä Liisan puhelinnumero on?

What is Liisa's telephone number?

SAAB

Liisa Salo

Kalle Oksanen

puh. 163220 os. Simonkatu 15 A 4

os. Meritie 47 C 11
puh. 780568

1. Mikä Liisan puhelinnumero on?

Liisan numero on

2. Mikä Kallen osoite on?

3. Mikä on Paavon sukunimi?

4. Mikä on rouva Laakson etunimi?

5. Mikä on herra John Smithin kotimaa?

6. Mikä John Smithin auto on?

1. What's Liisa's telephone number?
2. What's Kalle's address?
3. What's Paavo's family name?
4. What's Mrs. Laakso's first name?
5. What's Mr. John Smith's home country?
6. What is John Smith's car?

7. Sano mikä on Suomen pääkaupunki!

____

____

7. Tell me what is Finland's capital?

8. Entä Englannin?

____

8. And England's?

■■■

9. Onko Liisa tytön vai pojan nimi?

____

9. Is Liisa a girl's or a boy's name?

10. Onko Tapio miehen vai naisen nimi?
En tiedä.
Se on miehen nimi.

10. Is Tapio a man's or a woman's name? I don't know.
It's a man's name.

■■■

11. Kenen auto on Saab?
Kalle Oksasen.
12. Kenen puhelinnumero on 780568?
Laakson perheen.
13. Tiedätkö kenen romaani on Seitsemän veljestä? Aleksis Kiven.

14. Tiedätkö kenen sävellys on Finlandia? Se on Sibeliuksen sävellys.

11. Whose car is a Saab?
Kalle Oksanen's.
12. Whose telephone number is 780568?
It's the number of the Laakso family.
13. Do you know whose novel is ''The Seven Brothers''? It's a novel by Aleksis Kivi.
14. Do you know whose composition is ''Finlandia''? It is a composition by Sibelius.

■■■

Tämän miehen auto on Saab.
Sairaan tytön nimi on Anna.

This man's car is a Saab.
The sick girl's name is Anna.

tai/vai?
''you'' on suomeksi sinä **tai** te.
Onko ''hyvin'' englanniksi good **vai** well?

Kielioppia — Structural notes

1. Genitive singular

Kalle/n auto	Kalle's car
tytö/n osoite	the girl's address, the address of the girl
Englanni/n pääkaupunki	the capital of England

The ending of the genitive sing. in Finnish is **-n**.
The word in the genitive (except in poetry) invariably **precedes** the thing possessed. (In English the prepositional construction with *of* comes after it.)

The **stem** to which the genitive ending is added may differ from the basic form. As the genitive stem is widely used in the inflection of nouns, it will be listed in the vocabularies from now on and should be memorized along with the basic form.

When added to foreign names ending in a consonant, the gen. ending (and other endings as well) is preceded by a "link vowel" **-i-**:

Jamesi/n puhelinnumero	James's telephone number
New Yorki/n poliisi	the New York police

The title remains uninflected when followed by a name:

herra/n osoite	the gentleman's address, but:
herra Matti Suomela/n koti	Mr. Matti Suomela's home

An adjective or a pronoun preceding an inflected noun agrees with it, that is, has the same ending:

tuo/n karta/n hinta	the price of that map
vanha/n miehe/n poika	the old man's son
suomalaise/n naise/n nimi	the name of the Finnish woman

Note 1. Many pronouns have more or less irregular genitive forms. You already know (*minä*) *minun*, (*sinä*) *sinun*, (*te*) *teidän*. Note also:

hän hänen *kuka? kenen?* *mikä? minkä?*

Note 2. If the word has a poss. suffix, the gen. sing. and the basic form are identical:

(Minun) poikani on pieni.	My son is small.
(Minun) poikani nimi on Eero.	My son's name is Eero.

Note 3. The explanations given in this note are meant for those students who, instead of memorizing the words individually from vocabularies, prefer a more systematic approach.

The gen. stem may differ from the basic form for two reasons:
a) Words with **k**, **p**, or **t** undergo changes which will be explained in detail in 23:3. Examples: *kauppa*, gen. *kaupan*; *koti*, gen. *kodin*.
b) On the basis of how the words end, there are a number of inflectional types which the student will learn to recognize by and by. Examples: *Suomi*, gen. *Suomen*; *suomalainen*, gen. *suomalaisen*.
The gen. stem will differ from the basic form
— always if the word ends in a consonant, e.g. *Sibelius*, gen. *Sibeliuksen*; *puhelin*, gen. *puhelimen*
— with just a couple of exceptions if the word ends in **-e**, e.g. *huone*, gen. *huoneen*
— fairly often if a 2-syllable word ends in **-i**, e.g. *Suomi*, gen. *Suomen*; *kieli*, gen. *kielen*

The list below will help illustrate the rules given here.

A list of the nouns in lessons 1—6 with their gen. sing. forms

(+ shows that the word is subject to **k p t** changes)

auto-n 1	lauantai-n 5	rouva-n 4
bussi-n 1	maa-n 3	Ruotsi-n 4
+Englanti Englannin 3	maanantai-n 1	sivu-n 1
herra-n 4	+musiikki musiikin 5	+suku suvun 5
huono-n 2	nolla-n 5	sunnuntai-n 5
iso-n 2	numero-n 1	talo-n 1
kahvi-n 5	opettaja-n 5	televisio-n 1
+kartta kartan 3	opiskelija-n 5	tie-n 6
+katu kadun 1	pallo-n 6	tiistai-n 2
+kauppa kaupan 1	perjantai-n 5	tohtori-n 4
+kaupunki kaupungin 6	+poika pojan 1	torstai-n 4
+keski/viikko-viikon 3	päivä-n 1	+tyttö tytön 1
+koti kodin 5	radio-n 1	vanha-n 2
kurssi-n 5	Ranska-n 3	+vasta/kohta-kohdan 6
kuva-n 1	romaani-n 6	Venäjä-n 4

i→e words	**mies** miehen 1	perhe perheen 6
+kaikki kaiken 4	**vastaus** words	(exception: +nukke nuken 6)
kieli kielen 3	kiitos kiitoksen 3	
kivi kiven 1	kysymys kysymyksen 2	
nimi nimen 5	Sibelius Sibeliuksen 1	**Pronouns:**
nuori nuoren 2	sävellys sävellyksen 6	minä minun 3
pieni pienen 2	vastaus vastauksen 2	sinä sinun 3
Suomi Suomen 1	**sairas** sairaan 2	hän hänen 2
uusi uuden 2	kaunis kauniin 2	te teidän 4
nainen words	**huone** words	tämä-n 1
nainen naisen 1	huone huoneen 1	tuo-n 1
(all words in **-nen**)	kappale kappaleen 1	se-n 1
puhelin puhelimen 5	+osoite osoitteen 5	mikä minkä 1
		kuka kenen 1

Sanasto — Vocabulary

+kaupunki kaupungin	city, town
kenen? (from *kuka*?)	whose?
perhe perheen	family
+pää/kaupunki -kaupungin	capital (city)
romaani-n (cp. *novelli* short story)	novel
sävellys sävellyksen	composition
tie-n	road, way
+tietää (tiedän tiedät tiedätte)	to know (facts) (cp. Fr. savoir, Germ. wissen)
vai? (cp. *tai*)	or (in questions)

☆

englanniksi	in English
+nukke nuken	doll
pallo-n	ball
suomeksi	in Finnish
+vasta/kohta-kohdan	opposite, contrast

Kappale 7 Lesson

Paljonko sanakirja maksaa?

Kirjakaupassa

1. Paljonko tämä sanakirja maksaa?
2. Se maksaa 19,75.
3. Anteeksi, kuinka? Olkaa hyvä ja puhukaa hitaasti.
4. Tämän sanakirjan hinta on yhdeksäntoista markkaa seitsemänkymmentä viisi penniä.
5. En ymmärrä. Olkaa hyvä ja kirjoittakaa se. — Ai, 19,75! Se ei ole kallis.
6. Ei, se on hyvin halpa. Ostakaa se vain, se on oikein hyvä.
7. Kuinka paljon Helsingin kartta maksaa?
8. Tämäkö? Sen hinta on 5,40.

How much does the dictionary cost?

In the bookstore

1. How much does this dictionary cost?
2. It costs 19,75.
3. Pardon? Please speak slowly.
4. The price of this dictionary is nineteen marks seventy-five pennies.
5. I don't understand. Please write it down. — Oh, 19,75! It isn't expensive.
6. No, it's very cheap. Go ahead and buy it, it's very good.
7. How much does a map of Helsinki cost?
8. This one? It costs 5,40.

Kenen sanakirja tuo on?
Onko se sinun?
Ei ole, se on Liisan tai Eevan.

Minkä hinta on 19,75? Sanakirjan.

Pekka, **ole hyvä ja puhu** hitaasti!
Professori Joki, **olkaa hyvä ja puhukaa** hitaasti!

n-nn nimeni — nime**nne**, taloni — talo**nne**, koti**ni** — koti**nne**
r ka**r**tta, ma**r**kka, he**rr**a O**r**an ki**r**ja, ki**r**joittakaa nume**r**o!
h **h**etkinen! **h**erra **H**ietanen, pu**h**ukaa **h**itaasti!
halpa **h**inta, **h**yvin **h**uono, **h**erra pu**h**uu **h**ollantia

Kielioppia — Structural notes

1. Basic form of verbs

The basic form (dictionary form, infinitive) of Finnish verbs always ends in **-a (-ä)**.

Haluan puhu/a ja ymmärtä/ä suomea.	I want to speak and understand Finnish.
Haluatko tul/la kurssille?	Do you want to come to the course?

The ending of the infinitive is
— **-a** (**-ä**) if the inf. ends in two vowels:
puhu/a, ymmärtä/ä, sano/a, otta/a, maksa/a
— the preceding consonant plus **-a** (**-ä**) if the inf. ends in one vowel:
ol/la, tul/la, men/nä to go, *halu/ta*

More about the basic form of verbs in 27:1.

2. Imperative plural (affirmative)

Puhu/kaa suomea, Bill ja Mary!	Speak Finnish, Bill and Mary!
Olkaa hyvä ja istu/kaa, rouva Oksanen!	Please sit down, Mrs. Oksanen!

Imperative pl. is used when speaking to many people or, formally, to one person whom you address with his title, family name, and *te*. It is formed by dropping the inf. ending and adding **-kaa (-kää)** to the stem:

puhu/a	to speak	*puhu/kaa!*	speak!
ol/la	to be	*ol/kaa hyvä ja*	please (lit. "be good and")
istu/a	to sit	*istu/kaa!*	sit down!

More about the imperative pl. in 30:1.
(The imperative sing. was explained in 5:2.)

3. Adverbs from adjectives

millainen?	*kuinka?*	
huono bad	*Puhun huono/sti ranskaa.*	I speak French badly.
kaunis beautiful (gen. *kaunii/n*)	*Tanssit kaunii/sti.*	You dance beautifully.
hidas slow (gen. *hitaa/n*)	*Puhukaa hitaa/sti!*	Speak slowly!

Adverbs of manner are formed from adjectives by means of the suffix **-sti** (cp. **-ly** in English). The suffix is added to the genitive stem whenever it differs from the basic form.

Sanasto — Vocabulary

ai	oh, ah, ouch
+halpa halvan	cheap, inexpensive
+hinta hinnan	price
hitaasti (from *hidas hitaan*)	slowly
kallis kalliin	expensive, dear
kirja-n	book
maksa/a (maksa/n-t-tte)	to pay, cost
+markka markan	mark
olkaa hyvä!	please; here you are; help yourself (to many people or, formally, to one person)
osta/a (osta/n-t-tte)	to buy, purchase
paljon	much, a lot, lots of, a great deal
paljonko? = kuinka paljon?	how much?
penni-n	penny (one 100th of a mark)
sana-n	word
sana/kirja-n	dictionary (lit. ''word-book'')
+ymmärtä/ä (ymmärrä/n-t-tte)	to understand
en ymmärrä	I don't understand

☆

halu/ta (halua/n-t-tte)	to want, wish, desire
+kuppi kupin	cup
lasi-n	glass
laula/a (laula/n-t-tte)	to sing
men/nä (mene/n-t-tte)	to go
nopea-n (≠ *hidas*)	fast, quick, rapid
tee-n	tea

Numerals

yksi (yhden)	1
kaksi (kahden)	2
kolme (-n)	3
neljä (-n)	4
viisi (viiden)	5
kuusi (kuuden)	6
seitsemän (seitsemän)	7
kahdeksan (kahdeksan)	8
yhdeksän (yhdeksän)	9
kymmenen (kymmenen)	10
yksi/toista (yhden/toista)	11
kaksi/toista	12
kolme/toista	13
kaksi/kymmentä (kahden/kymmenen)	20
kaksi/kymmentä/yksi	21
+sata (sadan)	100
sata/kymmenen	110
viisi/sataa	500
tuhat (tuhannen)	1000
neljä/tuhatta	4000
miljoona (-n)	1 000 000

In colloquial Finnish many numerals have short quick-speech forms: *yks*, *kaks*, *viis*, *kuus*, *kaks/kyt/yks*, *kol/kyt/viis* etc.

Kappale **8** Lesson

Oikealla ja vasemmalla

Right and left

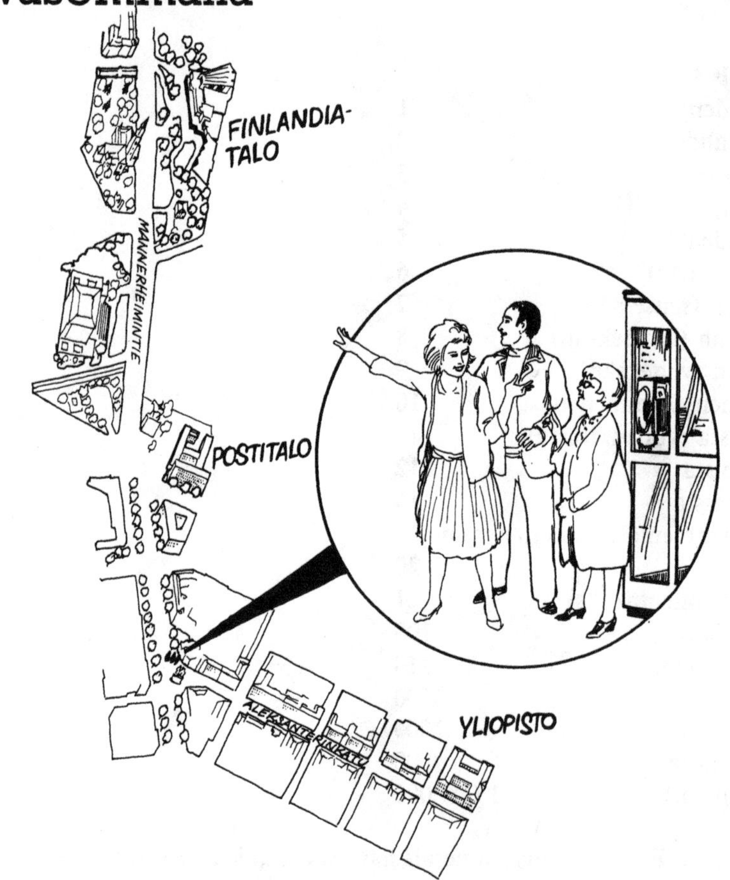

1. Rouva Hill. Hyvää huomenta!
2. Neiti Salo. Huomenta!
3. Rva H. Kaunis ilma tänään.
4. Nti S. Mutta vähän kylmä
5. Rva H. Saanko esitellä: mieheni — neiti Salo.

6. Hra H. Neiti Salo, missä lähin posti on?
7. Nti S. Mannerheimintiellä. Se on tuo talo tuolla.

1. Mrs Hill. Good morning!
2. Miss Salo. Good morning!
3. Mrs. H. Fine weather today.
4. Miss S. But a little cold.
5. Mrs. H. May I introduce you? My husband — Miss Salo. (They shake hands and say ''päivää''.)
6. Mr. H. Miss Salo, where is the nearest post-office?
7. Miss S. On Mannerheim Road. It's that building over there.

8. Rva H. Ja millä kadulla Finlandia-talo on?	8. Mrs. H. And on what street is Finlandia Hall?
9. Nti S. Myös Mannerheimintiellä, tuolla oikealla.	9. Miss S. Also on Mannerheim Road, over there, on the right.
10. Hra H. Missä yliopisto on?	10. Mr. H. Where is the University?
11. Nti S. Se on Aleksanterinkadulla. "Aleksi" on tämä katu täällä vasemmalla.	11. Miss S. It's on Alexander Street. "Aleksi" is this street here, on the left.
12. Rva H. Kiitoksia, neiti Salo, ja näkemiin!	12. Mrs. H. Thank you very much, Miss Salo, and goodbye.

Missä auto on? Kadu**lla**.
Millä sinä kirjoitat? Kynä**llä**.
Millä te tulette kurssille? Bussi**lla**. Metro**lla**. Auto**lla**.

uo	h**uo**menta, n**uo**ri mies, t**uo** s**uo**malainen t**uo**lla
uo-yö	**tuo** myös, myös **tuo**, myös Suomi, **Suo**mi myös
uo-yö-ie	myös mies, **tuo** mies myös, myös **tuo** tie

Keep stress on first syllable:
huomenta, **an**teeksi, **ka**dulla, **Hel**sinki, esitellä, **Fin**landia-talo, **Man**nerheimintie, yliopisto

Kielioppia — Structural notes

1. The "on" case (adessive)

		missä?	where?
katu (gen. *kadu/n*)	street	*kadu/lla*	on the street
hyvä tie	a good road	*hyvä/llä tie/llä*	on a good road
ovi (gen. *ove/n*)	door	*ove/lla*	at the door

In local expressions answering the questions "where?", "wherefrom?", "whereto?" Finnish very often uses noun endings, not prepositions as in English.

The ending roughly corresponding to "on, at" is **-lla (-llä)**. Whenever the basic form and the genitive stem are different, use the gen. stem before this ending.

Note: *tämä katu* but *tä/llä kadu/lla*
mikä katu? *mi/llä kadu/lla?*
se katu *si/llä kadu/lla*

Local cases may also have non-local functions. Thus, the ending **-lla (-llä)** has also the meaning ''with, by means of (something)'':

Kirjoitan kynä/llä.	I write with a pen (pencil).
Mi/llä sinä maksat kaupassa? Raha/lla tai seki/llä.	What do you pay with in the shop? With money or with a check.
Tule taksi/lla!	Come by taxi!

When you use poss. suffixes with the different cases, the poss. suffix always follows the case ending:

Istun tuolilla/ni.	I'm sitting on my chair.
Tuletko sinä kurssille autolla/si?	Do you come to the course by car?

(The ''in'' case will be explained in 10:1.)

Finlandia-talo. Vasemmalla Eduskuntatalo, oikealla Kansallismuseon torni

Sanasto — Vocabulary

+esitel/lä (esittele/n-t-tte)	to introduce
huomenta (= *hyvää h.*)	good morning
ilma-n	air; weather
kiitoksia	thank you, thanks
kylmä-n (≠ *lämmin* warm)	cold
lähin lähimmän	nearest, closest
missä?	where?
myös	also, too
+neiti neidin	Miss
oikealla	on the right
posti-n	post, mail; post-office; mailman, postman
saa/da (saa/n-t-tte)	to be allowed, may; to get, receive
saanko?	may I? may I have?
tuolla (from *tuo*)	over there
täällä (from *tämä*)	here
vasemmalla	on the left
yli/opisto-n	university

☆

hotelli-n	hotel
+konsertti konsertin	concert
kynä-n	pen, pencil
metro-n	subway
millä? (from *mikä?*)	what with? by what means?
ovi oven	door
raha-n	money; coin
rahaa	some money
+sekki sekin	check
taksi-n	taxi
teatteri-n	theater
turisti-n	tourist
vaimo-n	wife

Kappale 9 Lesson

Onko sinulla rahaa?

Do you have any money?

Rouva Hill haluaa soittaa

Mrs. Hill wants to make a phone call

1. Rva H. Minä haluan soittaa. Missä on lähin puhelin?
2. Hra H. Tuolla on kioski. Onko sinulla markka? Minulla ei ole.
3. Rva H. Minä luulen, että minulla on pikkurahaa. Hetkinen, minä katson. Ei ole!
4. Hra H. Katso, neiti Salo on vielä tuolla. Ehkä hänellä on rahaa. Anteeksi, neiti Salo! Onko teillä markka? Vaimoni haluaa soittaa.
5. Nti S. Hetkinen vain, minä katson. Ei ole. Mutta tuolla tulee Ville Vuori. Ehkä hänellä on. Hei, Ville! Onko sinulla markka? Rouva Hill haluaa soittaa.
6. V. Hetkinen! Ei ole, minulla on vain viisikymmentä penniä.
7. Rva H. No, sitten minä en voi soittaa. Minulla on aina huono onni.

1. Mrs. H. I want to make a phone call. Where's the nearest telephone?
2. Mr. H. There's a booth. Do you have a mark? I don't.
3. Mrs. H. I think (that) I have some small change. One moment, I'll see. No, I haven't any!
4. Mr. H. Look, Miss Salo is still there. Perhaps she has some money. Excuse me, Miss Salo! Do you have a mark? My wife wants to make a phone call.
5. Miss S. Just a moment, I'll see. No, I haven't. But there comes Ville Vuori. Maybe he has some. Hello, Ville! Do you have a mark? Mrs. Hill wants to make a phone call.
6. V. One moment! No, I only have fifty pennies.
7. Mrs. H. Well, then I can't make my phone call. I always have bad luck.

"that"
Tuo on kaunis valssi.
Minä luulen, **että** se on Sibeliuksen Valse triste.

pikku/pieni
Pikku Liisa on vielä **pieni**.

pieni/vähän
Rauma on **pieni** kaupunki (ei iso).
Minulla on **vähän** rahaa (ei paljon).

Kenellä on markka?
Minulla.

3

Kielioppia — Structural notes

1. Personal pronouns

The six personal pronouns in Finnish are:

	Gen.		Gen.
minä I	*minun* my, mine	*me* we	*meidän* our(s)
sinä you	*sinun* your(s)	*te* you	*teidän* your(s)
hän he/she	*hänen* his/her(s)	*he* they	*heidän* their(s)

2. "to have" in Finnish

Finnish has no specific verb corresponding to the English "to have". Instead, the verb *olla* "to be" is used in the following way:

Affirmative			**Negative**		
minu/lla	*on*	I have	*minu/lla*	*ei ole*	I do not have
sinu/lla		you have	*sinu/lla*		you do not have
häne/llä		he/she has	*häne/llä*		he/she does not have
mei/llä		we have	*mei/llä*		we do not have
tei/llä		you have	*tei/llä*		you do not have
hei/llä		they have	*hei/llä*		they do not have

Questions:

onko	*minu/lla?*	do I have?
	sinu/lla?	do you have?
	häne/llä?	does he/she have?
	mei/llä?	do we have?
	tei/llä?	do you have?
	hei/llä?	do they have?

Thus, the ending **-lla (-llä)** also signifies "in someone's possession" (*minulla on kirja* I have a book, lit. "in my possession is a book").

More about the Finnish "to have" in 17:2.

Sanasto — Vocabulary

aina	always
ehkä	maybe, perhaps
että (must not be omitted!)	that (when starting a clause)
luulen, että voin	I think I can
hetkinen hetkisen (= *hetki hetken*)	moment, while
katso/a (katso/n-t-tte)	to look, watch; to have a look
katso! (colloq. *kato!*)	look! see!
kioski-n	stand, booth, kiosk
luul/la (luule/n-t-tte)	to think, suppose, presume
no	well, now
onni onnen	happiness; luck, fortune
pikku (indeclinable)	little
pikku/raha	small change
sitten	then, after that; ago
vielä	still, yet; more, also
voi/da (voi/n-t-tte)	to be able, can

☆

he heidän	they (human beings)
kello-n	watch, clock; the time; bell
koira-n	dog
+lamppu lampun	lamp
me meidän	we
valssi-n	waltz

Missä te asutte?

1. Missä te asutte, herra Lake?
2. Minä asun nyt Helsingissä. Mutta kotini on Skotlannissa (Englannissa, Amerikassa, New Yorkin valtiossa).
3. Missä kaupungissa?
4. Edinburghissa. Se on Skotlannin pääkaupunki.
5. Skotlanti on kaunis maa.
6. Niin on. Siellä on kiva asua.
7. Asuuko teidän perheenne myös Suomessa?
8. Asuu. Me asumme täällä kaikki. Meillä on oikein mukava asunto.
9. Missä teidän asuntonne on?
10. Töölössä, Hesperiankadulla.
11. Vai niin! Siellä asuvat myös Juhani ja Riitta Metsä.
12. Niin, he asuvat samassa talossa. Heillä on kaunis koti. Juhani Metsä on hyvä ystäväni. Hän on oikein mukava ihminen.

Where do you live?

1. Where do you live, Mr. Lake?
2. I live in Helsinki now. But my home is in Scotland (England, America, New York State).
3. In what city?
4. In Edinburgh. It's the capital of Scotland.
5. Scotland is a beautiful country.
6. Yes, it is. It's nice to live there.
7. Does your family also live in Finland?
8. Yes, they do. We all live here. We have a very nice apartment.
9. Where is your apartment?
10. In Töölö, on Hesperia Street.
11. I see. Juhani and Riitta Metsä also live there.
12. Yes, they live in the same building. They have a pretty home. Juhani Metsä is a good friend of mine. He's a very nice person.

tuolla/siellä

— Missä Kalle on?
— **Tuolla.**

— Missä Maija on?
— Teatterissa. **Siellä** on Hamlet.

Mitä merkitsee *metsä*? Se merkitsee 'forest, woods'.

Kielioppia — Structural notes

1. The "in" case (inessive)

		missä?	where?
talo	house	*talo/ssa*	in a house
metsä	forest	*metsä/ssä*	in the forest
Suomi (gen. *Suome/n*)	Finland	*Suome/ssa*	in Finland
uusi kauppa (gen. *uude/n kaupa/n*)	a new shop	*uude/ssa kaupa/ssa*	in a new shop

The ending **-ssa (-ssä)** corresponds roughly to the English preposition "in".
Whenever the basic form and the gen. stem are different, use the gen. stem before this ending.

Note: *mikä maa?* but *mi/ssä maa/ssa?*
tämä maa? — *tä/ssä maa/ssa*
se maa — *siinä maa/ssa*

Note also:

Missä sinä olet?	Where are you?
Mi/ssä huonee/ssa sinä olet?	In which room are you?

The poss. suffix comes after the case ending:

Oletko sinä huoneessa/si?	Are you in your room?
Istun autossa/ni.	I'm sitting in my car.

n
Bad mistake: *Kurssi on Helsingissä yliopistossa.*
"Helsingin" is a gen. form ("Helsinki's, of Helsinki"), and is not an adjective or pronoun, which would agree with the following noun.

2. Present tense of verbs (affirmative)

asu/a to live		*tul/la* to come	
(minä) asu/n	I live, am living	*(minä) tule/n*	I come
(sinä) asu/t	you live, are living	*(sinä) tule/t*	you come
hän asu/u	he/she lives, is living	*hän tule/e*	he/she comes
(me) asu/mme	we live, are living	*(me) tule/mme*	we come
(te) asu/tte	you live, are living	*(te) tule/tte*	you come
he asu/vat	they live, are living	*he tule/vat*	they come

The ending of the 3rd pers. sing. is made by prolonging the final vowel of the stem. It may be any of the eight vowels (in these examples **u**, **e**). If there is already a long vowel or a diphthong, no ending is added: *(voi/n, voi/t) hän voi* he/she can, *(saa/n, saa/t) hän saa* he/she is allowed; he/she receives.

The ending of the 3rd pers. pl. is **-vat (-vät)**.

The pronouns *minä, sinä, me, te* may be omitted (cp. 3:1).

Some verbs have **k p t** changes in their conjugation. For some time, therefore, the entire present tense of each new verb will be given in the vocabulary.

In casual everyday speech you may hear forms which differ from the standard conjugation. For instance, the 3rd pers. sing. is often used instead of the 3rd pers. pl.: *Kalle ja Ville puhuu* ("puhuvat") *englantia.*

The negative present tense will be explained in 12:2.

Present tense of the verbs covered in lessons 1—10

(For inflection types like *voida, puhua* etc. see 27:1.)

voida verbs

saa/da 8	saa/n -t saa saa/mme -tte -vat
voi/da 9	voi/n -t voi voi/mme -tte -vat

puhua verbs

asu/a 10	asu/n -t -u -mme -tte -vat
istu/a 5	istu/n -t -u -mme -tte -vat
katso/a 9	katso/n -t -o -mme -tte -vat
+kirjoitta/a 5	kirjoita/n -t kirjoittaa kirjoita/mme -tte kirjoittavat
laula/a 7	laula/n -t -a -mme -tte -vat
maksa/a 7	maksa/n -t -a -mme -tte -vat
osta/a 7	osta/n -t -a -mme -tte -vat
+otta/a 5	ota/n -t ottaa ota/mme -tte ottavat
puhu/a 3	puhu/n -t -u -mme -tte -vat
sano/a 5	sano/n -t -o -mme -tte -vat
+soitta/a 5	soita/n -t soittaa soita/mme -tte soittavat

tanssi/a 5	tanssi/n -t -i -mme -tte -vat
+tietä/ä 6	tiedä/n -t tietää tiedä/mme -tte tietävät
+ymmärtä/ä 7	ymmärrä/n -t ymmärtää ymmärrä/mme -tte ymmärtävät
tulla verbs	
+esitel/lä 8	esittele/n -t -e -mme -tte -vät
luul/la 9	luule/n -t -e -mme -tte -vat
men/nä 7	mene/n -t -e -mme -tte -vät
ol/la 1	ole/n -t **on** ole/mme -tte **ovat**
tul/la 5	tule/n -t -e -mme -tte -vat
haluta verbs	
halu/ta 7	halua/n -t -a -mme -tte -vat
merkitä verbs	
merki/tä 10	merkitse/n -t -e -mme -tte -vät

Sanasto — Vocabulary

asu/a (asu/n-t-u-mme-tte-vat)	to live, reside, dwell; stay
+asunto asunnon	place to live, apartment
ihminen ihmisen	human being, man, person; pl. people
kiva-n (= *hauska, mukava*)	nice, fun (colloq.)
metsä-n	forest, woods
mukava-n	nice, pleasant; comfortable
niin	so; yes
nyt	now
sama-n	same
siellä	there
vai niin	I see, really? is that so?
valtio-n	state
ystävä-n	friend

☆

baari-n	bar; cafeteria
hauska-n	nice, interesting, fun
kotona	at home
merki/tä (merkitse/n-t-e-mme-tte -vät)	to mean, signify, denote; to mark
sauna-n	sauna
sohva-n	sofa, couch
yksin	alone, by oneself

Mitä te teette? / What do you do?

Henkilöt: Marja, Kari, James.	Characters: Marja, Kari, James.
1. Kari. Terve, Marja!	1. Kari. Hello, Marja!
2. Marja. Hei, Kari!	2. Marja. Hi, Kari!
3. K. Marja, tämä on amerikkalainen poika, James Brown.	3. K. Marja, this is James Brown, he's American.
4. M. Hei, James. Mitä sinä teet Suomessa?	4. M. Hi, James. What do you do in Finland?
5. James. Minä olen opiskelija.	5. James. I am a student.
6. M. Mitä sinä opiskelet?	6. M. What are you studying?
7. J. Nyt minä opiskelen suomea. Minä olen suomen kielen kurssilla yliopistossa.	7. J. I'm studying Finnish now. I'm attending a Finnish course at the University.
8. M. No, opitko sinä?	8. M. Well, are you learning it?
9. J. En tiedä. Minä olen vähän laiska.	9. J. I don't know. I am rather lazy.
10. K. Kyllä hän oppii. Hän puhuu jo aika hyvin.	10. K. Yes, he *is* learning it. He already speaks it quite well.
11. M. Niin puhuu. No, onko suomi helppo vai vaikea kieli?	11. M. Yes, he does. Well, is Finnish an easy or a difficult language?
12. J. Minusta aika vaikea.	12. J. Rather difficult, I think.
13. K. James on myös työssä.	13. K. James is also working.
14. M. Mitä hän tekee?	14. M. What is he doing?
15. K. Hän opettaa englantia kielikoulussa.	15. K. He's teaching English in a Language School.
16. M. Vai niin! Oletko sinä hyvä opettaja?	16. M. Really? Are you a good teacher?
17. J. En tiedä. Minä toivon niin.	17. J. I don't know. I hope so.

kyllä/niin

(asking with the verb)	Asutteko te Oulussa?	Asun (**kyllä**). **Kyllä** (asun).
(not asking with the verb)	Oulussako te asutte?	Oulussa. **Niin** (asun).
(agreeing to a statement)	Te asutte Oulussa. —	**Niin** asun.

Milloin teillä on suomen kurssi?
Maananta**ina** ja keskiviikko**na**.

"I think that"
Luulen, että tuo kasetti maksaa 55,—. (*assumption*)
Minusta se on kallis kasetti. (*opinion*)

nk-ng Helsi**nk**i — Helsi**ng**issä, kaupu**nk**i — kaupu**ng**in
y-ä kyllä kyllä, hyvä ystävä
y-ö Töölö, Töölön tyttö, tyttö on työssä

Kielioppia — Structural notes

1. Present tense of k p t verbs

a) +*otta/a* to take

(minä)	*ota*	*n*	I take
(sinä)		*t*	you take
hän	*otta/a*		he takes
(me)	*ota*	*mme*	we take
(te)		*tte*	you take
he	*otta/vat*		they take

+*tietä/ä* to know

(minä)	*tiedä*	*n*	I know
(sinä)		*t*	you know
hän	*tietä/ä*		he knows
(me)	*tiedä*	*mme*	we know
(te)		*tte*	you know
he	*tietä/vät*		they know

The most common type of Finnish verbs has a basic form which ends in two vowels: *puhu/a*, *sano/a*, *maksa/a*, +*otta/a* etc.

When such "puhua" verbs have **k p t** changes, their present tense always follows the same pattern:
— the 3rd pers. has the same consonant(s) as the infinitive;
— the 1st and 2nd pers. have a different consonant.

Two verbs with exceptional infinitives, +*tehdä* (*teen*) "to do" and +*nähdä* (*näen*) "to see" are, in the present, like *puhua* verbs:

tee	*n*	*tee*	*mme*
	t		*tte*
teke/e		*teke/vät*	

b) *tulla* verbs (and *haluta* verbs, see 27:1) have a different pattern:

+*esitel/lä* to introduce

(minä) esittele	*n*	I introduce
(sinä)	*t*	you introduce
hän	*e*	he introduces
(me)	*mme*	we introduce
(te)	*tte*	you introduce
he	*vät*	they introduce

2. No future tense in Finnish

The Finnish language has no specific tense for the future, which is simply expressed by the present. Thus, *minä menen* means:
a) I go
b) I am going
c) I shall (will) go
d) I shall (will) be going

Sanasto — Vocabulary

aika (adv.) (cp. *aika* time)	quite, rather, fairly
+helppo helpon	easy
henkilö-n (cp. *ihminen*)	person; character (in a play)
jo	already
koulu-n	school
laiska-n (≠ *ahkera*)	lazy
milloin?	when?
minu/sta (kuva on kaunis) (cp. *sinusta, hänestä, meistä* etc.)	in my opinion, I think that
+opetta/a opeta/n-t ope**tt**aa opeta/mme-tte ope**tt**avat	to teach, instruct
opiskel/la (opiskele/n-t-e-mme-tte -vat)	to study
+oppi/a opi/n-t o**pp**ii opi/mme-tte o**pp**ivat	to learn
+teh/dä **tee**/n-t te**k**ee **tee**/mme-tte te**k**evät	to do; to make
terve terveen (≠ *sairas*)	healthy, well; hello, cheerio
toivo/a (toivo/n-t-o-mme-tte-vat)	to hope
työ-n olla työssä	work, job to be working, be employed
vaikea-n	difficult, hard

☆

+kasetti kasetin	cassette
kerran	once; some time (in the future)
stipendi-n	scholarship, grant
tuoli-n	chair

James ja Jamesin naapurit

James and James's neighbors

Mattilat asuvat Presidentinkatu 11 B 4:ssä.

1. Kuinka sinä opit niin nopeasti suomea, James?
2. Minulla on huone suomalaisessa perheessä. Heidän nimensä on Mattila. Me puhumme vain suomea, me emme puhu yhtään englantia.
3. Mitä Mattilat tekevät?
4. Matti Mattila on insinööri, joka on työssä isossa firmassa. Hänellä on hyvä palkka. Hänen vaimonsa on lääkäri. Lapset ovat koulussa. He ovat oikein onnellinen perhe.
5. Tunnetko sinä myös naapurit?
6. No, minä tunnen lähimmät naapurit, Niemiset, Uusitalot ja Lindit. Arto Nieminen on liikemies. Vaimo ei ole työssä,

1. How do you learn Finnish so fast, James?
2. I have a room with a Finnish family. Their name is Mattila. We only speak Finnish, we don't speak any English at all.
3. What do the Mattilas do?
4. Matti Mattila is an engineer who works in a big firm. He has a good salary. His wife is a doctor. The children are at school. They are a very happy family.
5. Do you know the neighbors, too?
6. Well, I know the nearest neighbors, the Nieminens, the Uusitalos, and the Linds. Arto Nieminen is a businessman.

hän on kotona. Pojat eivät ole enää koulussa, he opiskelevat yliopistossa. Ville Uusitalo on automekaanikko. Ville ja minä olemme hyvät ystävät. Minä olen usein heillä, koska Ville haluaa oppia englantia.

His wife does not work, she stays at home. The sons are no longer at school, they study at the university. Ville Uusitalo is a car mechanic. We are great friends, Ville and I. I often visit them because Ville wants to learn English.

7. Lind ei ole suomalainen nimi. Ovatko he ulkomaalainen perhe?

7. Lind is not a Finnish name. Are they a foreign family?

8. Eivät. Lindin perhe on suomenruotsalainen. Mutta he puhuvat myös suomea. Rouva Lind on pianisti ja hänen miehensä oopperalaulaja. Lindit soittavat ja laulavat paljon — liian paljon, sanovat muut. Ja Mattilan lapset kysyvät: ''Miksi te ette soita rokkia?''

8. No, the Lind family are Swedish-speaking Finns. But they speak Finnish, too. Mrs. Lind is a pianist and her husband an opera singer. The Linds play and sing a great deal — too much, the others say. And the Mattila children ask, ''Why don't you play rock?''

Missä James asuu? Mattilan **perheessä** = Mattila**lla**

Ketkä ovat Jamesin naapurit?
Mikä perhe puhuu ruotsia?
Mitkä perheet puhuvat suomea?
Mitkä ovat viikonpäivät?

''who''
Kuka tuo mies on? Hän on Matti Mattila, **joka** on insinööri.

minun ystävä	**ni**	my	friend(s)
sinun	**si**	your	
hänen	**nsä**	his	
teidän	**nne**	your	
heidän	**nsä**	their	

Kielioppia — Structural notes

1. Basic form (nominative) plural

kirja	book	*kirja/t*	the books
Brown	(gen. *Browni/n*)	*Browni/t*	the Browns
pieni maa	(gen. *piene/n maa/n*) a small country	*piene/t maa/t*	the small countries

The ending of the basic form plural is **-t.**
If the basic form sing. and the gen. stem are different, the gen. stem is used.

Note: *mikä kirja?* which book? *mi/t/kä kirja/t?*
kuka? who? *ke/t/kä?*

The plurals of *tämä*, *tuo*, *se* are irregular:

tämä	*kirja* this book	*nämä*	*kirja/t* these books
tuo	that book	*nuo*	those books
se	the, that book	*ne*	the, those books

Colloquial variants of *nämä* and *nuo* are *nää* and *noi.*
kaikki is both sing. (''everything'') and pl. (''all, all people, everybody'').

Note also:
Sing. *Liisan ystävä on täällä.* Liisa's friend is here.
Hänen ystävänsä on täällä. Her friend is here.
Pl. *Liisan ystävät ovat täällä.* Liisa's friends are here.
Hänen ystävänsä ovat täällä. Her friends are here.

When followed by a poss. suffix, the basic form sing. and pl. are identical.

2. Present tense negative

olla to be — *minä ole/n*

Negative present		**Negative question**	
(minä) en	*ole* I am not	*en/kö (minä)*	*ole?* am I not?
(sinä) et	you are not	*et/kö (sinä)*	are you not?
hän ei	he is not	*ei/kö hän*	is he not?
(me) emme	we are not	*emme/kö (me)*	are we not?
(te) ette	you are not	*ette/kö (te)*	are you not?
he eivät	they are not	*eivät/kö he*	are they not?

Note that
— the negation changes like a verb: **en, et, ei, emme, ette, eivät;**
— the verb itself does not change: **ole**. This stem is derived from the 1st pers. present tense by dropping the ending **-n.**

Colloquial short forms: *mä en oo* (= *minä en ole*), *sä et oo* (= *sinä et ole*), *et(kö) sä oo* (= *etkö sinä ole*), *eik(ö) se oo* (= *eikö se ole*) etc.

Sanasto — Vocabulary

enää: ei enää	no longer, no more
firma-n	firm, concern, company
insinööri-n	engineer, graduate in engineering
joka jonka (relat. pron.)	who, which, that
koska	because, as, since; when?
kysy/ä (kysy/n-t-y-mme-tte-vät)	to ask (questions)
lapsi lapsen	child, infant
laulaja-n	singer
liian	too, excessively
+liike liikkeen	shop, store; business; motion, movement
liike/mies-miehen	businessman
lääkäri-n	physician, doctor
+mekaanikko mekaanikon	mechanic
miksi?	why?
muu-n	other, else
naapuri-n	neighbor
onnellinen onnellisen (≠ *onneton*)	happy
+palkka palkan	salary; wages; pay
+rokki rokin (= *rock*)	rock music
+tunte/a tu**nne**/n-t tu**nt**ee tu**nne**/mme-tte tu**nt**evat	to know, recognize; to feel (cp. Fr. connaître, Germ. kennen)
usein	often, frequently
yhtään: ei y.	not any, none at all

☆

kissa-n	cat
mitään: ei mitään	nothing
tänne (cp. *täällä*)	here, to this place
vasta/ta (vastaa/n-t vastaa vastaa/mme-tte-vat	to answer, reply; to be responsible
+viikko viikon	week
yhteensä	altogether, in total

Kappale **13** Lesson

Salaisuus — The secret

(Noin vuodelta 1920)

Sirkka tulee ovelta kukkapaketti kädessä.

1. Äiti. Kenelle nuo kukat ovat?
2. S. Nämä kukat? Ne ovat minulle.
3. Ä. Sinulle? Keneltä? Jussiltako taas?
4. S. Niin, häneltä ... Äiti, mihin minä panen nämä kukat?
5. Ä. Mihin? Tälle pöydälle. Tai tuolle pöydälle. Tai tuolille. Tai sohvalle. Tai lattialle, jos haluat. Tai ikkunalle. Mihin vain!
6. S. Äiti, miksi sinä olet minulle vihainen? Siksikö että nämä kukat ovat Jussilta? (Ottaa kirjat pieneltä pöydältä, panee ne tuolille ja kukat pöydälle.)
7. Ä. Mihin sinä menet? Tule tänne ja istu. Minä haluan puhua sinun kanssasi.
8. S. No, mitä nyt?

(From about the year 1920)

Sirkka comes from the door with a package of flowers in her hand.

1. Mother. Who are those flowers for?
2. S. These flowers? They are for me.
3. M. For you? From who? From Jussi again?
4. S. Yes, from him ... Mother, where shall I put these flowers?
5. M. Where? On this table. Or on that table. Or the chair. Or the sofa. Or the floor if you like. Or on the window sill. Anywhere!
6. S. Mother, why are you angry with me? Because these flowers are from Jussi? (She takes the books off the little table, puts them on a chair, and the flowers on the table.)
7. M. Where are you going? Come here and sit down. I want to talk to you.
8. S. Well, what is it now?

9. Ä. Sinä olet joka ilta ulkona Jussin kanssa.
10. S. Niin olen. Entäs (= entä) sitten?
11. Ä. Minä olen sinun äitisi. Minä haluan tietää, mitä te aiotte tehdä.
12. S. Mutta äiti, se on salaisuus!
13. Ä. Kerro minulle. Kyllä sinä voit kertoa äidille kaikki.
14. S. En kerro! Jos minä kerron sinulle, sinä kerrot rouva Lahtiselle ja rouva Lahtinen kertoo rouva Virtaselle ja rouva Virtanen kertoo neiti Laaksolle ja neiti Laakso kertoo kaikille, että minä olen salakihloissa Jussi Lehtisen kanssa!

9. M. You go out every evening with Jussi.
10. S. Yes, I do. So what?
11. M. I'm your mother. I want to know what you intend to do.
12. S. But mother, it's a secret!
13. M. Tell me. Why, you can tell everything to your mother.
14. S. No, I can't. If I tell you, you'll tell Mrs. Lahtinen and Mrs. Lahtinen will tell Mrs. Virtanen and Mrs. Virtanen will tell Miss Laakso and Miss Laakso will tell everybody that I am secretly engaged to Jussi Lehtinen!

Anna minu**lle** anteeksi!

say/tell
Sano ''aa''!
Sano (minulle) mikä päivä tänään on!
Kerro (minulle) mitä sinä teet huomenna!

Kysykää Ville**ltä**!
Ville ei vastaa mei**lle**.

Kielioppia — Structural notes

1. The ''(on)to'' case (allative)

		mihin?	where(to)?
pöytä	*(pöydä/n)*	*pöydä/lle*	on(to) the table
uusi pöytä	*(uude/n pöydän)*	*uude/lle pöydälle*	on(to) the new table
ovi	*(ove/n)*	*ove/lle*	to the door

The ending **-lle** corresponds to the English prepositions ''(on)to'', ''on(to)'', ''to''.
When the gen. stem and the basic form are different, the gen. stem is used.

Note: *mikä pöytä?* — *mi/lle pöydä/lle?*
tämä pöytä — *tä/lle pöydä/lle*
se pöytä — *si/lle pöydä/lle*

The "(on)to" case is also used with verbs denoting giving or telling something to someone:

Minä annan tei/lle kahvia.	I'll give you some coffee.
Kene/lle maksamme kaupassa?	Who do we pay in the shop (= to whom do we give money)?
Ostakaa tämä kirja Liisa/lle!	Buy this book for Liisa!
Voitteko sanoa minu/lle . . . ?	Can you tell me . . . ?
Lapsi vastaa äidi/lle.	The child answers his mother.

Note also:

Pane kukat pöydälle/si!	Put the flowers on your table!
Kerron ystävälle/ni, että . . .	I'll tell my friend that . . .

As always, the poss. suffix follows after the case ending.

2. The "from" case (ablative)

		mistä?	where from?
pöytä	*(pöydä/n)*	*pöydä/ltä*	from, off the table
pieni pöytä	*(piene/n pöydän)*	*piene/ltä pöydältä*	from the small table
ovi	*(ove/n)*	*ove/lta*	from the door

The case ending **-lta (-ltä)** roughly corresponds to the English prepositions "from", "off" (that is, away from somewhere or something).

When the gen. stem and the basic form are different, the gen. stem is used.

Note:	*mikä pöytä?*	*mi/ltä pöydä/ltä?*
	tämä pöytä	*tä/ltä pöydä/ltä*
	se pöytä	*si/ltä pöydä/ltä*

This case is also used with verbs which denote taking or getting something from someone:

Tyttö saa rahaa äidi/ltä.	The girl gets money from her mother.
Kene/ltä nämä kukat ovat?	Who are these flowers from?

In Finnish, people also ask questions "from" someone:

Kysy Liisa/lta, mitä hän tekee huomenna.	Ask Liisa what she's going to do tomorrow.

Note also:

Nämä kukat ovat poikaystävältä/ni.	These flowers are from my boyfriend.
Kysykää opettajalta/nne, miksi. . .	Ask your teacher why. . .

The poss. suffix always follows after the case ending.

Sanasto — Vocabulary

+aiko/a (cp. *aikomus* intention)	to intend, be going to
aio/n-t ai**k**oo	
aio/mme-tte ai**k**ovat	
ikkuna-n	window
+ilta illan	evening
joka (indecl. indef. pron.)	every
jos	if
kanssa	with, in the company of
Jussi/n kanssa	with Jussi
minu/n kanssa/ni	with me
+kerto/a (cp. *kertomus* story)	to tell, relate, narrate
ke**rr**o/n-t ke**rt**oo	
ke**rr**o/mme-tte ke**rt**ovat	
kihloissa	engaged to be married
+kukka kukan	flower, blossom, bloom
käsi käden	hand
lattia-n	floor
mihin?	where to?
mihin vain	anywhere, no matter where (to)
missä vain	anywhere, no matter where
mikä vain	anything, no matter what
milloin vain	anytime, no matter when
noin (abbr. *n.*)	about, approximately; so, like that
+paketti paketin	parcel, package, packet
pan/na (pane/n-t-e-mme-tte-vat)	to put, place
+pöytä pöydän	table
salaisuus salaisuuden	secret
siksi (cp. *miksi*?)	therefore, for that reason
siksi että (= *koska*)	for the reason that, because
taas	again; on the other hand
ulkona (≠ *sisällä*)	outside, out of doors
vihainen vihaisen	angry, cross
vuosi vuoden	year
+äiti äidin	mother, mommy

☆

+anta/a	to give; to let, allow
anna/n-t **ant**aa	
anna/mme-tte **ant**avat	
mistä?	where from? from where?

Kappale **14** Lesson

Ravintolassa on hyvää kalaa

Ilta helsinkiläisessä ravintolassa. James Brown syö tavallisesti täällä.

1. B. Hyvää iltaa, neiti. Onko tämä pöytä vapaa?

2. Tarjoilija. On kyllä. Ruokalista, olkaa hyvä.

3. B. Kiitos. — Ensin tomaattikeittoa. Sitten lihaa tai kalaa. Onko teillä tänään hyvää kalaa?

4. T. Meillä on oikein hyvää paistettua kalaa.

5. B. Hyvä on, minä otan sitä. Sitten leipää ja voita. Ja maitoa.

6. T. Iso vai pieni lasi?

7. B. Iso. Ei, hetkinen ... Mitä olutta teillä on?

8. T. Meillä on "Hippiä" ja "Hoppia".

9. B. Pullo olutta sitten, minä otan Hoppia. Saanko myös kylmää vettä?

10. T. Tuon kyllä.

11. B. Sitten jälkiruokaa. Jäätelöä ja pieni kuppi kahvia.

James syö ja juo. Sitten hän sanoo tarjoilijalle:

12. B. Neiti, lasku! (Maksaa.) Hyvää yötä! (James lähtee.)

There's good fish at the restaurant

An evening in a restaurant in Helsinki. James Brown usually eats here.

1. B. Good evening. Is this table free?

2. Waitress. Yes, it is. Here's the menu, sir.

3. B. Thank you. — First tomato soup. Then meat or fish. Do you have good fish today?

4. W. We have very good fried fish.

5. B. Good, I'll take that ("some of it"). Then bread and butter. And milk.

6. W. A large glass or small?

7. B. Large, please. No, just a moment ... What beer do you have?

8. W. We have "Hippi" and "Hoppi".

9. B. A bottle of beer, then; I'll take Hoppi. May I have some cold water, too?

10. W. Yes, I'll bring you some.

11. B. Then the dessert. Ice-cream and a small cup of coffee.

James eats and drinks. Then he says to the waitress:

12. B. Waitress, the check, please! (He pays.) Good night! (James leaves.)

Mitä ruokaa te otatte?
Matti. Minä otan **tätä** (= some of this).
Jussi. Minä otan **tuota** (= some of that).
Pekka. Minä otan myös **sitä** (= some of it).
Liisa. Minä **en** ota **mitään**.

Haluatko kahvia? Ei kiitos.
Otatko teetä? (Kyllä) kiitos.

Saanko kylmää vettä?
Ole hyvä/Olkaa hyvä (said when you give something to someone)!

öy-yö-uo y**ö**p**öy**tä, t**yö**p**öy**tä, **tuo** p**öy**tä, **ruo**kap**öy**tä
s**yö**kää ja **juo**kaa, pöydällä on **ruo**kaa!

Kielioppia — Structural notes

1. Partitive singular

Basic form		**Partitive**	
Onko sinulla auto?	Do you have a car?	*Onko sinulla raha/a?*	Do you have money?
Kahvi on kuuma juoma.	Coffee is a hot beverage.	*Saanko kahvi/a?*	May I have some coffee please?
Tämä maa on Suomi.	This country (land) is Finland.	*Virtaset ostavat maa/ta.*	The Virtanens will buy (some) land.
Onko olut jääkaapissa?	Is the beer in the refrigerator?	*Ahaa, sinä haluat olut/ta.*	I see, you want some beer.

The basic meaning of the partitive sing. is indefinite quantity (in English often ''some'', ''any'', or a noun without an article) in contrast to the basic form which denotes definite quantity (''the beer'') or entity (''a car''; ''coffee'', the whole category).

In its basic meaning, the partitive sing. is used of material nouns and other uncountables. Uncountable words have no plural, they cannot be counted (you cannot say ''the butters'' or ''five musics''). Countables can have pl. forms (''the cups'' or ''five songs'').

However, all Finnish nouns and adjectives have their part. forms, as the part. is a frequently used form with several different functions. Some of these will be discussed in lessons 14—17, others will come later, and they will be reviewed after lesson 39, p. 207.

Structure

The ending is	**-a (-ä)** after one vowel: *kahvi/a, leipä/ä*
	-ta (-tä) after two vowels or a consonant: *maa/ta, olut/ta*

The stem may differ from the basic form if the word ends in **-i**, **-e**, or a consonant. Otherwise the part. sing. ending can be added directly to the basic form. From now on, the part. sing. of each new noun will be included in the vocabulary and should be memorized along with the basic form and the gen. sing. (The irregular part. sing. forms of the nouns covered up to now are listed on p. 70. The part. sing. forms of the nouns in lessons 1—21 can be looked up in a list arranged by inflection types on p. 99.)

Note. The following word types have part. sing. stems which differ from the basic form:

— **i→e** words, e.g.	*onni*	*(onnen)*	*onne/a*
	pieni	*(pienen)*	*pien/tä*
	vesi	*(veden)*	*vet/tä*
— **huone** words	*huone*	*(huoneen)*	*huonet/ta*
— **nainen** words	*nainen*	*(naisen)*	*nais/ta*
— **salaisuus** words	*salaisuus*	*(salaisuuden)*	*salaisuut/ta*

As usual, adjectives and pronouns agree with the noun:

Millais/ta kahvi/a haluat?	What kind of coffee do you want?
Hyvä/ä, kuuma/a kahvi/a.	Good hot coffee.
Onko teillä minulle helppo/a työ/tä?	Do you have some easy work for me?

Note also:	*mikä leipä?*	*mi/tä leipä/ä?*
	tämä leipä	*tä/tä leipä/ä*
	tuo leipä	*tuo/ta leipä/ä* (colloq. *to/ta*)[1]
	se leipä	*si/tä leipä/ä*

Possessive suffixes, as always, come after the partitive ending:

Haluatko suklaata/ni?	Do you want some of my chocolate?
Pöydällä on sinun rahaa/si.	Some of your money is on the table.

Important to remember:
The partitive is not used as the subject of the sentence (except in "there is" sentences, 17:1).

---

[1] The form *tuota (tota)* is generally used as a fill-in word to start or to interrupt a statement:

Tuota — mitä minä nyt teen?	Well — what shall I do now?
Voit sä — tota tota — lainata kaks sataa?	Can you — well — lend me 200 marks?

KAHVI
Bad mistake: ~~*Kahvia*~~ *maksaa paljon.*

(The part. pl. will be explained in 21:1.)

2. Special uses of partitive

The partitive is used after words indicating measure or quantity:

lasi vet/tä	a glass of water
iso kuppi kahvi/a	a large cup of coffee
vähän musiikki/a	a little music
paljon työ/tä	a lot of work

The partitive is used in greetings, wishes, and exclamations:

Hyvä/ä yö/tä!	Good night!
Hauska/a ilta/a!	Have a nice evening!
Ihana/a!	How wonderful!

Sanasto — Vocabulary

ensin	(at) first
juo/da (juo/n-t juo juo/mme-tte -vat)	to drink
+jälki/ruoka-a-ruoan or -ruuan (always pronounced *ruuan*)	dessert (''after-food'')
jäätelö-ä-n (cp. *jää* ice)	icecream
kala-a-n	fish
+keitto-a keiton	soup
lasku-a laskun	check, bill
+leipä-ä leivän	bread, loaf
liha-a-n	meat; flesh
+lähte/ä läh**d**e/n-t läh**t**ee läh**d**e/mme-tte läh**t**evät	to leave, depart, go
+maito-a maidon	milk
olut-ta oluen	beer
+paistettu-a paistetun	fried, roasted
pullo-a-n	bottle
ravintola-a-n	restaurant
ruoka/lista-a-n	menu (''food-list'')
syö/dä (syö/n-t syö syö/mme-tte -vät)	to eat
tarjoilija-a-n (from *tarjoilla* to serve, wait)	waiter, waitress

tavallisesti	usually, ordinarily
+tomaatti-a tomaatin	tomato
tuo/da (tuo/n-t tuo tuo/mme-tte-vat) (≠ *viedä*)	to bring; to import
vapaa-ta-n	free; vacant
vesi vettä veden	water
voi-ta-n	butter
yö-tä-n	night

☆

ihana-a-n	wonderful, lovely
+salaatti-a salaatin	salad; lettuce

Irregular part. sing. forms of nouns in lessons 1—13

i→e words
+kaikki kaikkea kaiken 4
kivi kiveä kiven 1
nimi nimeä nimen 5
onni onnea onnen 9
ovi ovea oven 8
Suomi Suomea Suomen 1

kieli kieltä kielen 3
nuori nuorta nuoren 2
pieni pientä pienen 2
lapsi lasta lapsen 12

käsi kättä käden 13
uusi uutta uuden 2
vuosi vuotta vuoden 13

huone words
huone-tta huoneen 1
kappale-tta kappaleen 1
+liike-ttä liikkeen 12
+osoite-tta osoitteen 5
perhe-ttä perheen 6
terve-ttä terveen 11
Exception:
+nukke-a nuken 6

nainen words
nainen naista naisen 1
hetkinen hetkistä hetkisen 9
ihminen ihmistä ihmisen 10
millainen millaista millaisen 2
onnellinen onnellista onnellisen 12
suomalainen suomalaista suomalaisen 3
vihainen vihaista vihaisen 13

salaisuus words
salaisuus salaisuutta salaisuuden 13

Pronouns:
minä minua minun 3
sinä sinua sinun 3
me meitä meidän 9
te teitä teidän 4
he heitä heidän 9

tämä tätä tämän (pl. nämä) 1
se sitä sen (pl. ne) 1

mikä mitä minkä (pl. mitkä) 1
kuka ketä kenen (pl. ketkä) 1
joka jota jonka (pl. jotka) 12

Numerals:
yksi yhtä yhden 7
kaksi kahta kahden 7
kolme-a kolmen 7
viisi viittä viiden 7
kuusi kuutta kuuden 7
seitsemän seitsemää seitsemän 7
kahdeksan kahdeksaa kahdeksan 7
yhdeksän yhdeksää yhdeksän 7
kymmenen kymmentä kymmenen 7
yksi/toista yhtä/toista yhden/toista 7
kaksi/kymmentä kahta/kymmentä kahden/kymmenen 7

Vaikea asiakas

1. Asiakas. Neiti, mikä tämä on?
2. Tarjoilija. Se on lautanen.
3. A. Ei, *tämä* tässä! Mikä tämä on, sanokaa!
4. T. Se on pihvi.
5. A. Hyvä neiti, se ei ole pihvi. Se ei ole lihaa.
6. T. Mitä se sitten on?
7. A. Se on nahkaa. Vanhaa nahkaa. Viekää se pois! Heti! Ja sanokaa, mitä tuo on?
8. T. Se on kahvia.
9. A. Kahvia kahvia. Mutta millaista se on?
10. T. Hyvää kai. Tämän ravintolan kahvi on aina hyvää.
11. A. Ja kuumaa?
12. T. Ja kuumaa, aivan niin.
13. A. Mutta tämä kahvi on huonoa. Ja aivan kylmää. Viekää se pois! Millainen ravintola tämä on: tuoli on kova, tarjoilija on huono, liha on vanhaa, kahvi on kylmää, vesi on lämmintä, kaikki ruoka on kallista. Viekää kaikki pois. Hyvästi!

A difficult customer

1. Customer. Waitress, what is this?
2. Waitress. It's a plate.
3. C. No, *this* here! What is this, tell me?
4. W. It's a steak.
5. C. Young lady, it isn't a steak. It isn't meat.
6. W. What is it then?
7. C. It is leather. Old leather. Take it away! At once! And tell me what that is?
8. W. It's coffee.
9. C. Coffee, of course. But what's it like?
10. W. Good, I suppose. Coffee is always good in this restaurant.
11. C. And hot?
12. W. And hot, yes.
13. C. But this coffee is bad. And completely cold. Take it away! What kind of restaurant is this? The chair is hard, the waitress is bad, the meat is old, the coffee is cold, the water is warm, all the food is expensive. Take everything away. Goodbye!

long vowels in later syllables	olk**aa** hyvä ja sanok**aa** **aa**, olk**aa** hyvä ja sanok**aa** **ää**! hyv**ää** ilt**aa**, s**aa**nko lih**aa**, kal**aa** ja leip**ää**? tän**ää**n hän ott**aa** hyv**ää** j**ää**telöä
diphthongs in -i	**lei**pä ja **voi** v**ai**n m**ai**toa, n**ei**ti **ei** k**ai** **ai**van **oi**kein on **ai**na v**ai**kea sanoa **ei**
yö-uo	hän s**yö** ja j**uo**, **yö**t**yö**, t**uo** t**yö**, t**uo** **yö**, t**uo** mies j**uo** m**yö**s
hv	pi**hv**i ja ka**hv**i **hv**yää ka**hv**ia

Tarjoilija **tuo** keittoa.

Tarjoilija **vie** lasit pois.

Kielioppia — Structural notes

1. "What is this?" — "What is it like?"

Mikä tämä on?	*Millainen se on?*	*Mi/tä tämä on?*	*Millais/ta se on?*
Se on kuppi.	*Se on pieni.*	*Se on kahvi/a.*	*Se on kuuma/a.*
What is this?	What is it like?	What is this?	What is it like?
It's a cup.	It's small.	It's coffee.	It's hot.

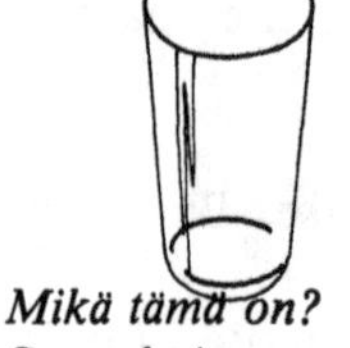

Mikä tämä on?	*Millainen se on?*	*Mi/tä tämä on?*	*Millais/ta se on?*
Se on lasi.	*Lasi on iso.*	*Se on maito/a.*	*Maito on kylmä/ä.*
It's a glass.	The glass is big.	It's milk.	The milk is cold.

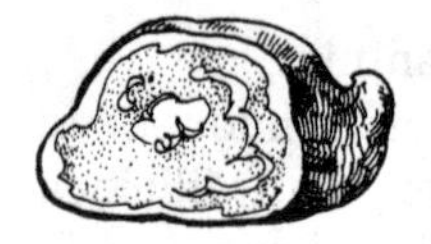

Mikä tuo on?	*Millainen se on?*	*Mi/tä tuo on?*	*Millais/ta se on?*
Se on pihvi.	*Se on hyvä.*	*Se on liha/a.*	*Se on hyvä/ä.*
It's a steak.	It's good.	It's meat.	It's good.

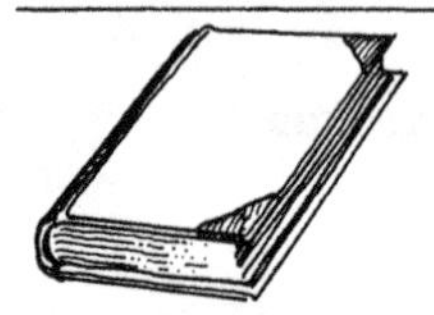

Mikä tämä on?	*Millainen se on?*	*Mi/tä tämä on?*	*Millais/ta se on?*
Se on kirja.	*Se on halpa.*	*Se on paperi/a.*	*Se on halpa/a.*
It's a book.	It's cheap.	It's paper.	It's cheap.

Mikä tämä on?	*Minkälainen se on?*	*Mi/tä tämä on?*	*Minkälais/ta se on?*
Se on laulu.	*Se on kaunis.*	*Se on musiikki/a.*	*Se on kaunis/ta.*
It's a song.	It's beautiful.	It's music.	It's beautiful.

mitä is the partitive of *mikä*.

When, in questions of the type ''what is this?'' you ask about a single object, a countable, use *mikä* (answer: *kuppi*). When asking about a substance or material, or other uncountables, use *mitä* (answer: *kahvia*).

When, in questions of the type ''what is this like?'' you ask about a single object, a countable, use *millainen* or *minkälainen* (answer: *pieni*). When asking about a substance or material, or other uncountables, use *millaista* or *minkälaista* (answer: *kuumaa*).

LIHA
Bad mistake: ~~*Lihaa*~~ *on hyvää.*

(More about the complement of the verb ''to be'' in 22:1 and 34:2.)

Sanasto	Vocabulary
aivan	quite, exactly, precisely
aivan niin	exactly, just so, that's it
+asiakas-ta asiakkaan	customer, client
heti	at once, immediately
hyvästi!	goodbye
kai	probably, very likely, I suppose
kova-a-n (≠ *pehmeä*)	hard (not soft); severe, strict
kuuma-a-n (≠ *kylmä*)	hot
lautanen lautasta lautasen	plate
lämmin-tä lämpimän (≠ *kylmä*)	warm
minkä/lainen-laista-laisen? (= *millainen?*)	what ... like? what kind of?
+nahka-a nah(k)an	leather, skin
pihvi-ä-n	steak
pois	away, off
tässä (cp. *täällä*)	right here
vie/dä (vie/n-t vie vie/mme-tte-vät) (≠ *tuoda)*	to take (somewhere); to export

☆

kuin	as; than

Kuinka monta?

James Brown on tavallinen mukava nuori mies, joka on 20 vuotta vanha. Hän on 180 senttiä pitkä ja painaa 75 kiloa. Hänellä on rahaa 10 markkaa 50 penniä.

Jamesilla on niin vähän rahaa, koska hän oli juuri ostoksilla.

■■■

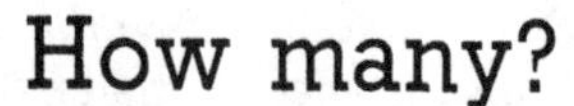

James Brown is an ordinary, nice young man, who is twenty years old. He is 180 cm tall and weighs 75 kg. He has 10 marks 50 pennies.

James has so little money because he just went shopping.

■■■

Nyt James tekee ruokaa Mattilan keittiössä. Mutta hän ei ole siellä yksin. Mattilan Tapani on myös siellä, ja Tiina, perheen toinen lapsi, tulee juuri sisään. Tapani on kymmenen ja Tiina seitsemän vuotta vanha. Tiinalla on kaksi kissaa. Toinen on valkoinen, toinen musta. Ne juovat maitoa keittiössä. Lapset syövät jäätelöä ja puhuvat Jamesin kanssa.

Montako huonetta Mattilan perheellä on? Neljä huonetta ja keittiö.

■■■

Now James is cooking in Mattila's kitchen. But he is not there alone. Tapani Mattila is also there, and Tiina, the other child of the family, is just coming in. Tapani is ten and Tiina seven years old. Tiina has two cats, one of them white, the other one black. They are drinking milk in the kitchen. The children are eating icecream and talking to James.

How many rooms does the Mattila family have? Four rooms and a kitchen.

■■■

Liisalla on 15 mk ja Lailalla 28 mk. Paljonko rahaa heillä on yhteensä?

Liisa has 15 marks and Laila 28 marks. How much money do they have altogether?

Kuinka monta (= montako) autoa?

yksi auto

pari autoa
(pari autoa = 2—3)

monta autoa

Kielioppia — Structural notes

1. Partitive singular with cardinal numbers

Partitive singular is used after cardinal numbers (except *yksi* one) and after the word *monta* many:

yksi kirja	but: *kaksi kirja/a*	two books
yksi talo	*kolme talo/a*	three houses
yksi mies	*sata mies/tä*	a hundred men
yksi omena	*kuinka monta omena/a?*	how many apples?
yksi salaisuus	*monta salaisuut/ta*	many secrets

If the subject of a sentence consists of a cardinal number + noun, the verb will be in the singular:

(Yksi) kirja maksaa 30 markkaa.
Kaksi kirjaa maksaa 60 markkaa.
Kolme autoa tulee Mikonkadulle.

2. About foreign loanwords in Finnish

Finnish, like all languages, has borrowed words from other tongues during the different periods of its history, mostly from the neighboring Indo-European languages.

Most loanwords from other languages (except for the most recent) have been ''Finnicized''
— by changing foreign consonants to their domestic equivalents, esp. **b, d, g** to **p, t, k** (e.g. *kulta* gold);

— by dropping initial consonants except for the last (e.g. *koulu* school, *Ranska* France);
— by adding a final vowel, most typically **-i**, to words ending in a consonant (e.g. *pommi* bomb, *lasi* glass).

Examples: viikko, minuutti, numero, pankki, metalli, passi, silkki, nailon, sokeri, kakku, riisi, vitamiini, konsertti, orkesteri, sirkus, tennis, kulttuuri, akateeminen, fysiikka, matematiikka, teksti, tyyli, arkkitehtuuri, huumori, normaali, romanttinen, romantiikka, atomi, tekniikka, politiikka, ministeri, prinssi, senaatti, sosialisti, kommunismi, kameli, tiikeri, tulppaani, kaktus, temppeli, alttari, paratiisi.

Sanasto — Vocabulary

gramma-a-n (abbr. *g*)	gram
juuri	just, exactly
juusto-a-n	cheese
keittiö-tä-n	kitchen
kilo-a-n (abbr. *kg*)	kilogram
litra-a-n (abbr. *l*)	liter
makkara-a-n	sausage
moni monta monen	many
montako? = kuinka monta?	how many?
muna-a-n	egg
musta-a-n	black
myyjä-ä-n (from *myy/dä* to sell)	salesclerk; vendor
+nakki-a nakin	frankfurter
ostoksilla:	
olla o.	to be shopping
mennä ostoksille	to go shopping
paina/a (paina/n-t-a-mme-tte-vat)	to weigh (= have a certain weight); to press; to print
pitkä-ä-n (≠ *lyhyt*)	long; tall
puoli puolta puolen	half; side
+sentti-ä sentin (abbr. *cm*)	centimeter; cent
sisään (≠ *ulos*)	in; "come in!"
tavallinen tavallista tavallisen	usual, ordinary, frequent
toinen toista toisen	other, another; second; one of the two
toinen . . . toinen	one . . . the other
vuoro-a-n	turn; shift (at work)

☆

+pankki-a pankin	bank
pari-a-n	pair; couple; two or three

Jamesilla on radio, mutta ei televisiota

Tässä kuvassa on James Brownin huone. Kuten näet, huoneessa on kirjoituspöytä. Oikealla on sänky ja vasemmalla mukava tuoli. Kun James on kotona, hän istuu siinä ja lukee. Tuolin lähellä on kirjahylly ja siinä monta kirjaa. Kirjat ovat Jamesin. Huoneen toisella puolella on pari muuta tuolia. Jamesilla ei ole televisiota, mutta pöydällä on pieni radio.

James has a radio but no television

This is a picture of James Brown's room. As you can see, there is a writing-desk in the room. On the right there is a bed and on the left a comfortable chair. When James is at home, he sits in it and reads. Near the chair there is a book-shelf with many books. The books belong to James. On the other side of the room there are two or three other chairs. James has no television but there is a little radio on the desk.

17

Huone ei ole suuri, mutta se on tarpeeksi suuri Jamesille. Tällä nuorella miehellä ei ole vielä perhettä, ei vaimoa eikä lasta. Ja hän aikoo olla Suomessa vain puolitoista vuotta. Mistä hän saa rahaa? Onko hän työssä vai onko hänellä rikas perhe? James ei ole enää työssä, koska hänellä ei nyt ole työlupaa. Hänen perheensä ei ole rikas eikä köyhä, mutta hänellä on pieni stipendi, ja joskus perhe lähettää hänelle vähän rahaa.

The room is not large, but it is large enough for James. This young man has no family as yet, neither wife nor child. And he intends to stay in Finland for only a year and a half. Where does he get his money from? Does he work, or has he got a rich family? James no longer works because he does not have a work permit now. His family is neither rich nor poor, but he has a small scholarship, and his family sometimes sends him a little money.

iso — suuri
iso t. suuri huone *(concrete)*
suuri ja vaikea kysymys *(abstract)*

''stay''

Peter on Turussa kaksi päivää. — Peter will stay in Turku for two days.

Hän asuu Grand-hotellissa. — He will be staying at the Grand Hotel.

(About **stay** remain, not go away, see 34.)

Minulla on kiire!	Minulla on jano.	Minulla on nälkä.	Minulla on kylmä.	Minulla on kuuma (lämmin).	Minulla on hyvä olla.	Minulla on paha olla.

Kielioppia — Structural notes

1. ''there is, there are'' sentences

Pöydällä on kuppi.	There is a cup on the table.
Kupissa on tee/tä.	There is tea in the cup.
Pöydällä ei ole kuppi/a.	There is no cup on the table.
Kupissa ei ole tee/tä.	There is no tea in the cup.

''there is, there are'' in Finnish is simply **on**, negative **ei ole.**
The thing that is not there is generally in the partitive. The word-order differs from that of an English sentence:

1. place	2. ''there is''	3. the thing that is there
pöydällä	*on*	*kuppi*
(''on the table	there is	a cup'')

The Finnish word-order shows that it is *a* cup, something that has not been mentioned before; its existence is introduced here for the first time. (Such sentences are called **introductory** or **existential sentences.**)

If the word-order changes, the meaning changes, too:

Kuppi on pöydällä.	The cup is on the table.
Kuppi ei ole pöydällä.	The cup is not on the table.

Question:

Onko pöydällä kuppi?	Is there a cup on the table?
(kuppi/a?)	(''Is there on the table a cup?'')

The partitive is fairly common in the question. It implies that even a negative answer will not be unexpected.

Negative question:

Eikö pöydällä ole kuppi/a?	Isn't there any cup on the table?
	(''Isn't there on the table any cup?'')

Note: Remember that outside the ''there is, there are'' type of sentences, the subject is rarely in the partitive.

2. ''have'' sentences

Miehellä on markka.	The man has a mark.
Hänellä on pikkuraha/a.	He has small change.
Naisella ei ole markka/a.	The woman does not have a mark.
Hänellä ei ole pikkuraha/a.	She doesn't have small change.

The thing **not** possessed is generally in the partitive.

Question:

Onko tytöllä markka? *(markka/a?)*	Does the girl have a mark?

The partitive in the question implies that even a negative answer will not be unexpected.

Negative question:

Eikö pojalla ole markka/a?	Doesn't the boy have a mark?

Note:

Minulla on nälkä, kylmä etc.	I am hungry, cold etc.
Minulla ei ole nälkä, kylmä etc.	I am not hungry, cold etc.
Onko sinulla/eikö sinulla ole jano?	Are you/are you not thirsty?

In certain expressions using ''have'' (but not expressing possession), the partitive is not used in the negative sentence.

Note also:
As the sentence *hänellä on rahaa* actually means ''there is money in his possession'', the Finnish ''have'' structure is mostly limited to subjects who can possess something, esp. to human beings. Otherwise, the ''there is'' structure is preferred:

Huoneessa on iso ikkuna.	The room has a large window.
Suomessa on noin 5 000 000 asukasta.	Finland has about 5,000,000 inhabitants.

Sanasto — Vocabulary

Sanasto	Vocabulary
ei ... eikä	neither ... nor
hylly-ä-n	shelf
joskus	some time; sometimes
+kirjoitus/pöytä-ä-pöydän	writing-desk
kun	when; (sometimes also:) because
kuten	like, as, such as
köyhä-ä-n	poor (= not rich)
+luke/a	to read
l**ue**/n-t lu**k**ee	
l**ue**/mme-tte lu**k**evat	
lähellä	near, close to, close by
pöydä/n lähellä	near the table
+lähettä/ä	to send
lähe**t**ä/n-t lähe**tt**ää	
lähe**t**ä/mme-tte lähe**tt**ävät	
+näh/dä	to see
n**äe**/n-t nä**k**ee	
n**äe**/mme-tte nä**k**evät	
puoli/toista	one and a half
(cp. *kaksi ja puoli*	2 1/2)
+rikas-ta rikkaan	rich
siinä ("in" case of *se*)	in it; (right) there
suuri suurta suuren (≠ *pieni*)	big, large; great
+sänky-ä sängyn	bed
tarpeeksi	enough
+työ/lupa-a-luvan	work permit

☆

jano-a-n	thirst
kiire-ttä-en	haste, hurry
minulla on kiire	I'm in a hurry, I'm busy
paha-a-n (≠ *hyvä*)	bad, ill, evil, wicked
minulla on paha olla	I feel bad, I feel ill
+nälkä-ä nälän	hunger
puu-ta-n	tree; wood

Kappale **18** Lesson

Toinen vaikea asiakas

1. Asiakas. Tämä kamera täytyy vaihtaa. Se ei toimi.
2. Nuori mies. Vai niin. Mikä vika siinä on?
3. A. En minä tiedä. Se ei toimi, se on rikki, kuuletteko?
4. N. Kuulen, minulla on hyvät korvat. Mutta ...
5. A. Katsokaa itse, filmi ei liiku. Näettekö?
6. N. Näen, minulla on hyvät silmät. Mutta miksi ...
7. A. Minulla on kiire. Antakaa minulle heti toinen, parempi kamera! Vai onko teillä jalat?
8. N. On, minulla on kaksi jalkaa.
9. A. Ja kaksi kättä? Jos on, niin ottakaa tämä kamera ja tuokaa minulle toinen. Nopeasti!
10. N. Kuulkaa nyt, hyvä herra ...
11. A. No mitä te vielä haluatte sanoa? Puhukaa! Onko teillä suu, onko teillä kieli? Ettekö te ymmärrä mitään! Minkälainen myyjä te oikein olette?
12. N. En minä ole myyjä. Minä olen asiakas!

Another difficult customer

1. Customer. This camera must be changed. It doesn't work.
2. Young man. I see. What's wrong with it?
3. C. I don't know. It doesn't work, it's broken, do you hear?
4. Y. Yes, I do, I've got good ears. But ...
5. C. Look for yourself, the film doesn't move. Do you see?
6. Y. Yes, I do, I've got good eyes. But why ...
7. C. I'm in a hurry. Give me another, better camera at once! Have you got legs?
8. Y. Yes, I've got two legs.
9. C. And two hands? If so, take this camera and bring me another one. Quick!
10. Y. Now listen, sir ...
11. C. Well, what else do you want to say? Speak up! Have you got a mouth, have you got a tongue? Don't you understand anything? What kind of a sales assistant are you?
12. Y. I'm not a sales assistant. I'm a customer!

hyvä — parempi — paras

"when"
Milloin tulet meille?
Kun tulet meille, saat kahvia ja kakkua.

Sanasto — Vocabulary

Sanasto	Vocabulary
itse-ä-n	self; myself, yourself etc.
+jalka-a jalan	foot; leg
kamera-a-n	camera
korva-a-n	ear
kuul/la (kuule/n-t-e-mme-tte-vat) (cp. *kuulo* hearing)	to hear
+liikku/a (cp. *liike* motion) lii**k**u/n-t lii**kk**uu lii**k**u/mme-tte lii**kk**uvat	to move, be in motion
mikään mitään minkään	any, anything
ei mikään	no, not any, nothing
paras-ta parhaan	best
+parempi parempaa paremman	better
rikki	broken; in pieces
silmä-ä-n	eye
suu-ta-n	mouth
toimi/a (toimi/n-t-i-mme-tte-vat)	to act; to function, work, operate
täytyy	must
+vaihta/a vaih**d**a/n-t vaih**t**aa vaih**d**a/mme-tte vaih**t**avat	to change, exchange
+vika-a vian	fault, defect, something wrong

Kappale 19 Lesson

Bussissa ja raitiovaunussa

Ystävämme James nousee bussiin. Hänen täytyy mennä Eiraan. Hänen uusi työpaikkansa on siellä.

1. J. Meneekö tämä bussi keskustaan? — Mitä lippu maksaa?
2. Kuljettaja. Kertalippu . . . , kymmenen matkan lippu . . . markkaa.
3. J. Antakaa minulle kymmenen matkan lippu. Mikä raitiovaunu menee Eiraan?
4. K. Numero 3.
5. J. Ja missä minun täytyy vaihtaa?
6. K. Stockmannin pysäkillä.
7. J. Monesko pysäkki se on?
8. K. Neljäs.

Koska on aamu, bussi on täynnä. Jamesin täytyy seisoa koko matka. Mihin kaikki menevät? Yksi menee työhön, toinen kauppaan, kolmas kouluun, neljäs yliopistoon . . .

James vaihtaa raitiovaunuun numero 3.

9. J. Menen Eiraan, osoite on Tehtaankatu 23. Voitteko sanoa minulle milloin minun täytyy nousta pois. Onko se pitkä matka?
10. K. Ei, aivan lyhyt, noin viisi minuuttia.

On the bus and streetcar

Our friend James gets on a bus. He has to go to Eira. His new job is there.

1. J. Does this bus go to the Center? — What does a ticket cost?
2. Bus driver. A single ticket is . . . , a ten-trip card is . . . marks.
3. J. Give me a ten-trip card. Which streetcar goes to Eira?
4. B. Number three.
5. J. And where do I have to change?
6. B. At the Stockmann stop.
7. J. How many stops is it from here?
8. B. The fourth.

Because it is morning, the bus is full. James has to stand all the way. Where are all the people going? One goes to work, another to a store, a third to school, a fourth to the university . . .

James changes to streetcar number three.

9. J. I'm going to Eira, the address is Tehtaankatu 23. Can you tell me please when I have to get off. Is it a long way?
10. B. No, quite short, about five minutes.

James istuu ja katselee ulos. Hän ajattelee: ''Kaunis päivä. Tänään lähden Porvooseen Ritvan kanssa.''
Vaunu tulee Eiraan, Tehtaankadulle.

James sits and looks out. He thinks, ''Fine day. Today I'll go to Porvoo with Ritva.''
The streetcar comes to Tehtaankatu in Eira.

11. K. Seuraava pysäkki!
12. J. Paljon kiitoksia, näkemiin.

11. B. Next stop, sir!
12. J. Thanks a lot, goodbye.

ensimmäinen — ensin
Näetkö nuo pojat? **Ensimmäinen** on Eero, toinen Leo, kolmas Ari. He nousevat bussiin. **Ensin** nousee Eero, sitten Leo ja Ari.

minun koti	**ni**	meidän koti	**mme**
sinun	**si**	teidän	**nne**
hänen	**nsa**	heidän	**nsa**

rt	kertalippu, ka**rt**ta, postiko**rt**ti
ht-hd	vai**hd**an bussia, lä**hd**en La**ht**een, **Aht**i vai**ht**aa, **Aht**i lä**ht**ee La**ht**een
äy-au	vaunu on **täy**nnä, **Tau**non **täy**tyy vaihtaa **vau**nua

Kielioppia — Structural notes

1. The ''into'' case (illative)

a)

maa	country	*maa/han*	to a country
työ	work	*työ/hön*	to work
tiistai	Tuesday	*tiistai/hin*	until Tuesday

One-syllable words have the ''into'' ending **h + vowel + n**, the vowel being the same as the one before **h**.
All stems ending in a diphthong also take this ending.

b)

Porvoo			*Porvoo/seen* to Porvoo
huone	*(huonee/n)*	room	*huonee/seen* into the room
kaunis	*(kaunii/n)*	beautiful	*kaunii/seen*
hidas	*(hitaa/n)*	slow	*hitaa/seen*

Longer stems ending in a **long vowel** have the ending **-seen**; the stem comes from the genitive.

c) *talo*		house	*talo/on*	into a house
sauna			*sauna/an*	into a sauna
Suomi	*(Suome/n)*		*Suome/en*	to Finland
toinen	*(toise/n)*	other	*toise/en*	
mies	*(miehe/n)*	man	*miehe/en*	into the man

The largest group of Finnish nouns have a stem ending in **one short vowel**. Their "into" case ending is **a prolongation of the final vowel of the stem + n.**

However, if their gen. stem differs from the basic form in regard to the **k p t** changes, the consonant of the basic form must be used:

koti	*(kodi/n)*	home	*koti/in*	(into the) home
Turku	*(Turu/n)*		*Turku/un*	to Turku
kirkko	*(kirko/n)*	church	*kirkko/on*	to church
Lahti	*(Lahde/n)*		*Lahte/en*	to Lahti
parempi	*(paremma/n)*	better	*parempa/an*	

Note: *vesi (vede/n) vete/en* into water
käsi (käde/n) käte/en into the hand

mikä maa? *mi/hin maa/han?*
tämä maa *tä/hän maa/han*
se maa *sii/hen maa/han*

Note also:

Menen kotii/ni.	I'm going to my home.
Mene huoneesee/si!	Go to your room!
Panetteko sokeria teehe/nne?	Do you put sugar in your tea?

The "into" case ending drops its final **-n** before possessive suffixes.
(About the "into" form see also 24:2.)
The "into" case is used extensively of place-names (city districts, towns and cities, countries, continents etc.):

James Brown tulee Töölö/ön,	James Brown comes to Töölö,
Helsinki/in,	Helsinki,
Suome/en,	Finland,
Eurooppa/an.	Europe.

(More about the place-names in 27:3.)

2. Ordinal numbers

Kuinka mones? = Monesko? Which in order ("the how-manieth")?

ensimmäinen (ensimmäistä ensimmäisen) the 1st
toinen (toista toisen) 2nd

kolmas (kolmatta kolmannen)	3rd
neljäs (neljättä neljännen)	4th
viides (viidettä viidennen)	5th
kuudes (kuudetta kuudennen)	6th
seitsemäs (seitsemättä seitsemännen)	7th
kahdeksas (kahdeksatta kahdeksannen)	8th
yhdeksäs (yhdeksättä yhdeksännen)	9th
kymmenes (kymmenettä kymmenennen)	10th
yhdes/toista (yhdettä/toista yhdennen/toista)	11th
kahdes/toista	12th
kolmas/toista	13th
kahdes/kymmenes	20th
kahdes/kymmenes/yhdes	21st
kahdes/kymmenes/kahdes	22nd
sadas (sadatta sadannen)	100th
kolmas/sadas/kuudes/kymmenes/viides	365th
tuhannes (tuhannetta tuhannennen)	1000th
miljoonas (miljoonatta miljoonannen)	1 000 000th

Note:
Turku, 10. syyskuuta 1985 (= 10.9.1985)
Ranskan Napoleon I ja III, Englannin Elisabet I ja II
Eilen oli Helsinki-maraton. Meidän Pekka oli 236:s.

3. "minun täytyy lähteä"

minun	*täytyy lähteä*	I	must go
sinun		you	
hänen		he	
meidän		we	
teidän		you	
heidän		they	

Kallen täytyy soittaa kotiin.	Kalle must call home.
Perheen täytyy ottaa laina.	The family must take a loan.
Tämän opiskelijan täytyy saada stipendi.	This student must get a scholarship.
Kenen täytyy viedä koira ulos tänään?	Who must take the dog out today?

Question: *Täytyy/kö* | *sinun lähteä?*
meidän vaihtaa bussia?
perheen ottaa laina?

Note: *Sinun täytyy kertoa hänelle.* You must tell her.
Sinä et saa kertoa hänelle. You must not tell her.

Sanasto — Vocabulary

aamu-a-n	morning
+ajatel/la (ajattele/n-t-e-mme-tte-vat)	to think, think over, consider (cp. Fr. penser, Germ. denken)
Meillä on aivot, voimme ajatella.	We have brains, we can think.
Cp. Luulen, että sataa.	I think it's raining.
Minusta filmi oli hyvä.	I think the film was good.
katsel/la (katsele/n-t-e-mme-tte-vat) (= *katsoa*)	to watch, look
+kerta-a kerran	time (in telling how many times)
kerran/kaksi kertaa	once/twice
keskusta-a-n	center
koko (indecl.)	whole, all, entire
kuljettaja-a-n	driver
+lippu-a lipun	ticket; flag
lyhyt-tä lyhyen (≠ *pitkä*)	short, brief
matka-a-n	distance, way; trip, journey
+minuutti-a minuutin	minute
mones/ko? = kuinka mones? (monetta monennen)	which in order?
nous/ta (nouse/n-t-e-mme-tte-vat)	to rise, get up, arise; to get on, off
+paikka-a paikan	place, location, site; seat; job
+pysäkki-ä pysäkin (from *pysähtyä* to stop)	stop (for bus, streetcar, train)
raitio/vaunu-a-n	streetcar, tram
seiso/a (seiso/n-t-o-mme-tte-vat)	to stand
seuraava-a-n (from *seurata*)	following, the next
+työ/paikka-a-paikan	job, situation
täynnä	full
+täyty/ä	to have to, must
minun, sinun, hänen täytyy, meidän, teidän, heidän täytyy	
ulos (≠ *sisään*)	out
+vaihto-a vaihdon	change, exchange, transfer
vaunu-a-n	carriage, (street)car

☆

hissi-ä-n	lift, elevator
joulu-a-n	Christmas
kerros-ta kerroksen	floor, storey
+kirkko-a kirkon	church
sokeri-a-n	sugar

Tapaaminen kadulla

Annikki tulee kaupasta, Linda metrosta.

1. A. Hei, Linda. Mihin sinä olet menossa?
2. L. Tuohon pankkiin tuolla.
3. A. Mutta pankki on jo suljettu. Kello on melkein viisi.
4. L. Minä luulin, että pankit ovat auki yhdeksästä viiteen, kuten kaupat.
5. A. Ei ei. Vain viisitoista yli neljään maanantaista perjantaihin, ja lauantaina ne ovat kiinni.
6. L. Voi voi. No, minun täytyy mennä pankkiin huomenna. Mistä sinä olet tulossa? Sinulla on uusi kiva käsilaukku.
7. A. Se on tuosta liikkeestä, siellä on tällä viikolla ale.
8. L. Minusta se on ihana. Mitä te teette ensi viikonloppuna?
9. A. Me menemme kai maalle, Hollolaan. Matti on kotoisin Hollolasta. Meillä on siellä kesämökki ja sauna pienen järven rannalla.
10. L. Ai kuinka kivaa! Missä päin Hollola on?
11. A. Vähän yli sata kilometriä Helsingistä Jyväskylään päin.
12. L. Minusta sauna on todella ihana paikka. Meillä on sauna omassa talossa, ja meidän perheellä on saunavuoro joka keskiviikko. Mutta hei nyt, Annikki, minun täytyy lähteä. Oli hauska tavata. Terveisiä kaikille ja hauskaa viikonloppua!
13. A. Kiitos samoin. Terveisiä Billille!

■■■

Meeting on the street

Annikki comes out of a shop, Linda from the subway.

1. A. Hello, Linda. Where are you going?
2. L. To that bank over there.
3. A. But the bank is already closed. It's almost five o'clock.
4. L. I thought that banks are open from nine to five, like shops.
5. A. No, no. Only until quarter past four from Monday to Friday, and on Saturday they are closed.
6. L. Oh dear. Well, I must go to the bank tomorrow. Where are you coming from? You've got a nice new handbag.
7. A. It's from that store, there's a sale there this week.
8. L. I think it's lovely. What will you do next weekend?
9. A. We'll probably go to the country, to Hollola. Matti is from Hollola. We have a summer cottage and sauna there on a little lake.
10. L. Oh how nice! In what direction is Hollola?
11. A. A little more than a hundred kilometers from Helsinki in the direction of Jyväskylä.
12. L. I think the sauna is really a wonderful place. We have one in our own building, and our family has a sauna time every Wednesday. Goodbye now, Annikki, I have to go. It was nice to meet you. Love to everybody, and have a nice weekend!
13. A. Thanks, the same to you. Remember me to Bill!

■■■

20

Paljonko kello on? **What's the time?**

Kello on yksi (13).

Kello on puoli kolme (14.30).

Kello on viisitoista yli (neljännestä yli) kuusi (6.15, 18.15).

Kello on viittä vaille kaksitoista (11.55, 23.55).

"maa"

Missä **maassa** asutte? Belgiassa.	(in a country, land)
Me asumme **Maassa,** ei Marsissa.	(on Earth)
Me liikumme **maassa,** ei ilmassa.	(on the ground)
Matti asuu **maalla,** ei kaupungissa.	(in the country)
Maalla ja merellä.	(on land)

l	**kello kolme, kello neljä, suljettu kolmesta neljään Helsingistä Hollolaan kallis kello, luulen kylmä ilma**
r	**järven rannalla, kilometri Turusta, terveisiä Eerolle, mikä kerros? ymmärrätkö? torstaina ja perjantaina**
e-ä	**kesä on lähellä, vielä neljä päivää, hän ei ole täällä entä te? en tiedä vielä mitä tehdä**

Kielioppia — Structural notes

1. The "out of" case (elative)

		mistä?	
Turku (Turu/n)		*Turu/sta*	from T.
liike (liikkee/n)	store	*liikkee/stä*	from a store
uusi koti (uude/n kodi/n)	new home	*uude/sta kodi/sta*	from a new home

The case ending **-sta (-stä)** roughly corresponds to the English prepositions "out of", "from (within something)".
If the basic form and the gen. stem are different, the gen. stem is used.

Note: *mikä kaupunki?* — *mi/stä kaupungi/sta?*
tämä | se *kaupunki* — *tä/stä | siitä* *kaupungi/sta*

Non-locally, the **"ouf of" case** is, among other things, used

a) to denote the topic about (of, on) which something is said, written etc.:

Mi/stä ihmiset puhuvat?	What do people talk about?
Ilma/sta, työ/stä, viikonlopu/sta, raha/sta.	About weather, work, the weekend, money.
Helsingin Sanomissa on hyvä artikkeli Ranskan ulkopolitiika/sta.	The Helsingin Sanomat has a good article on French foreign policy.

b) to denote the thing we thank someone for:

Kiitos kahvi/sta!	Thanks for the coffee!
Kiitos viimeise/stä![1]	Thanks for last time!

c) together with the "into" case, to denote "from a point of time" (to a point of time):

Pekka on työssä yhdeksä/stä neljä/än.	Pekka works from nine to four.
Olimme Oulussa maanantai/sta keskiviikko/on.	We stayed in Oulu from Monday to Wednesday.

[1] Said when you meet your hosts after a visit or a party.

Note:

Minä kerron sinulle perheestä/ni.	I'll tell you about my family.
Lähdetkö pois työpaikasta/si?	Are you going to leave your job?

As always, the poss. suffix follows after the case ending.
(For a review of the six local cases see 24:2.)

2. Expressions of time

milloin?	*maanantai/na*	when? on Monday
	tä/nä maanantai/na	this Monday
	ensi (viime) maanantai/na	next (last) Monday
	maanantai-ilta/na	on Monday evening
	tä/llä (ensi, viime) viiko/lla	this (next, last) week
	joka maanantai, päivä, viikko	every Monday, day, week
	joka toinen (kolmas) päivä	every other (third) day
	maanantai/sta torstai/hin	from Monday to Thursday
	yhde/stä kahte/en (viite/en)	1—2 (5)
	seitsemä/stä kahdeksa/an	7—8
	puoli yhdeksä/stä puoli kymmene/en	from half past eight to half past nine
	kahde/sta/toista kahte/en-kymmene/en	12—20

Kesämökki on usein järven rannalla

Sanasto — Vocabulary

ale-a-n (= *alennus/myynti*)	sale
auki (= *avoinna*)	open
ensi (indecl.)	first; (of time) next
järvi järveä järven	lake
kesä-ä-n	summer
kiinni	closed, shut
kotoisin: olla kotoisin	be from, come from, be a native of
+laukku-a laukun	bag
melkein	nearly, almost
meno: olla menossa	to be going (somewhere)
+mökki-ä mökin	cottage, cabin, hut
oma-a-n	own (adj.)
päin: missä p.?	in what direction?
mennä Ouluun päin	go in the direction of O.
asua Oulussa päin	live in the direction of O.
tulla Oulusta päin	come from the direction of O.
+ranta-a rannan	shore, bank, (sea, river) side
samoin	likewise, in the same way
+suljettu-a suljetun (from *sulkea sul-jen*; cp. *kiinni*)	closed, shut
+tava/ta (t**a**paa/n-t t**a**paa t**a**paa/mme-tte-vat)	to meet
terveiset terveisiä (pl.)	greetings, regards, love
todella	really, indeed
tulo: olla tulossa	to be coming, arriving
+viikon/loppu-a-lopun	weekend
voi! voi voi!	oh, oh my, oh dear!

☆

neljännes-tä neljänneksen	one fourth; quarter
+politiikka-a politiikan	politics; policy
vailla (= *vaille*)	lacking, without; (in telling time:) to, of
viime (indecl.) (≠ *ensi*)	last
yli	over, across; (in telling time:) past

Kauppatorilla

In the Market Square

Rouva Hill menee tänään ostoksille Kauppatorille. Hänen täytyy ostaa hedelmiä, vihanneksia ja kukkia.

Mrs. Hill is going shopping in the Market Square today. She must buy fruit, vegetables, and flowers.

1. Myyjä. Hyviä hedelmiä, rouva! Omenia, appelsiineja, banaaneja!
2. H. Mitä hedelmät maksavat tänään?
3. M. Omenat maksavat ... markkaa, appelsiinit ... markkaa ja banaanit ... markkaa kilo.
4. H. No, minä otan puolitoista kiloa omenia. Ja muutamia banaaneja, viisi tai kuusi. Onko teillä viinirypäleitä?
5. M. On, meillä on hyviä espanjalaisia rypäleitä.
6. H. Antakaa minulle niitä puoli kiloa.
7. M. Entäs vihanneksia? Meillä on hyviä perunoita.

1. Market woman. Good fruit, madam! Apples, oranges, bananas!
2. H. What does the fruit cost today?
3. M. Apples cost ... marks, oranges ... marks, and bananas ... marks a kilo.
4. H. Well, I'll take one and a half kilos of apples. And a few bananas, five or six. Do you have any grapes?
5. M. Yes, we have some good Spanish grapes.
6. H. Give me half a kilo of them.
7. M. What about vegetables? We have good potatoes.

8. H. Ei kiitos, tänään minä en tarvitse perunoita. Mutta vähän salaattia ja tomaatteja.
9. M. Voi voi, rouva, salaatti on lopussa.
10. H. No, minä otan sitten vain tomaatteja.
11. M. Isoja vai pieniä?
12. H. Noita isoja.

Torilla on paljon vihanneksia ja hedelmiä. Siellä on paljon ostajia ja myyjiä, miehiä ja naisia, helsinkiläisiä ja turisteja, suomalaisia ja ulkomaalaisia, nuoria ja vanhoja. Ilma on ihana, aurinko paistaa. Rouva Hill kävelee ja katselee. Lopuksi hän ostaa vähän kukkia ja lähtee torilta.

8. H. No thanks, I don't need any potatoes today. But a little lettuce and tomatoes.
9. M. Oh dear, madam, the lettuce has all gone.
10. H. Well, I'll just take some tomatoes, then.
11. M. Big or small ones?
12. H. Some of those big ones.

There are lots of vegetables and fruit in the market. There are lots of customers and vendors, men and women, Helsinki people and tourists, Finns and foreigners, young and old. The weather is wonderful, the sun is shining. Mrs. H. walks about and looks around. Finally she buys some flowers and leaves the market place.

■■■

Mitä hedelmiä te otatte?
A. Minä otan **näitä**.
B. Minä otan **noita**.
C. Tässä on omenia, minä otan **niitä**.
D. Minä **en** ota **mitään**.

■■■

Which fruit will you take?
A. I'll take some of these.
B. I'll take some of those.
C. Here are some apples, I'll take some of them.
D. I won't take anything.

Kuinka paljon / **Paljonko** **autoja?**

muutamia auto**ja**

vähän auto**ja**

paljon auto**ja**

a-ä vähän s**a**l**a**attia, vähän parempi, **a**nt**a**k**a**a näitä b**a**n**a**aneja
u-y hyvä myyjä, tuo myyjä **myy** j**uu**stoa, mitä m**uu**ta myyjä **myy**? m**uu**tamia hyviä m**u**nia
r rouvan vuoro, torilla on perunoita, sata grammaa makkaraa koiralle

Kielioppia — Structural notes

1. Partitive plural

Part.pl.		**Basic form pl.**	
Kaupassa on radio/i/ta.	There are radios in the shop.	*Radiot maksavat paljon.*	Radios cost a lot.
Miehellä on laps/i/a.	The man has children.	*Lapset ovat koulussa.*	The children are in school.
Ostammeko omen/i/a?	Shall we buy some apples?	*Ostamme nämä omenat.*	We'll buy these apples.
Pekka myy silmälase/j/a.	Pekka sells glasses.	*Tarvitsen silmälasit.*	I need (a pair of) glasses.

The basic meaning of the partitive plural is **indefinite number** (in English often ''some'', ''any'', or a noun without an article), in contrast to the basic form which expresses definite number (''the children'', ''these children'', ''those children'' etc.) or entity (''glasses'' = a pair; ''radios'', ''all radios'', the whole category).

However, the part. pl. is an extremely common form with a number of different functions similar to those of the part. sing. These functions will be discussed mainly in lessons 21—22, 26:1, and 39:1. (There will be a review of the use of the partitive after lesson 39, p. 207.)

Structure

The ending is **-a (-ä)** or **-ta (-tä)** as in the sing. Each noun usually, but not always, has the same ending in the sing. and the pl. (cp. *radio/ta: radio/i/ta,* but *las/ta: laps/i/a*).

The **-i-** (between vowels **-j-**), which precedes the ending, is the plural marker used in the part. pl. and all other pl. cases except for the basic form pl. (*lapset*).

The stem comes from

— the basic form sing. if the word ends in a vowel

— the gen. sing. for words ending in a consonant, and for *huone* words.

The plural marker -i- may cause changes in the stem. The part. pl. of each new noun will from now on be listed in the vocabulary and should be memorized as the last of the four principal parts of nouns.

How to form the part. pl. can also be studied in the chart on p. 98. It is in your interest to familiarize yourself with this reference list as soon as possible. Remember, however, that the part. pl. is not learned in a day.

The part. pl. forms of the nouns covered in chapters 1—21 can be looked up in the list on p. 99. (The nouns are listed according to word types, following the order in a more detailed chart on p. 219.)

Adjectives and pronouns agree with the noun as usual:

Millais/i/a hedelm/i/ä haluatte?	What sort of fruit(s) do you want?
Iso/j/a, halpo/j/a appelsiine/j/a.	Big, cheap oranges.
Onko teillä hyv/i/ä peruno/i/ta?	Do you have good potatoes?

Note also:

mikä kukka?				*mi/tä kukk/i/a?*
tämä	*kukka*	*(nämä*	*kukat)*	*nä/i/tä* *kukk/i/a*
tuo		*(nuo*		*no/i/ta*
se		*(ne*		*ni/i/tä*

Possessive suffixes, as always, follow after the case ending:

Saat omenia/ni.	You can have some of my apples.
Ovatko he teidän ystäviä/nne?	Are they friends of yours?

Important to remember:
The partitive is rarely used as the subject, except in ''there is, there are'' type of sentences. Its place is generally at the end of the sentence.
If the sentence has a partitive subject, the verb is in the singular:

Kadulla on ihmisiä.	There are people on the street.
Tänne tulee lapsia.	There are children coming here.
Saunassa istuu miehiä.	There are men sitting in the sauna.

AUTOT
Bad mistake: ~~*Autoja*~~ *maksavat paljon.*

2. Special uses of the partitive plural

The part. pl. is used, among other things,
— after words indicating measure or amount:

Kilo rypäle/i/tä.	A kilo of grapes.
Vähän opettaj/i/a, paljon opiskeli-jo/i/ta.	Few teachers, many students.

— to indicate things that are not there and things not possessed:

Huoneessa ei ole ikkuno/i/ta.	There are no windows in the room.
Miehellä ei ole lase/j/a.	The man has no glasses.

— wishes and exclamations:

Kauni/i/ta un/i/a!	Sweet dreams!
Hyv/i/ä uutis/i/a!	Good news!

Sanasto — Vocabulary

appelsiini-a-n appelsiineja	orange
+aurinko-a auringon aurinkoja	sun
banaani-a-n banaaneja	banana
hedelmä-ä-n hedelmiä	fruit
kauppa/tori-a-n-toreja	market square, outdoor market
kävel/lä (kävele/n-t-e-mme-tte-vät)	to walk
+loppu-a lopun loppuja	end
olla lopussa	to be over, out, at an end, gone
lopuksi	finally, at last
muutama-a-n muutamia (usu. pl.)	a few, some
omena-a-n omenia (omenoita)	apple
ostaja-a-n ostajia	buyer, customer
paista/a (paista/n-t-a-mme-tte-vat)	to shine; to roast, fry
peruna-a-n perunoita	potato
tarvi/ta (tarvitse/n-t-e-mme-tte-vat)	to need
tori-a-n toreja	square, market place
vihannekset vihanneksia (usu. pl.)	vegetables
(viini)rypäle-ttä-en-itä	grape

☆

ruusu-a-n-ja	rose
tulppaani-a-n tulppaaneja	tulip

How to form the partitive plural

(V = vowel, C = consonant)

I. Words ending in a vowel (stem from the basic form)

1. Words ending in a long vowel or a diphthong

			(Part. sing.)	Partitive pl.	Notes
-VV	VV>V	*maa*	*(-ta)*	*ma/i/ta*	
-Vi	i>Ø	*tiistai*	*(-ta)*	*tiista/i/ta*	
-ie	ie>e	*tie*	*(-tä)*	*te/i/tä*	
-uo	uo>o	*suo*	*(-ta)*	*so/i/ta*	
-yö	yö>ö	*työ*	*(-tä)*	*tö/i/tä*	

2. 2-syllable words ending in one vowel (-**e** words: see II)

Ending	Change		Word	Part. sing.	Part. pl.
-o, -ö, -u, -y	no change		*auto*	*(-a)*	*auto/j/a*
			koulu	*(-a)*	*koulu/j/a*
-ä	ä>Ø		*päivä*	*(-ä)*	*päiv/i/ä*
-a 1)	a>Ø	if first vowel is **o, u**;	*poika*	*(-a)*	*poik/i/a*
			kuva	*(-a)*	*kuv/i/a*
		if not,			
2)	a>o		*kirja*	*(-a)*	*kirjo/j/a*
-i 1)	i>Ø	in **i→e** words	*ovi (oven)*	*(ovea)*	*ov/i/a*
			uusi (uuden)	*(uutta)*	*uus/i/a*
2)	i >e	if **no -e-** in sing.	*bussi*	*(-a)*	*busse/j/a*

3. Longer words ending in one vowel

-o, -ö, -u, -y	Like *auto*, but the ending **-ta (-tä)** may also occur, depending on the word type	(Sometimes parallel endings, e.g. *hotelle/j/a* or *hotelle/i/ta*)
-i	Like *bussi*, but the ending **-ta (-tä)** may also occur, depending on the word type	
	Exception: *parempi (parempaa) paremp/i/a*	(Comparatives)
-a, -ä	The word type decides what the part. plural will be like. See the chart on p. 219.	(Sometimes parallel endings, e.g. *omen/i/a* or *omeno/i/ta*)

II. Words ending in a short -e or a consonant (stem from the gen. sing.)

			(Part. sing.)	(Gen. sing.)	Part. pl.
-e	Long end-vowel of	*huone*	*(-tta)*	*huonee/n*	*huone/i/ta*
-C	stem shortens	*sairas*	*(-ta)*	*sairaa/n*	*saira/i/ta*
	Short end-vowel of	*nainen*	*(naista)*	*naise/n*	*nais/i/a*
	stem disappears	*mahdoton*	*(-ta)*	*mahdottoma/n*	*mahdottom/i/a*

For more examples and exceptional word types see the chart on p. 219.

Nouns in lessons 1—21 by inflection types

1. Words ending in a long vowel or a diphthong

maa words
maa-ta-n maita 3
muu 12
puu 17
suu 18
tee 7
vapaa 14

tiistai words
tiistai-ta-n-ta 2
lauantai 5
maanantai 1
perjantai 5
sunnuntai 5
torstai 4

voi 14

tie words
tie-tä-n teitä 6
työ-tä-n töitä 11
yö-tä-n öitä 14

2. 2-syllable words ending in a vowel

auto words
auto-a-n-ja 1
aamu 19
+helppo-a helpon helppoja 11
huono 2
hylly 17
iso 2
jano 17
juusto 16
+katu-a kadun katuja 1
+keitto-a keiton keittoja 14
kello 9
+kirkko-a kirkon kirkkoja 19
koulu 11
+lamppu-a lampun lamppuja 9
lasku 14
+laukku-a laukun laukkuja 20
+lippu-a lipun lippuja 19
+loppu-a lopun loppuja 21
+maito-a maidon maitoja 14
meno 20
metro 8
pallo 6
pullo 14
ruusu 21
sivu 1
+suku-a suvun sukuja 5
+sänky-ä sängyn sänkyjä 17
talo 1
tulo 20
+tyttö-ä tytön tyttöjä 1
+vaihto-a vaihdon vaihtoja 19
vaimo 8
vaunu 19
+viikko-a viikon viikkoja 12
vuoro 16

päivä words
päivä-ä-n päiviä 1
kylmä 8
kynä 8
köyhä 17
+leipä-ä leivän leipiä 14
metsä 10
myyjä 16
+nälkä-ä nälän 17
pitkä 16
+pöytä-ä pöydän pöytiä 13
silmä 18

kuva words
kuva-a-n kuvia 1
koira 9
korva 18
kova 15
+kukka-a kukan kukkia 13
kuuma 15
muna 16
musta 16
nolla 5
oma 20
+poika-a pojan poikia 1
rouva 4
sohva 10
+työ/lupa-a-luvan lupia 17
+vasta/kohta-a -kohdan-kohtia 6

kirja words
kirja-a-n kirjoja 7
firma 12
gramma 16
+halpa-a halvan halpoja 7
hauska 10
herra 4
+hinta-a hinnan hintoja 7
ilma 8
+ilta-a illan iltoja 13
+jalka-a jalan jalkoja 18
kala 14
+kartta-a kartan karttoja 3
+kauppa-a kaupan kauppoja 1
+kerta-a kerran kertoja 19
kissa 12
laiska 11
liha 14
litra 16
+markka-a markan markkoja 7
matka 19
+nahka-a nah(k)an nahkoja 15
paha 17
+paikka-a paikan paikkoja 19
+palkka-a palkan palkkoja 12
raha 8
+ranta-a rannan rantoja 20
ruoka/lista 14
sama 10
sana 7
vanha 2
+vika-a vian vikoja 18

bussi words
bussi-a-n busseja 1
baari 10
kahvi 5
+koti-a kodin koteja 5
+kuppi-a kupin kuppeja 7
kurssi 5

lasi 7
+mökki-ä mökin mökkejä 20
+nakki-a nakin nakkeja 16
+neiti-ä neidin neitejä 8
+pankki-a pankin pankkeja 16
pari 16
penni 7
pihvi 15
posti 8
+rokki-a rokin 12
+sekki-ä sekin sekkejä 8
+sentti-ä sentin senttejä 16
taksi 8
tori 21

tuoli 11
valssi 9
+äiti-ä äidin äitejä 13

i→e:

ovi words
ovi ovea oven ovia 8
järvi 20
+kaikki kaikkea kaiken kaikkia 4
kivi 1
nimi 5
onni 9

pieni words
pieni pientä pienen pieniä 2
kieli kieltä kielen kieliä 3

lapsi lasta lapsen lapsia 12
moni monta monen monia 16
nuori nuorta nuoren nuoria 2
puoli puolta puolen puolia 16
suuri suurta suuren suuria 17

uusi words
+uusi uutta uuden uusia 2
+käsi kättä käden käsiä 13
+vesi vettä veden vesiä 14
+vuosi vuotta vuoden vuosia 13

---

3. Longer words ending in a vowel

toimisto words
toimisto-a-n-ja
+asunto-a asunnon asuntoja 10
+aurinko-a auringon aurinkoja 21
+mekaanikko-a mekaanikon mekaanikkoja 12
+paistettu-a paistetun paistettuja 14
+suljettu-a suljetun suljettuja 20
yli/opisto 8

radio words
radio-ta-n-ita 1
keittiö 16
televisio 1
valtio 10
henkilö-ä 11
jäätelö-ä 14
numero-a 1

ostaja words
ostaja-a-n ostajia 21
kuljettaja 19
laulaja 12
opettaja 5
hedelmä 21
muutama 21
ihana 14
omena 21
mukava 10
seuraava 19
ystävä 10

opiskelija words
opiskelija-a-n opiskelijoita 5
tarjoilija 14
lattia 13
ravintola 14
ikkuna 5
(omena 21)
peruna 21
kamera 18

makkara 16

vaikea words
vaikea-(t)a-n vaikeita 11
nopea 7

hotelli words
hotelli-a-n hotelleja 8
appelsiini 21
banaani 21
insinööri 12
+kasetti-a kasetin kasetteja 11
+kaupunki-a kaupungin kaupunkeja 6
kioski 9
+konsertti-a konsertin konsertteja 8
+minuutti-a minuutin minuutteja 19
+musiikki-a musiikin 5
+paketti-a paketin paketteja 13

+pysäkki-ä pysäkin pysäkkejä 19
romaani 12
+salaatti-a salaatin salaatteja 14
stipendi 11
+tomaatti-a tomaatin tomaatteja 14
tulppaani 21
turisti 8

naapuri words
naapuri-a-n naapureita 11
lääkäri 12
sokeri 19
teatteri 8
tohtori 4

parempi words
+parempi parempaa paremman parempia 18
(and all other comparatives)

---

4. Words ending in a short -e or a consonant

huone words
huone-tta-en huoneita 1
kappale 1
kiire 17
+liike-ttä liikkeen liikkeitä 12
+osoite-tta osoitteen osoitteita 5
perhe 6
rypäle 21
terve 11
(Exceptions:
ale-a-n-ja 20
itse-ä-n 18
+nukke-a nuken nukkeja 6)

nainen words
nainen naista naisen naisia 1
hetkinen 9
ihminen 10
millainen 2
(and all other -nen words)

puhelin words
puhelin-ta puhelimen puhelimia 5

sairas words
sairas-ta sairaan sairaita 2
+asiakas-ta asiakkaan asiakkaita 15
+hidas-ta hitaan hitaita 7
paras-ta parhaan parhaita 18
+rikas-ta rikkaan rikkaita 17

kaunis words
kaunis-ta kauniin kauniita 2
kallis 7

vastaus words
vastaus-ta vastauksen vastauksia 2
kysymys 2
Sibelius 1
sävellys 6
kiitos 3
neljännes 20
vihannes 21

lyhyt words
lyhyt-tä lyhyen lyhyitä 19
olut 14

5. Exceptional or rare paradigms

+**lämmin**-tä lämpimän lämpimiä 15

lähin words
+lähin-tä lähimmän lähimpiä 8 (and all other superlatives)

mies-tä miehen miehiä 1

salaisuus words
+salaisuus salaisuutta salaisuuden salaisuuksia 13

kolmas words
+kolmas kolmatta kolmannen kolmansia 18 (and all other ordinals)

+**tuhat**-ta tuhannen tuhansia

Pronouns:

minä minua minun 3
sinä 3
hän häntä hänen 2
me meitä meidän 9
te 4
he 9
tämä tätä tämän 1
tuo tuota tuon 1
se sitä sen 1
nämä näitä näiden 12
nuo noita noiden 12
ne niitä niiden 12
kuka ketä kenen keitä 1
mikä mitä minkä mitä 1
(ei) mikään mitään minkään mitään 18
joka jota jonka joita 12

Mitä nämä ovat?

Ystävällinen vanha täti katselee kuvia pikku Pekan kanssa

1. T. No niin, Pekka, katsotaan nyt näitä kuvia. Tässä kuvassa on paljon eläimiä. Mikä eläin tämä on?
2. P. Se on lehmä.
3. T. No, minkälainen eläin lehmä on?
4. P. Se on ruskea. Ja siitä tulee maitoa.
5. T. Mitäs nämä ovat?
6. P. Nekin ovat lehmiä. Tuo on hevonen.
7. T. Se on iso ja kaunis. Mutta katsos millaisia nuo hevoset ovat! Miksi ne ovat niin pieniä?
8. P. Ne ovat poneja. Ponit ovat pieniä, tavalliset hevoset ovat suuria.
9. T. Entäs nämä muut eläimet, mitä ne ovat?
10. P. Tämä on lammas. Lampaasta tulee villaa. Tuo on sika, siasta tulee lihaa. Nuo ovat kanoja. Kanat munivat.

What are these?

A friendly old lady is looking at pictures with little Pekka

1. L. Well, Pekka, let's look at these pictures now. There are lots of animals in this picture. Which animal is this?
2. P. It's a cow.
3. L. Well, what kind of animal is a cow?
4. P. It's brown, and milk comes from cows.
5. L. What are these?
6. P. They're cows, too. That one is a horse.
7. L. It's big and beautiful. But see what those horses are like! Why are they so small?
8. P. They are ponies. Ponies are small, ordinary horses are big.
9. L. What about these other animals, what are they?
10. P. This one is a sheep. Wool comes from sheep. That one is a pig, meat comes from pigs. Those are hens. Hens lay eggs.

11. T. Ne munivat kauniita valkoisia munia, ja ihmiset syövät niitä ... Mikä tämä hirveä eläin on, joka on kuin iso kissa?

11. L. They lay pretty white eggs, and people eat them ... What's this terrible animal which looks like a big cat?

12. P. Se on tiikeri. Kuule Anna-täti, mennään joskus yhdessä eläintarhaan. Minä näytän sinulle, mitä eläimiä siellä on. Kun sinä et ymmärrä eläimistä yhtään mitään!

12. P. It's a tiger. Listen, Aunt Anna, let's go to the Zoo some time together. I'll show you what animals they have there. Since you don't understand anything about animals!

■■■

Minkävärinen ruusu on?	What color is a rose?
Se on punainen, keltainen tai valkoinen.	It's red, yellow, or white.
Minkävärisiä tulppaanit ovat?	What color are tulips?
Ne ovat punaisia, keltaisia tai valkoisia.	They are red, yellow, or white.
Hevoset ovat usein ruskeita.	Horses are often brown.
Kissa voi olla valkoinen, harmaa tai musta. Mutta yöllä kaikki kissat ovat harmaita.	A cat may be white, grey, or black. But at night all cats are grey.

the colloquial -s:

Mitäs kuuluu?	How's everything?
Onkos (onks) Pekka kotona?	Is P. at home?
Kukas tuolla tulee?	Who's coming there?
Annas tänne!	Give (it) here, will you?

Kielioppia — Structural notes

1. "What are these?" — "What are they like?"

Mi/tä nämä ovat?	What are these?
Ne ovat omeni/a.	They are apples.
Millaisi/a omenat ovat?	What are (the) apples like?
Omenat ovat hyvi/ä.	(The) apples are good.

Mi/tä nuo ovat?	What are those?
Ne ovat tulppaanej/a.	They are tulips.
Minkälaisi/a ne ovat?	What are they like?
Ne ovat kaunii/ta.	They are pretty.

mitä is also the part. pl. of *mikä*.

In questions of the type ''what are these?'' use *mitä* as the interrogative word. The answer will also be in the part. pl.: *omeni/a, tulppaanej/a.*

In questions of the type ''what are these like?'' use *millaisia* as the interrogative word. The answer will also be in the part. pl.: *hyvi/ä, kaunii/ta.*

However, when you ask about things which form an entity or series, use the words *mitkä* and *millaiset*. The answer will also be in the basic form pl.:

Mi/t/kä nämä ovat?	What are these?
Ne ovat silmälasi/t.	They are (a pair of) glasses.
Millaise/t ne ovat?	What are they like?
Ne ovat uude/t.	They are new.

Minkälaise/t Liisan silmät ovat?	What are Liisa's eyes like?
Liisan silmät ovat sinise/t.	Liisa's eyes are blue.
Mi/t/kä ovat viikonpäivät?	What are the days of the week?
Mi/t/kä ovat Suomen naapurimaat?	What are the neighboring countries of Finland?

OMENAT
Bad mistake: ~~*Omenia*~~ *ovat hyviä.*
(Subject)

2. Principal parts of nouns

By now you know the four key forms listed in the vocabulary for all nouns, adjectives, and pronouns. All the other cases are formed on the basis of these four. Memorizing them well after each lesson is strongly recommended. Thus, the principal parts for *mies* 'man' are:

mies miestä miehen miehiä

Tuolla on mies.	There is a man over there.
Miehen nimi on Lauri Leino.	The man's name is L.L.
Autossa on kaksi miestä.	There are two men in the car.
Kadulla on paljon miehiä.	There are lots of men on the street.

Sanasto — Vocabulary

eläin-tä eläimen eläimiä	animal
eläin/tarha-a-n-tarhoja	zoo
hevonen hevosta hevosen hevosia	horse
hirveä-(t)ä-n hirveitä	terrible
kana-a-n kanoja	hen
-kin (= *myös*)	also, too; sometimes an emphasizing suffix
+lammas-ta lampaan lampaita	sheep
lehmä-ä-n lehmiä	cow
minkä/väri/nen-stä-sen-siä?	what color?
muni/a (muni/n-t-i-mme-tte-vat)	to lay eggs
no niin	well, all right
+näyttä/ä näytä/n-t näyttää näytä/mme-tte näyttävät	to show; to point; to seem, look (like)
poni-a-n poneja	pony
-s	nearly meaningless suffix generally used in colloquial speech
Missäs Ville on? Tulkaas tänne! Eik(ö)s niin?	
+sika-a sian sikoja	pig, hog, swine
tiikeri-ä -n tiikereitä	tiger
+täti-ä tädin tätejä	aunt, auntie; (in children's language:) lady, woman
villa-a-n villoja	wool
väri-ä-n värejä	color
yhdessä	together (with)
ystävälli/nen-stä-sen-siä (≠ *epä/ys-tävällinen*)	friendly, kind

Värejä	**Colors:**
harmaa-ta-n harmaita	grey
keltai/nen-sta-sen-sia	yellow
punai/nen-sta-sen-sia	red
ruskea-(t)a-n ruskeita	brown
sini/nen-stä-sen-siä	blue
vaalean/punainen	pink
valkoi/nen-sta-sen-sia	white
vihreä-(t)ä-n vihreitä	green

Matti Suomelan päiväohjelma (I)

1. Mihin aikaan sinä nouset aamulla?
2. Minä nousen aina seitsemältä. Minä syön aamiaista puoli kahdeksalta.
3. Mitä sinä syöt aamiaiseksi?
4. Minä syön voileipää ja juon teetä.
5. Etkö sinä juo kahvia?
6. En. Minä en pidä kahvista, vaikka suomalaiset tavallisesti pitävät siitä.
7. Milloin sinä menet työhön?
8. Kello yhdeksän, samoin kuin vaimoni. Me olemme työssä samassa toimistossa.
9. Kuinka kauan sinä olet työssä?
10. Kolme tuntia aamupäivällä, neljä iltapäivällä. Lauantaina minä en ole työssä.
11. Syötkö sinä lounasta kotona?
12. Lounasta me emme syö koskaan kotona. Lapset syövät koulussa, me vanhemmat lähimmässä ravintolassa.
13. Milloin teidän perheessä on päivällinen?
14. Viideltä, paitsi sunnuntaina.
15. Mitä sinä teet päivällisen jälkeen?
16. Joskus minä teen työtä, joskus lepään. Usein minä autan vaimoani. Sitten minä luen sanomalehtiä tai kirjoja tai kirjoitan kirjeitä. Minusta lukeminen on hauskaa, minä pidän lukemisesta.

■■■

Matti Suomela's daily program (I)

1. What time do you get up in the morning?
2. I always get up at seven. I have breakfast at half past seven.
3. What do you eat for breakfast?
4. I eat bread and butter and I drink tea.
5. Don't you drink coffee?
6. No, I don't like coffee, although Finns usually like it.
7. When do you go to work?
8. At nine, like my wife. We work at the same office.
9. How long do you work?
10. Three hours in the morning, four in the afternoon. I don't work on Saturday.
11. Do you have lunch at home?
12. We never have lunch at home. The children eat at school; we parents eat at the nearest restaurant.
13. When do you have dinner in your family?
14. At five, except on Sunday.
15. What do you do after dinner?
16. Sometimes I work, sometimes I rest. I often help my wife. After that I read the papers or read books or write letters. I think reading is fun, I like reading.

■■■

Pidän kahvi**sta**, mutta en pidä	tee**stä**.
en välitä	

tehdä työtä to work, not to be idle
olla työssä to work outside the home, have a job (colloq. *olla töissä*)

Kielioppia Structural notes

1. More expressions of time

milloin? (koska?)

aamu	morning	*aamu/lla*	in the morning
päivä	day	*päivä/llä*	during the day
ilta (illa/n)	evening	*illa/lla*	in the evening
yö	night	*yö/llä*	at night

mihin aikaan? (at) what time?

(kello) kahde/lta *kello kaksi* (colloq.)	at two o'clock
puoli neljä/ltä *kello puoli neljä*	at half past three

But, according to the 24-hour system:

Bussi lähtee 14.30 (**ei** *puoli viisitoista!*). The bus will leave at 14.30 hours.

2. "to like" in Finnish

Mi/stä sinä pidät?	What do you like? What are you fond of?
Pidän musiiki/sta, työ/stä, matkustamise/sta ja perhee/stä/ni.	I like music, work, traveling, and my family.

With the verb *pitää* to like, be fond of, Finnish idiomatically uses the "out of" case; likewise with the verbs *tykä/tä* (*tykkään*) to like (colloq.) and *välittä/ä* (*välitän*) to care:

Tykkäätkö sinä saunasta?	Do you like the sauna?
En, minä en paljon välitä siitä.	No, I don't care for it much.

3. k p t changes ("consonant gradation")

k p t changes occur, as you will have noticed by now, in the inflection of both nouns and verbs and are very characteristic of the Finnish language.

k, **p**, and **t** are subject to these regular changes either alone or in combination with certain other consonants.

sp, **st**, **sk**, **tk** are not subject to **k p t** changes.

23

The **"strong grade"** occurs when the following syllable is **open** (ends in a vowel). The **"weak grade"** occurs when the following syllable is **closed** (ends in a consonant).

strong	weak	strong		weak
Changes of p				
pp	**: p**	kau**pp**a	shop	kau**p**at
p (lp, rp)	**: v (lv, rv)**	lei**p**ä	bread	lei**v**än
mp	**: mm**	ka**mp**a	comb	ka**mm**at
Changes of t				
tt	**: t**	o**tt**aa	to take	o**t**amme
t (ht)	**: d (hd)**	ka**t**u	street	ka**d**ut
lt, rt	**: ll, rr**	i**lt**a	evening	i**ll**alla
		ke**rt**oa	to tell	ke**rr**on
nt	**: nn**	hi**nt**a	price	hi**nn**at
Changes of k				
kk	**: k**	Mi**kk**o	Michael	Mi**k**on
k (lk, rk)	**: - (l-, r-)**	lu**k**ea	to read	luette
hk	**: h(k)**	na**hk**a	leather	nah(**k**)an
hke, lke, rke	**: hje, lje, rje**	su**lk**ea	to close	su**lj**ettu
nk	**: ng**	Helsi**nk**i		Helsi**ng**issä

Notes:

aika time :*ajan*
poika boy :*pojat*
vaaka scales :*vaa'at*; the apostrophe is used when **k** disappears between two identical vowels.
suku family :*suvut*; **k** changes to **v** (instead of disappearing) to avoid confusion with *suut* mouths; this is also the case with a few other nouns ending in **-uku (-yky)**.

Why *Turkuun*, *Helsinkiin*?
If the closed syllable contains a **long vowel**, there is always **strong grade**.

The principle of strong grade in the open, and weak grade in the closed syllable does not always apply in modern Finnish. If the student remembers the principal parts of the words and which stems are used to make the different forms, he will produce language with correct grades of **k p t** changes.

Sanasto — Vocabulary

aamiai/nen-sta-sen-sia	breakfast
aamu/päivä-ä-n-päiviä	(late) morning
+aika-a ajan aikoja	time
mihin aikaan?	(at) what time?
+autta/a	to help, aid, assist
auta/n-t auttaa	
auta/mme-tte auttavat	
autan sinu/a, hän/tä	I help you, him
ilta/päivä-ä-n-päiviä	afternoon
jälkeen (+ gen.)	after
päivällise/n jälkeen	after dinner
kauan	for a long time
kirje-ttä-en-itä	letter (in correspondence)
koskaan (= *milloinkaan*)	ever
ei koskaan (= *ei milloinkaan*)	never
+lehti lehteä lehden lehtiä	newspaper, magazine; leaf
+levä/tä (lepää/n-t lepää-mme-tte-vät) (cp. *lepo* rest)	to rest
lounas-ta lounaan lounaita	lunch; south-west
lukemi/nen-sta-sen-sia	reading, something to read
ohjelma-a-n ohjelmia	program
paitsi	besides; except
+pitä/ä	to like, be fond of
pidä/n-t pitää	
pidä/mme-tte pitävät	
minä pidän sinu/sta	I like you
päivälli/nen-stä-sen-siä	dinner
+sanoma/lehti	newspaper
+teh/dä työtä	to work
toimisto-a-n-ja	office, bureau
+tunti-a tunnin tunteja	hour; lesson, class
vaikka	although, even if
+vanhemmat vanhempia vanhempien (pl.) (from *vanhempi* older)	parents
+voi/leipä-ä-leivän-leipiä	bread and butter; sandwich

☆

+tykä/tä (tykkää/n-t tykkää/mme-tte-vät) (= *pitää*)	(colloq.) to like, be fond of
+välittä/ä	to care for, about
välitä/n-t välittää	
välitä/mme-tte välittävät	
en välitä lukemise/sta	I don't care for reading

Matti Suomelan päiväohjelma (II)

1. Kuinka te vietätte iltanne?
2. Minä katselen aika paljon televisiota. Vaimoni ei välitä siitä, paitsi kun on oikein hyvää ohjelmaa. Hän haluaa kuunnella radiota.
3. Menettekö te usein ulos?
4. Me olemme paljon kotona. Joskus me menemme teatteriin, elokuviin ja niin edelleen.
5. Pidättekö te musiikista?
6. Kyllä.
7. Minkälaisesta musiikista te pidätte?
8. Kaikesta hyvästä musiikista. Meillä on levysoitin ja paljon hyviä levyjä. Ja kasetteja. Me kuuntelemme niitä usein illalla, ennen kuin menemme nukkumaan.
9. Ja millä tavalla suomalaiset viettävät viikonloppua?
10. Eri ihmiset eri tavalla. Monet menevät maalle. Nuoret menevät tanssimaan lauantai-iltana. Sunnuntaina me emme nouse kovin aikaisin, vaan nukumme myöhään. Muutamat menevät kirkkoon. Iltapäivällä me menemme ehkä kylään, tai meille tulee vieraita. Jos ilma on kaunis, olemme paljon ulkona.

Matti Suomela's daily program (II)

1. How do you spend your evenings?
2. I watch television quite a lot. My wife doesn't care for it, except when there is a very good program. She wants to listen to the radio.
3. Do you often go out?
4. We stay a lot at home. Sometimes we go to the theater, the cinema, and so on.
5. Do you like music?
6. Yes, we do.
7. What kind of music do you like?
8. All good music. We have a record-player and many good records. And cassettes. We often listen to them in the evening before we go to bed.
9. And in what manner do Finns spend their weekends?
10. Different people in different ways. Many people go to the country. Young people go dancing on Saturday night. We don't get up very early on Sunday, we sleep late. Some people go to church. In the afternoon we may visit friends, or we have guests. If the weather is fine, we stay outdoors a great deal.

■■■

Ihmisellä on korvat, hän **kuulee**.
Ihmisellä on silmät, hän **näkee**.

Hän voi **kuunnella** musiikkia.
Hän voi **katsella** kuvia.

Hän on **sisällä**. Hän on **ulkona**. **Sisään!** **Ulos!**

Kielioppia — Structural notes

1. syömään, syömässä

Lapset, tulkaa syö/mään!	Children, come and eat!
(Cp. *Tulkaa keittiöön!*)	
Minä menen nukku/maan.	I'll go to bed (lit. "to sleep").
(Cp. *Menen sänkyyn.*)	
Mihin sinä menet? Tanssi/maan.	Where are you going? I'm going dancing.

Forms like *"syö/mään, tanssi/maan"* express what people will go and do. They occur in connection with verbs of motion like *mennä* and *tulla*.

Structure: stem from 3rd pers. pl. present tense + **maan (mään)**

nukkua	*nukku/vat*	*mennä nukku/maan*
tavata	*tapaa/vat*	*tulla tapaa/maan*

Missä lapset ovat? Syö/mässä.	Where are the children? They're eating.
(Cp. *He ovat keittiössä.*)	
Vauva on nukku/massa.	The baby is sleeping.
(Cp. *Hän on sängyssä.*)	

Forms like *"syö/mässä", "nukku/massa"*, usually in connection with the verb *olla*, express in what action people are engaged at the moment referred to.

Note that the use of this form is largely concentrated on certain concrete situations (*olla syömässä, nukkumassa, lepäämässä, uimassa* swimming, *hiihtämässä* skiing, *tanssimassa* etc.). It is far less frequent than the English "to be doing something". Remember that, most often, the Finnish for "I'm doing, reading, thinking" etc. is simply *"minä teen, luen, ajattelen"* etc.

Structure: stem from 3rd pers. pl. present tense + **massa (mässä)**

syödä	*syö/vät*	*olla syö/mässä*
tavata	*tapaa/vat*	*olla tapaa/massa*

(More about *syömään* and *syömässä* in Finnish for Foreigners 2.)

2. The six local cases

This is a review of the six local cases of nouns.
Three of them refer to the inside of things **(inner local cases)**:

lasi/ssa	*lasi/sta*	*lasi/in*
in the glass	out of the glass	into the glass

Three, on the other hand, refer to the outside of things **(outer local cases)**:

pöydä/llä	*pöydä/ltä*	*pöydä/lle*
on the table	from, off the table	on(to) the table

The picture below illustrates the difference between the inner and outer series of local cases.

Stem of the local cases:

Five of them use the gen. stem unmodified, e.g. *pöytä*: *pöydä/n* — *pöydä/llä, pöydä/ltä, pöydä/lle, pöydä/ssä, pöydä/stä.*

Now that you know the rules of **k p t** changes, it is possible to reformulate the rule concerning the sixth of the local forms. The ''into'' case also makes use of the gen. stem but it must always be in the strong grade.

Examples:

koti: kodi/n	*(koti-)*	*koti/in*	(to the) home
Turku: Turu/n	*(Turku-)*	*Turku/un*	to Turku
Lahti: Lahde/n	*(Lahte-)*	*Lahte/en*	to Lahti
vesi: vede/n	*(vete-)*	*vete/en*	into water
kaksi: kahde/n	*(kahte-)*	*kahte/en*	to two
parempi: paremma/n	*(parempa-)*	*parempa/an*	into a better ...
kolmas: kolmanne/n	*(kolmante-)*	*kolmante/en*	into the third ...

Sanasto — Vocabulary

aikaisin (≠ *myöhään*)	early (= at an early hour)
edelleen	on, onward, further
ja niin edelleen (jne.)	and so on (etc.)
elo/kuva-a-n-kuvia	moving picture, movie, film
ennen kuin	before (when beginning a clause)
eri (indecl.) (≠ *sama*)	different (= not the same)
kovin (= *hyvin, oikein*)	very
+kuunnel/la (kuuntele/n-t-e-mme-tte -vat)	to listen to, listen in
kuuntelen musiikki/a, radio/ta	I listen to music, to the radio
kylä-ä-n kyliä	village
mennä kylään	go and visit people, friends
levy-ä-n-jä	plate; disc; record
+levy/soitin-ta-soittimen-soittimia	record-player
myöhään (≠ *aikaisin*)	late
+nukku/a	to sleep
nuku/n-t nukkuu	
nuku/mme-tte nukkuvat	
mennä nukkumaan	to go to bed
tanssi-a-n tansseja	dance, dancing
+tapa-a tavan tapoja	way, manner; habit, custom
millä tavalla?	in what manner, what way?
vaan	but (only after neg. sentence)
vieras-ta vieraan vieraita	unknown; guest; pl. party
+viettä/ä	to spend, pass time; celebrate
vietä/n-t viettää	
vietä/mme-tte viettävät	

Muistatko sinä minut vielä?

Vanhat toverit tapaavat

1. Arto. Terve, Veikko!
2. Veikko. No terve, terve! Pitkästä aikaa!
3. A. Tunnetko sinä minut vielä?
4. V. Totta kai tunnen. Sinä olet vanha luokkatoverini Koskisen Arto. Mitä sinä teet Oulussa?
5. A. Minä olen täällä työmatkalla Kari Peltosen ja Heikki Lampion kanssa. Muistatko sinä heidät?
6. V. Kari Peltonen ... hänet minä kyllä muistan. Mutta Heikki Lampio — häntä minä en muista.
7. A. Voi olla, että sinä et tunne häntä. Hän oli eri koulussa. Tai ainakin eri luokalla.
8. V. Kauanko sinä olet Oulussa?
9. A. Kolme päivää.
10. V. Minä haluaisin kutsua sinut meille, jos sinulla on aikaa. Meidän asunto ei ole kaukana keskustasta. Kävelet Kauppakatua suoraan eteenpäin puoli kilometriä ja käännyt sitten oikealle, Isokadulle. Sinä löydät sinne helposti. Tule päivälliselle huomenna. Päivi haluaisi varmasti myös tavata sinut.
11. A. Ja minä haluaisin tavata teidät molemmat. Kiitos vain, mutta en tiedä vielä, onko minulla aikaa. Anna minulle puhelinnumerosi, niin minä soitan sinulle.
12. V. Tässä on minun korttini, siinä on osoite ja puhelinnumero.
13. A. Minä soitan sitten teille. Terveisiä Päiville!

■■■

Do you still remember me?

Old friends meet

1. Arto. Hello, Veikko!
2. Veikko. Well, hello! It's been a long time!
3. A. Do you still recognize me?
4. V. Of course I do. You're my old classmate, Arto Koskinen. What are you doing in Oulu?
5. A. I'm here on a business trip with Kari Peltonen and Heikki Lampio. Do you remember them?
6. V. Kari Peltonen ... I do remember him. But Heikki Lampio — I don't remember him.
7. A. It's possible that you don't know him. He was in a different school. Or at least in a different class.
8. V. How long are you staying in Oulu?
9. A. Three days.
10. V. I'd like to invite you to my home if you have time. Our apartment is not far from the center. You walk straight along Kauppakatu for half a kilometer and then turn right into Isokatu. You'll find it easily. Come and have dinner with us tomorrow. Päivi would certainly like to meet you, too.
11. A. And I'd like to see both of you. Thank you, but I don't know yet if I'll have the time. Give me your phone number, I'll call you.
12. V. Here's my card with my address and telephone number.
13. A. I'll call you then. Love to Päivi!

■■■

Kenet tapaat illalla? Hänet.
Kenelle kirjoitat? Hänelle.

missä? **täällä tuolla siellä**
mistä? **täällä tuolta sieltä**
mihin? | **tänne tuonne sinne**
minne? |

kuka? **ei kukaan**
mikä? **ei mikään**
missä? **ei missään**
milloin? **ei milloinkaan**
koska? **ei koskaan**

Kielioppia — Structural notes

1. Object forms of personal pronouns and "kuka"

In the English sentence "We often invite him for dinner" *him* indicates a person directly affected by the action of the verb and is therefore called the **direct object**.

Kene/t rouva Virtanen kutsuu?		Who will Mrs. V. invite?	
Rva V. kutsuu	*minu/t,*	Mrs. V. will invite	me,
	sinu/t,		you,
	häne/t,		him/her,
	meidä/t,		us,
	teidä/t,		you,
	heidä/t.		them.

The six personal pronouns and the pronoun *kuka* have a special object form (**accusative**) which ends in **-t**. It is only used in affirmative sentences.

Ke/tä rouva Virtanen ei kutsu?		Whom won't Mrs. V. invite?	
Rva V. ei kutsu	*minu/a,*	Mrs. V. won't invite	me,
	sinu/a,		you,
	hän/tä,		him/her,
	mei/tä,		us,
	tei/tä,		you,
	hei/tä.		them.

In negative sentences, the direct object is in the **partitive**.

Note: For various reasons, the partitive may occur in affirmative sentences as well, for instance with verbs generally used with the partitive:

Voinko auttaa tei/tä? — Can I help you?
Minä rakastan sinu/a. — I love you.

(More about this in lesson 29:3.)

Note also:
Do not mix up the direct object with what English grammar calls the **indirect object.** It answers the question "to whom", "for whom" and corresponds to the Finnish "onto" case:

Anna minulle kylmää vettä! — Give me some cold water!
Minä esittelen heidät sinulle. — I'll introduce them to you.
Kertokaa meille kaikki! — Tell us everything!

2. Words ending in -nen ("nainen" words)

Olen niin onnellinen! — I'm so happy!
Onnellista uutta vuotta! — Happy New Year!
Onnellisen elämän salaisuus. — The secret of a happy life.
On ilo nähdä onnellisia ihmisiä. — It is a pleasure to see happy people.

Finnish has a large number of nouns and adjectives which end in **-nen** in their basic form. Note the following points about this word type:

— The element **-nen** only appears in the basic form;
— All other forms have the element **-s-**, and the principal parts are *nainen naista naisen naisia*;
— The stem form *nais-* is used as the first part of compound words:

nais/poliisi, nais/lääkäri
helsinkiläis/perhe = helsinkiläinen perhe
ruotsalais-suomalainen sanakirja

Sanasto — Vocabulary

ainakin	at least
eteen/päin	forward, ahead
haluaisin	I'd like to
kaukana (≠ *lähellä*)	far away, at a distance
+kortti-a kortin kortteja	card
kutsu/a kutsun	to call, invite
+käänty/ä	to turn, be turned
käänny/n-t kääntyy	
käänny/mme-tte kääntyvät	
+luokka-a luokan luokkia	class
+löytä/ä	to find, discover
löydä/n-t löytää	
löydä/mme-tte löytävät	
+molemmat molempia (molempien)	both, the two
muista/a muistan (≠ *unohtaa*)	to remember, recall
pitkästä aikaa!	it's been a long time!
sinne (cp. *siellä*, *sieltä*)	there(to), to that place
suoraan (from *suora* straight, direct)	straight, directly
totta kai (= *tietysti*)	of course, naturally
toveri-a-n tovereita (= *kaveri* colloq.)	companion, friend, pal, comrade
varma-a-n varmoja (≠ *epä/varma*)	sure, certain

ei kukaan ketään kenenkään keitään	nobody, no one, none
ei missään	nowhere

Liisa Salo lähtee matkalle

Liisa Salon täytyy matkustaa Vaasaan. Mutta kuinka? Lentäminen on nopeaa, mutta kallista. Liisa ajattelee asiaa: parempi matkustaa yöjunalla.

— Minulla on kai aikataulu ... Joo, mutta tämä on liian vanha. Paras kysyä asemalta.

1. L. Mihin aikaan Vaasan yöjuna lähtee Helsingistä?
2. Neuvonta. Hetkinen ... Lähtöaika on 22.00, laituri 3.
3. L. Ja koska se saapuu Vaasaan?
4. N. Kello 6.35.
5. L. Selvä on, kiitos, kuulemiin.

Liisa pakkaa matkatavaransa ja soittaa taksin lähimmältä taksiasemalta. Taksi vie Liisan ja Liisan tavarat asemalle.
Liisa ostaa matkalipun.

Liisa Salo takes a trip

Liisa Salo has to go to Vaasa. But how? Flying is quick but expensive. Liisa thinks it over; better travel by night train.

— I probably have the timetable ... Yes, but this one is too old. The best thing is to inquire at the station.

1. L. What time does the night-train to Vaasa leave Helsinki?
2. Information. Just a moment ... The time of departure is 22.00, platform 3.
3. L. And when does it arrive in Vaasa?
4. I. At 6.35.
5. L. All right, thank you, goodbye.

Liisa packs her baggage and rings for a taxi from the nearest taxi station. The taxi takes Liisa and her things to the station.
Liisa buys the ticket.

6. L. Vaasa, meno. Onko makuupaikkoja jäljellä?
7. Lipunmyyjä. Ei ole.
8. L. No, sitten pikajunan paikkalippu. Ei-tupakkavaunu. Ikkunapaikka, jos on.
9. Lipunmyyjä. Katsotaan. Kyllä täällä on. (Antaa Liisalle paikkalipun.)

Liisa ostaa vielä postimerkin ja panee kirjeen postilaatikkoon. Sen jälkeen hän ostaa lukemista: iltalehden ja pari naistenlehteä. Hän löytää helposti oikean junan ja vaunun. Ja nyt hän istuu junassa. Kello on 22.00. Matka voi alkaa.

6. L. A single to Vaasa, please. Are there any sleeping berths left?
7. Ticket clerk. No, there aren't.
8. L. A seat-ticket, then, for the express train. A non-smoker. A window seat, if there is one.
9. Clerk. Let's see. Yes, there is. (Gives Liisa the seat-ticket.)

Liisa also buys a stamp and drops a letter in the mailbox. After this she buys something to read: an evening paper and a couple of women's magazines. She easily finds the right train and car. And now she is sitting on the train. It is ten o'clock. The journey can begin.

■■■

Ihmiset ostavat matkalippuja:
— Espoo, meno-paluu.
— Kauniainen, kymmenen matkan lippu.
— Korso—Helsinki, kuukausilippu.
Juna- ja metrolippuja saa myös automaatista.

Ota omenia!
Saanko **yhden?**
Saanko **kaksi?**

Kielioppia — Structural notes

1. The direct object of nouns

In the English sentence "We often invite Mr. Bradley for dinner" or "I'm giving the book to her", "Mr. Bradley" and "book" are directly affected by the action of the verb, that is, they are **direct objects**.

Unlike personal pronouns, Finnish nouns have no specific accusative forms. Instead, the direct object of nouns is expressed as follows.

	Affirmative sentence		Negative sentence	
Sing.	*Otan kirja/n.*	I take a/the book.	*En ota kirja/a.*	I do not take a/ the book.
Cp.	*Otan raha/a.*	I take some money.	*En ota raha/a.*	I do not take any money.
Pl.	*Otan kirja/t.*	I take the books.	*En ota kirjoj/a.*	I do not take the books.
Cp.	*Otan kirjoj/a.*	I take some books.	*En ota kirjoj/a.*	I do not take any books.

Note the following points:

— In negative sentences, the direct object is always in the **partitive**
— If the direct object expresses indefinite amount or number, it is always in the **partitive** (*raha/a, kirjoj/a*)
— If the direct object is one countable thing (or definite amount, e.g. *the* money), it is in the **genitive** (*kirja/n*)
— If the direct object expresses definite number, it is in the **basic form pl.** (*kirja/t*)

(When the genitive and the basic form are used as direct objects, they are often called accusatives.)

The basic form is used instead of the genitive in **imperative** and **täytyy** sentences:

Ota kirja! (cp. *Ota rahaa!*) Take a/the book!
Sinun täytyy ottaa kirja (rahaa). You must take a/the book.

Note.	Sing.	*Otan kirja/n.*	I take a/the book.
		Otan kirja/ni.	I take my book. (See 6:1.)
	Pl.	*Otan kirja/t.*	I take the books.
		Otan kirja/ni.	I take my books. (See 12:1.)

Note also: *Otan yhde/n (omena/n).* I take one (apple).
Otan kaksi (omena/a). I take two (apples).

(There will be a review of the direct object in 39:1.)

Important to remember: In a sentence with a direct object, the subject must never be in the partitive:

LAPSET
~~*Lapsia*~~ *syövät omenia.*

2. "Aion olla Suomessa vuoden"

Kuinka kauan sinä aiot olla Suomessa?	How long are you going to stay in Finland?
Vuode/n. (Kaksi vuotta.)	A year. (Two years.)
Kuinka kauan sinä olet ollut täällä?	How long have you been here?
Kuukaude/n. (Kolme kuukautta.)	A month. (Three months.)
Kuinka usein teillä on suomea?	How often do you have Finnish?
Kerra/n (kaksi kertaa) viikossa.	Once (twice) a week.
Kuinka pitkä/n matka/n kävelet joka päivä?	What distance do you walk every day?
Kilometri/n. (Kolme kilometriä).	One kilometer. (Three kilometers).

When answering the questions "how long? how many times? what distance?" the forms used are the same as for the direct object.

Note:

Ostan kirjan.	*En osta kirjaa.*	Partitive
Kävelen kilometrin.	*En kävele kilometriä.*	in the
Pöydällä on kirja.	*Pöydällä ei ole kirjaa.*	negative
Pojalla on kirja.	*Pojalla ei ole kirjaa.*	sentence

but:

Tämä on kirja.	*Tämä ei ole kirja.*
Kirja on kallis.	*Kirja ei ole kallis.*

Sanasto — Vocabulary

aika/taulu-a-n-ja	timetable, schedule
asema-a-n asemia	station; position, location
asia-a-n asioita	thing, matter; errand; question, point
+automaatti-a automaatin automaatteja	automatic, automate

juna-a-n junia	train
jäljellä	left, remaining
+kuu/kausi-kautta-kauden-kausia	month
kuulemiin (cp. *näkemiin*)	goodbye (in telephone conversations)
+laatikko-a laatikon laatikkoja	box; drawer
laituri-a-n laitureita	platform, pier, landing, wharf
+lentä/ä	to fly
lennä/n-t lentää	
lennä/mme-tte lentävät	
+lähtö-ä lähdön lähtöjä	leaving, going away, departure
+makuu/paikka-a-paikan-paikkoja	sleeping berth
+matka/lippu-a-lipun-lippuja	ticket
matka/tavara-a-n-tavaroita	baggage, luggage
matkusta/a matkustan	to travel, go, tour
+neuvonta-a neuvonnan (from *neuvo* advice, *neuvo/a* to advise)	guiding, information
+paka/ta pakkaan	to pack
paluu-ta-n (from *pala/ta* to return)	return, coming back, going back
pika/juna	express train
+posti/merkki-ä-merkin-merkkejä	(postage) stamp
+saapu/a	to arrive, come
saavu/n-t saapuu	
saavu/mme-tte saapuvat	
Juna saapuu Ouluun, asemalle	The train arrives in Oulu, at the station
selvä-ä-n selviä (≠ *epä/selvä*)	clear, distinct; plain, apparent
selvä on	I see, all right, okay
tavara-a-n tavaroita	thing, article, goods
+tupakka-a tupakan	tobacco; cigarettes

Viime viikonloppu

Jussi Salo tapaa Matti Suomelan

1. J. Terve, Matti! Mitäs sinulle kuuluu?
2. M. Kiitos, ei erikoista.
3. J. Miten viikonloppu meni? Olitteko te kaupungissa?
4. M. Kirsti ja lapset olivat kotona, mutta minä kävin Turussa.
5. J. Oliko se työmatka?
6. M. Oli, meillä oli tärkeä kokous. Näin paljon vanhoja tuttavia. Söimme yhdessä lounasta, ja meillä oli oikein hauskaa. Mitä sinä itse teit?
7. J. Minullakin oli mukava viikonloppu. Me kävimme Tampereella. Me lähdimme Helsingistä toissapäivänä ja tulimme takaisin eilen illalla.
8. M. Oliko tiellä paljon liikennettä?
9. J. Ei menomatkalla. Me ajoimme Tampereelle kahdessa ja puolessa tunnissa. Mutta tulomatka kesti kolme ja puoli tuntia.
10. M. Mitä te teitte Tampereella?
11. J. Meillä on siellä tuttavia. Kävimme heillä. Sitten me katselimme vähän kaupunkia. Lapset olivat ensi kertaa Tampereella. Ja siellä on paljon nähtävää.
12. M. Minäkin pidän Tampereesta. Se on siisti ja kaunis, vaikka onkin tehdaskaupunki. Minä käyn siellä usein. Ostitteko te jotakin?
13. J. Ei mitään erikoista. Lapset ostivat pari pientä matkamuistoa.

Last weekend

Jussi Salo meets Matti Suomela

1. J. Hello, Matti! How's everything?
2. M. All right, thank you.
3. J. How was the weekend? Did you stay in town?
4. M. Kirsti and the children stayed at home but I went to Turku.
5. J. Was it a business trip?
6. M. Yes, we had an important meeting. I saw many old friends. We had lunch together and had a very good time. What did you do yourself?
7. J. I had a nice weekend too. We went to Tampere. We left Helsinki the day before yesterday and came back last night.
8. M. Was there much traffic on the road?
9. J. Not on the way there. We drove to Tampere in two and a half hours. But the journey back took three and a half hours.
10. M. What did you do in Tampere?
11. J. We've got some friends there. We visited them. Then we looked at the city a bit. The children were in Tampere for the first time. And there is a great deal to see.
12. M. I like Tampere, too. It's clean and pretty, although it is a factory town. I often go there. Did you buy something?
13. J. Nothing special. The children bought a couple of little souvenirs.

meillä meidän talossa, perheessä; meidän maassamme
Voit asua meillä, Timo.
Tulkaa meille kylään!
Meillä (= Suomessa) ihmiset puhuvat paljon englantia.

27

ystävä **tuttava** (less close)
toveri (colloq. **kaveri**): hyvä toveri, vanha toveri, koulu-, luokka-, opiskelutoveri, työtoveri, huonetoveri, kirjeenvaihtotoveri

käydä

Kello käy (ei seiso).

Moottori ei käy normaalisti.

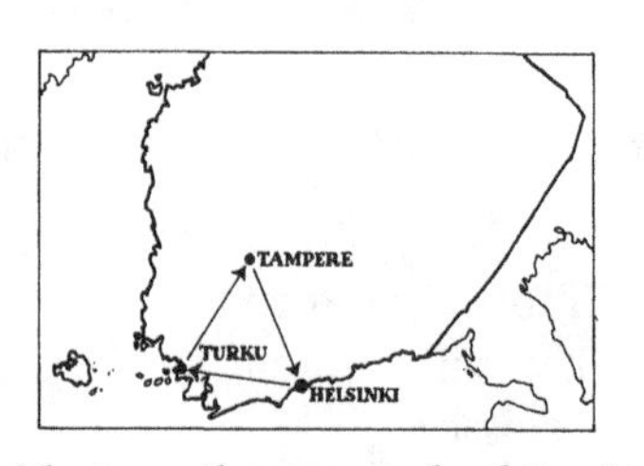

Ahot matkustavat, he käyvät **Turussa** ja **Tampereella**.

Rouva Aho käy **kaupassa**.

Mutta: Rouva A. menee **kauppaan**.

Matkustatteko Helsinkiin? Voitte mennä sinne

linja-autolla

junalla

lentokoneella

laivalla

polkupyörällä

jalan

Kielioppia — Structural notes

1. About the Finnish verb types: from basic form to present

The basic form of verbs in Finnish ends in

a)	b)	c)	d)
-da (-dä)	vowel + **a (ä)**	**-la, -na, -ra** (**lä, -nä, -rä**) **-s + ta (tä)**	vowel + **ta (tä)**
voi/da to be able	*puhu/a* to speak	*tul/la* to come	*halu/ta* to want
tuo/da to bring	*anta/a* to give	*men/nä* to go	**-ita (-itä)**
jää/dä to remain	*etsi/ä* to look for	*sur/ra* to grieve	*merki/tä*
		nous/ta to rise	to mean

How to obtain the present tense from the basic form:

voida verbs: Remove the inf. ending and use the stem as such: *voi/da — voi/n, voi/t, voi* etc.
No **k p t** changes.

puhua verbs: Remove the inf. ending and use the stem considering the **k p t** changes: *puhu/a — puhu/n puhu/t, puhu/u* etc., *anta/a — anna/n, anna/t, anta/a* etc.

tulla verbs: Remove the inf. ending and add **-e** to the stem: *tul/la — tule/n, tule/t, tule/e* etc., *nous/ta — nouse/n, nouse/t, nouse/e* etc.
k p t changes: **strong grade** in the whole present tense: *ajatel/la* to think — *ajattele/n, ajattele/t, ajattele/e* etc.

haluta verbs: Remove the inf. ending and add **-a (-ä)** to the stem: *halu/ta — halua/n, halua/t, halua/a* etc., *vasta/ta* to answer — *vastaa/n, vastaa/t, vastaa* etc.
k p t changes: **strong grade** in the whole present tense: *tava/ta* to meet — *tapaa/n, tapaa/t, tapaa* etc.

merki/tä verbs: Remove the inf. ending and add **-tse** to the stem: *merki/tä — merkitse/n, merkitse/t, merkitse/e* etc.
No **k p t** changes.
(More about *haluta* and *merkitä* verbs in 36:4.)

2. Past tense of verbs (affirmative)

a) *sano/a* to say

Present			Past		
(minä)	*sano/n*	I say	*(minä)*	*sano/i/n*	I said, was saying
(sinä)	*sano/t*	you say	*(sinä)*	*sano/i/t*	you said, were saying
hän	*sano/o*	he/she says	*hän*	*sano/i*	he/she said, was saying
(me)	*sano/mme*	we say	*(me)*	*sano/i/mme*	we said, were saying
(te)	*sano/tte*	you say	*(te)*	*sano/i/tte*	you said, were saying
he	*sano/vat*	they say	*he*	*sano/i/vat*	they said, were saying

teh/dä to do, to make

Present			Past		
(minä)	*tee/n*	I do	*(minä)*	*te/i/n*	I did, was doing
(sinä)	*tee/t*	you do	*(sinä)*	*te/i/t*	you did, were doing
hän	*teke/e*	he/she does	*hän*	*tek/i*	he/she did, was doing
(me)	*tee/mme*	we do	*(me)*	*te/i/mme*	we did, were doing
(te)	*tee/tte*	you do	*(te)*	*te/i/tte*	you did, were doing
he	*teke/vät*	they do	*he*	*tek/i/vät*	they did, were doing

Questions: *sano/i/ko hän?* did he/she say?
te/i/t/kö (sinä)? did you do? etc.

Compare the present and the past tense with each other. Note the following points:

— The past tense is formed from the present by inserting the past tense marker **-i-** between the verb stem and the personal ending;

— The endings are the same as in the present, except in the 3rd pers. sing., which has no ending;

— The past tense marker **-i-** may effect changes in the final vowel of the stem. The past tense of each new verb will be given in the vocabularies from now on and may be memorized from there. These changes can also be studied in the chart on p. 131. It is in your interest to familiarize yourself with this reference list as soon as possible. (There is a more detailed chart on the different types of verbs on p. 221.)

— As for the **k p t** changes, each person in the past tense has the same grade, weak or strong, as the corresponding person in the present tense (see *tehdä* above.)

Note, however, that most verbs with the combinations **-lt-**, **-nt-**, **-rt-** in their stem will have **-s-** all through their past tense:

kieltä/ä to forbid
Present *kiellä/n kiellä/t kieltä/ä kiellä/mme kiellä/tte kieltä/vät*
Past *kielsi/n kielsi/t kielsi kielsi/mme kielsi/tte kielsi/vät*

Similarly also *löytä/ä* to find, *pyytä/ä* to request, *tietä/ä* to know etc.:

Present *tiedä/n tiedä/t tietä/ä tiedä/mme tiedä/tte tietä/vät*
Past *tiesi/n tiesi/t tiesi tiesi/mme tiesi/tte tiesi/vät*

b) *haluta* verbs have a longer past tense marker **-si**.
k p t changes are the same as in the present tense.

halu/ta to want		*tava/ta* to meet	
Present	Past	Present	Past
halua/n	*halusi/n*	*tapaa/n*	*tapasi/n*
halua/t	*halusi/t*	*tapaa/t*	*tapasi/t*
halua/a	*halusi*	*tapaa*	*tapasi*
halua/mme	*halusi/mme*	*tapaa/mme*	*tapasi/mme*
halua/tte	*halusi/tte*	*tapaa/tte*	*tapasi/tte*
halua/vat	*halusi/vat*	*tapaa/vat*	*tapasi/vat*

The past tense of the verbs covered in lessons 1—26 can be looked up in the list on p. 132 (following this chapter). (The past tense negative will be introduced in 31:1.)

3. Turussa — Tampereella

Ingrid asuu Ruotsi/ssa, Ivan Venäjä/llä. — Ingrid lives in Sweden, Ivan in Russia.
Asun Turu/ssa (Tamperee/lla). — I live in Turku (Tampere).
Menkää Turku/un (Tamperee/lle)! — Go to Turku (Tampere)!
Olen tulossa Turu/sta (Tampe- ree/lta). — I'm coming from Turku (Tampere).

With some place-names, outer local cases are used instead of the more common inner local cases.

Almost all foreign place-names are used with inner local cases. An exception to this rule is *Venäjä* Russia.

Among Finnish place-names, most are used like *Turku* but quite a few are used like *Tampere*. No rules can be given, as it is the local usage that finally decides whether **-ssa** or **-lla** is preferred.

However, the outer local cases are often used if the place name ends in *-mäki (mäen)* hill; *-niemi (niemen)* peninsula, cape, point; *-järvi (järven)* lake; *-joki (joen)* river; *-koski (kosken)* rapids, waterfall etc. (that is, words with which the outer local endings are natural: *mäellä* on a hill). Examples: *Riihi/mäki — Riihi/mäellä, Rova/niemi — Rova/niemellä, Valkea/koski — Valkea/koskella, Vantaa/lla* (from a river name).

(Note, however, that names of city districts are mostly used in the inner local cases: *Lautta/saaressa, Munkki/niemessä, Kannel/mäessä* etc.)

Sanasto — Vocabulary

aja/a ajan ajoi	to drive; to ride
erikoi/nen-sta-sen-sia	special, particular
hauska: olla hauskaa (*mukavaa, kivaa*)	to have fun, a good time; to enjoy oneself
jo/kin jota/kin (= *jotain*) jon/kin joita/kin	some; something
kestä/ä kestän kesti	to last, take (of time); to stand, endure
kokous-ta kokouksen kokouksia	meeting, assembly
käy/dä käyn kävi	to go; to run, function; to walk; to visit, call on
käydä jossakin (Suome/ssa, Tamperee/lla)	to visit some place (Finland, Tampere)
mutta: tyttö käy koulu/a	but: the girl attends school, goes to school
+liikenne-ttä liikenteen	traffic
matka/muisto-a-n-ja (*muisto* memory; keepsake, from *muistaa* to remember)	souvenir
miten? (*miten/kä?*) (= *kuinka?*)	how?
nähtävä-ä-n nähtäviä	something to see
siisti-ä-n siistejä (≠ *epäsiisti*)	neat, clean
takaisin	back
+tehdas-ta tehtaan tehtaita	factory, mill, works
toissa/päivänä	(on) the day before yesterday
tuttava-a-n tuttavia	acquaintance, friend
tärkeä-(t)ä-n tärkeitä	important

☆

jalan	on foot
+joki jokea joen jokia	river
kaveri-a-n kavereita (= *toveri*)	(colloq.) friend, pal
kone-tta-en-ita	machine, engine
laiva-a-n laivoja	ship, boat
lento/kone-tta-en-ita	airplane
linja-auto-a-n-ja (= *bussi*)	bus
+mäki mäkeä mäen mäkiä	hill
normaali-a-n normaaleja (≠ *epänormaali*)	normal
polku/pyörä-ä-n-pyöriä	bicycle, bike
saari saarta saaren saaria	island, isle

27

Past tense of verbs (affirmative)
Vowel changes caused by the past tense marker -i-

		Present		Past	
Present stem ends in					
-o, -ö, -u, -y	no change	*katso/n*	*katso/o*	*katso/i/n*	*katso/i*
		nuku/n	*nukku/u*	*nuku/i/n*	*nukku/i*
-e	e>Ø	*lue/n*	*luke/e*	*lu/i/n*	*luk/i*
-ä	ä>Ø	*lähetä/n*	*lähettä/ä*	*lähet/i/n*	*lähett/i*
-i	i>Ø	*opi/n*	*oppi/i*	*op/i/n*	*opp/i*
-a	1. a>o in two-syllable verbs if first vowel is **a**	*maksa/n*	*maksa/a*	*makso/i/n*	*makso/i*
		auta/n	*autta/a*	*auto/i/n*	*autto/i*
	2. a>Ø in two-syllable verbs if 1st vowel is not **a**; in longer verbs	*soita/n*	*soitta/a*	*soit/i/n*	*soitt/i*
		matkusta/n	*matkusta/a*	*matkust/i/n*	*matkust/i*
-VV	VV>V	*saa/n*	*saa*	*sa/i/n*	*sa/i*
-ie	ie>e	*vie/n*	*vie*	*ve/i/n*	*ve/i*
-uo	uo>o	*juo/n*	*juo*	*jo/i/n*	*jo/i*
-yö	yö>ö	*syö/n*	*syö*	*sö/i/n*	*sö/i*
-Vi	i>Ø	*voi/n*	*voi*	*vo/i/n*	*vo/i*

Note:

— *käydä käyn/käy kävin/kävi*

— Present and past of **-i-** verbs are identical except for the 3rd pers. sing.:
Present *opin opit oppii opimme opitte oppivat*
Past *opin opit oppi opimme opitte oppivat*

— Present and past of **-Vi-** verbs are entirely identical: *voin voit voi voimme voitte voivat.*

27

A list of the verbs in lessons 1—26 by verb types

1.
voida verbs
juo/da-n joi 14
saa/da-n sai 8
syö/dä-n söi 14
tuo/da-n toi 14
vie/dä-n vei 15
voi/da-n voi 9

2.
puhua verbs
+aiko/a aion aikoi 13
asu/a-n-i 10
istu/a-n-i 5
katso/a-n-i 9
+kerto/a kerron kertoi 13
kutsu/a-n-i 25
kysy/ä-n-i 12
+käänty/ä käännyn kääntyi 25
+liikku/a liikun liikkui 18
+nukku/a nukun nukkui 24
puhu/a-n-i 3
+saapu/a saavun saapui 26
sano/a-n-i 5
seiso/a-n-i 19
toivo/a-n-i 11
+täyty/ä täytyy täytyi 19

+**luke/a** luen luki 17
+lähte/ä lähden lähti 14
muni/a-n muni 22
+oppi/a opin oppi 11
tanssi/a-n tanssi 5
toimi/a-n toimi 18

+**lähettä/ä** lähetän lähetti 17
+näyttä/ä näytän näytti 22
+pitä/ä pidän piti 23
+viettä/ä vietän vietti 24
+välittä/ä välitän välitti 23

+**kirjoitta/a** kirjoitan kirjoitti 5
matkusta/a-n matkusti 26
muista/a-n muisti 25
+opetta/a opetan opetti 11
osta/a-n osti 7
+otta/a otan otti 5
+soitta/a soitan soitti 5

+**anta/a** annan antoi 13
+autta/a autan auttoi 23
laula/a-n lauloi 7
maksa/a-n maksoi 7
paina/a-n painoi 16
paista/a-n paistoi 21
+vaihta/a vaihdan vaihtoi 18

+**lentä/ä** lennän lensi 26
+löytä/ä löydän löysi 25
+tietä/ä tiedän tiesi 6
+tunte/a tunnen tunsi 12
+ymmärtä/ä ymmärrän ymmärsi 7

3.
tulla verbs
+ajatel/la ajattelen ajatteli 19
+esitel/lä esittelen esitteli 8
katsel/la katselen katseli 19
kuul/la kuulen kuuli 18
+kuunnel/la kuuntelen kuunteli 24
kävel/lä kävelen käveli 21
luul/la luulen luuli 9
men/nä menen meni 7
nous/ta nousen nousi 19
ol/la olen (on) oli 1
opiskel/la opiskelen opiskeli 11
pan/na panen pani 13
tul/la tulen tuli 5

4.
haluta verbs
halu/ta haluan halusi 7
+levä/tä lepään lepäsi 23
+paka/ta pakkaan pakkasi 26
+tava/ta tapaan tapasi 20
vasta/ta vastaan vastasi 4

merkitä verbs
merki/tä merkitsen merkitsi 10
tarvi/ta tarvitsen tarvitsi 21

5.
Irregular verbs
+**näh/dä** näen näki 17
+**teh/dä** teen teki 11

Puhelinkeskustelu

Rouva Whitney soittaa neiti Jalavalle

(Puhelin soi. Joku vastaa puhelimeen.)

1. Jalavalla.
2. W. Täällä on rouva Whitney. Onko Kaarina Jalava tavattavissa?
3. Hetkinen, olkaa hyvä.

■■■

4. J. Kaarina Jalava puhelimessa.
5. W. Hyvää iltaa, täällä puhuu Jane Whitney. Anteeksi, että minä häiritsen näin myöhään.
6. J. Ei se mitään.
7. W. Tehän annatte suomen kielen tunteja ulkomaalaisille?
8. J. Niin annan. Mutta tehän osaatte puhua suomea.
9. W. Minä osaan vähän, mutta en tarpeeksi. Ja minä ymmärrän huonosti, varsinkin jos ihmiset puhuvat nopeasti. Minä haluaisin ottaa keskustelutunteja.
10. J. Montako tuntia viikossa te ottaisitte?
11. W. Voisinkohan minä saada kaksi tuntia?
12. J. Kyllä se sopii. Te voitte tulla päivällä, eikö niin?
13. W. Valitettavasti en. Minä olen työssä neljään saakka.
14. J. Sopisiko teille sitten kahdeksalta tiistaina ja perjantaina?

Telephone conversation

Mrs. Whitney is calling Miss Jalava

(The telephone rings. Somebody answers the phone.)

1. Hello (''At the Jalava's.'')
2. W. This is Mrs. W. May I speak to Miss Kaarina Jalava (''Is Miss K.J. to be met?'')?
3. Just a minute, please.

■■■

4. J. Kaarina Jalava speaking.
5. W. Good evening, this is Mrs. Jane Whitney calling. Excuse me for disturbing you as late as this.
6. J. Never mind.
7. W. You give Finnish lessons to foreigners, don't you?
8. J. Yes, I do. But you *can* speak Finnish.
9. W. Yes, I can a little, but not enough. And I understand poorly, especially if people speak quickly. I'd like to take conversation lessons.
10. J. How many lessons a week would you like to take?
11. W. I wonder if I could have two lessons?
12. J. Yes, that's all right. You can come during the day, can't you?
13. W. Unfortunately not. I work until four.
14. J. Would eight o'clock on Tuesday and Friday suit you, then?

15. W. Anteeksi, minä en ymmärrä. Voisitteko te toistaa? — Perjantai ei sovi oikein hyvin, me menemme silloin usein maalle. Jos teillä olisi aikaa esimerkiksi torstaina, se olisi parempi.
16. J. Selvä, torstai-iltana samaan aikaan. Kuinka pian te tahtoisitte aloittaa, ylihuomennako jo?
17. W. Se sopisi oikein hyvin. Saisinko kysyä, paljonko yksi tunti maksaa?
18. J. ... markkaa. Te voitte maksaa joka kerta tai kerran viikossa tai kerran kuussa, aivan kuten te itse tahdotte.
19. W. No, sitten kai kaikki on selvää. Olen siellä ylihuomenna tasan kello kahdeksan.
20. J. Näkemiin, tervetuloa!

15. W. Sorry, I don't understand. Could you repeat that please? — Friday doesn't suit me very well, we often go to the country then. If you had time on Thursday, for instance, it would be better.
16. J. OK, Thursday evening at the same time. How soon would you like to start, the day after tomorrow already?
17. W. That would suit me very well. May I ask how much a lesson costs?
18. J. ... marks. You can pay every time or once a week, or once a month, just as you wish yourself.
19. W. Well, then I suppose everything is settled. I'll be there at eight o'clock sharp the day after tomorrow.
20. J. I'm looking forward to seeing you, Mrs. W.

■■■

Kun soitat firmaan:
— Suksi Oy, hyvää päivää.
— Saanko johtaja Lammio.
— Numero on varattu, voitteko odottaa?
— Kyllä kiitos.

■■■

When calling a firm:
— Suksi Co., good morning.
— May I speak with Mr. Lammio, please.
— The line's busy, can you wait?
— Yes, thanks.

Lintu **osaa** lentää (can, has the skill).

Ihminen ei osaa. Mutta hän **voi** lentää lentokoneella (can, is able).

kerran/kaksi kertaa **päivässä**, **viikossa**, **kuussa**

sitten — silloin
Klo 7 nousen, **sitten** (= sen jälkeen) syön.
Soittakaa klo 18, **silloin** (= siihen aikaan, sillä hetkellä) olen kotona.

Kielioppia — Structural notes

1. Principal parts of verbs

Now you know the three key forms of verbs. All other verb forms can be formed on the basis of these three.

	1) **basic form**	2) **present**	3) **past**
puhua verbs	*laulaa*	*laulan*	*lauloi*
	nukkua	*nukun*	*nukkui*
	tietää	*tiedän*	*tiesi*
tulla verbs	*ajatella*	*ajattelen*	*ajatteli*
haluta verbs	*tavata*	*tapaan*	*tapasi*

With *puhua* verbs, no. 1 (*nukkua*) shows the **k p t** grade for the 3rd person present and past (*nukkuu/nukkui*, *nukkuvat/nukkuivat*); no. 2 shows the **k p t** grade for the rest of the two tenses (*nukun/nukuin*, *nukut/nukuit* etc.).

No. 3 shows the vowel changes and the eventual change of **t** to **s** in the past tense (*tietää* verbs).

With *tulla* and *haluta* verbs, no. 2 (*ajattelen*) shows the **k p t** grade for the entire present and past.

Note: *tehdä* and *nähdä* are exceptions to these rules.

Memorizing the principal parts of each verb is strongly recommended.

2. Some auxiliary verbs

As in English, certain verbs in Finnish require the basic form of another verb to complete their meaning. Among such auxiliaries are:

aikoa aion aikoi	to intend	*Aion lähteä.*	I intend to leave.
haluta haluan halusi	to want	*Haluatko syödä?*	Do you want to eat?
tahtoa tahdon tahtoi	to want	*Tahdotko syödä?*	
osata osaan osasi	to know how, can	*Osaako hän uida?*	Can he swim?
voida voin voi	to be able, can	*En voi auttaa.*	I cannot help.
saada saan sai	to be allowed, may	*Saanko selittää?*	May I explain?
		Et saa unohtaa.	You must not forget.
täytyä täytyy täytyi	to have to, must	*Meidän täytyy lähteä heti.*	We must leave at once.

3. Conditional present

Affirmative		Negative		
sano/isi/n	I should (would, I'd) say	*en*	*sano/isi* I should	not say
sano/isi/t	you would (you'd) say	*et*	you would	
sano/isi	he/she would (he'd) say	*ei*	he/she would	
sano/isi/mme	we should (would, we'd) say	*emme*	we should	
sano/isi/tte	you would (you'd) say	*ette*	you would	
sano/isi/vat	they would (they'd) say	*eivät*	they would	

Question:
sano/isi/ko hän? would he say? etc.

Negative question:
eikö hän sano/isi? wouldn't he say? etc.

The conditional present is formed by inserting **-isi-** between the stem and the personal ending.

The personal endings are the same as in the ordinary present tense except that the 3rd pers.sing. has no ending.

The stem is obtained from the 3rd pers. sing. present tense by dropping the last vowel:

(sanoa)	*sanoo*	he says	*sano/isi*	he would say
(tilata)	*tilaa*	he orders	*tila/isi*	he would order
(löytää)	*löytää*	he finds	*löytä/isi/mme*	we'd find
(voida)	*voi*	he can	*vo/isi/n*	I'd be able, I could

If the 3rd pers. sing. present tense ends in **-ee** or **-ii**, drop both before adding **-isi-**:

(nähdä)	*näkee*	he sees	*näk/isi/n*	I should see
(oppia)	*oppii*	he learns	*opp/isi/tte*	you would learn

The conditional of the following verbs does not follow these main rules:

(olla)	*on*	he is	*ol/isi*	he would be	(cp. *oli*)
(käydä)	*käy*	he visits	*käv/isi*	he would visit	*(kävi)*
(juoda)	*juo*	he drinks	*jo/isi*	he would drink	*(joi)*
(syödä)	*syö*	he eats	*sö/isi*	he would eat	*(söi)*
(viedä)	*vie*	he takes (something somewhere)	*ve/isi*	he would take (something somewhere)	*(vei)*

tuoda to bring, *suoda* to give, grant, *luoda* to create, are similar to *juoda; lyödä* to beat, strike, is similar to *syödä.*

"If" clauses

Jos minulla olisi rahaa, ostaisin talon.	If I had money, I'd buy a house.
Jos tietäisitte kaiken, ymmärtäisitte häntä.	If you knew everything, you would understand her.

The Finnish language uses the conditional also in the *jos* clause of a conditional sentence. (Note that English normally uses the simple past tense instead.)

The "polite" conditional

Voisinko saada lasin kylmää vettä?	Could I have a glass of cold water?
Etkö haluaisi levätä vähän?	Wouldn't you like to rest a little?
Haluaisin kilon tätä lihaa.	I'd like a kilo of this meat.

The conditional is also used to make questions and requests sound more hesitant and therefore more polite.

Sanasto — Vocabulary

+aloitta/a aloitan aloitti (≠ *lopettaa*)	to begin, start
eikö niin? (colloq. *eiks niin?*)	isn't it? doesn't it? haven't you? etc. (cp. Fr. n'est-ce pas?)
+esi/merkki-ä-merkin-merkkejä	example
esi/merkiksi (abbr. *esim.*)	for example, for instance (e.g.)
-han (-hän)	a suffix added to the first word (group of words) in a sentence to create different shades of emphasis:
Pekka/han sen teki, en minä.	Pekka did it, not me.
Sinä/hän tiedät sen.	You know it, don't you?
Koska/han kurssi alkaa?	I wonder when the course starts?
Onko/han Ville kotona?	I wonder whether V. is at home?

häiri/tä-tsen-tsi	to disturb, bother, interfere
joku jota/kuta jon/kun joita/kuita	somebody, someone
keskustel/la-en-i	to converse, discuss, talk
keskustelu-a-n-ja	conversation, discussion, talk
kuu-ta-n kuita	moon; (= *kuu/kausi*) month
näin	like this, in this way, so
näin iso	as big as this, so big
osa/ta-an-si	to know how, can
pian	soon
saakka (= *asti*)	until, up to, as far as; ever since
ilta/an saakka	until the evening
Turku/un, Tamperee/lle s.	as far as Turku, Tampere
tammikuu/sta saakka	(ever) since January
silloin	then, at that time
soi/da-n soi	to ring, give a ringing sound
+sopi/a sovin sopi	to suit, be all right; to suit, fit, become; to agree
+tahto/a tahdon tahtoi (cp. *tahto* will)	to want, will
tasan	evenly, equally; just, precisely, sharp
tavattavissa (from *tavata*)	to be met, within reach
toista/a-n toisti	to repeat, say/do once more
valitettavasti (≠ *onneksi*)	unfortunately
varsinkin	especially, particularly
yli/huomenna	(on) the day after tomorrow

☆

johtaja-a-n johtajia (from *johtaa* to lead, direct)	director, leader, manager, conductor
+lintu-a linnun lintuja	bird
+odotta/a odotan odotti (jotakin)	to wait for, expect (something)
+osake/yhtiö-tä-n-itä (abbr. *oy*) (*osake* share, stock)	(joint-stock) company
+varattu-a varatun varattuja (≠ *vapaa*)	reserved, engaged, taken

Liisa ja Kalle katselevat perhekuvaa

Liisa and Kalle are looking at a family picture

Henkilöt:
Kalle Oksanen, nuori maisteri, 25-vuotias.
Liisa Salo, 19-vuotias, Kallen hyvä ystävä.
Meeri Vaara, 22-vuotias, Kallen serkku.

Characters:
Kalle Oksanen, a young M.A., 25 years old.
Liisa Salo, 19 years old, Kalle's good friend.
Meeri Vaara, 22 years old, Kalle's cousin.

1. K. No niin, tässä on minun perheeni. Minä otin tämän kuvan vuosi sitten, isoisän syntymäpäivänä.

Tuossa ovat minun vanhempani. Oikealla on isä, vasemmalla äiti, edessä Jaana-sisko, takana Olli-veli ja keskellä isoisä. Tämä on Ville-setä ja tuo Martta-täti.

1. K. Well, here's my family. I took this picture a year ago, on Grandfather's birthday.

There are my parents. On the right is my father, on the left my mother, in the front my sister Jaana, at the back my brother Olli, and in the center is my grandfather. This is my uncle Ville and that is my aunt Martha.

Meeri tulee.

Meeri enters.

2. L. Hei, Meeri! Tunnetko sinä Kallen perheen? Tässä on heidän kuvansa.

2. L. Hello, Meeri! Do you know Kalle's family? Here is their picture.

3. M. Tunnen kyllä. Tässä ovat hänen vanhempansa, edessä on hänen sisarensa, takana hänen veljensä ja keskellä hänen isoisänsä. Tämä on hänen setänsä ja tuo hänen tätinsä.

3. M. Yes, I do. Here are his parents, in the front is his sister, at the back his brother, and in the center his grandfather. This is his uncle and that is his aunt.

4. L. Kylläpä sinä tunnetkin Kallen perheen hyvin.

4. L. You do know Kalle's family well, don't you?

5. M. Totta kai minä tunnen heidät, mehän olemme sukulaisia. Kalle on minun serkkuni.

5. M. Why, of course I know them, we're relatives. Kalle is my cousin.

6. L. Ai niinkö, no, se selittää asian. — Minä pidän teidän isoisästänne. Kuinka vanha hän on?

6. L. Oh, is that so? Well, that explains it. — I like your grandfather. How old is he?

7. K. 70 vuotta. Hän on syntynyt vuonna 1923.

7. K. 70 years. He was born in 1923.

8. L. Elääkö teidän isoäitinne vielä?

8. L. Is your grandmother still alive?

9. M. Ei, isoäiti on kuollut. Hän kuoli jo monta vuotta sitten.

9. M. No, she isn't. Grandmother is dead. She died many years ago.

10. L. Katsotaan muitakin kuvia. Kuka tuo kaunis nainen tuossa on? Serkku vai täti?

10. L. Let's look at some other pictures too. Who's that pretty woman there? A cousin or an aunt?

11. K. Eräs vanha ystävä vain. Et sinä tunne häntä.

11. K. Just an old friend. You don't know her.

12. L. Sinunko vanha ystäväsi?

12. L. Your old friend?

13. M. Anteeksi, minun täytyy nyt lähteä. Näkemiin, Liisa. Hei sitten, Kalle. (Menee.)

13. M. Excuse me, I've got to go now. Goodbye, Liisa. Bye bye, Kalle. (Exit Meeri.)

14. L. *Sinunko* vanha ystäväsi??

14. L. *Your* old friend??

15. K. Ei minun, rakas Liisa! *Meidän* ystävämme, *perhe*ystävä. Hänen nimensä on Sirkka Sipi, hän on naimisissa ja hänellä on kuusi lasta. Liisa, sinä tiedät, että minä rakastan sinua. Vain sinua! (Liisa ja Kalle eivät enää katsele kuvia.)

15. K. Not mine, dear Liisa! *Our* friend, a *family* friend. Her name is Sirkka Sipi, she is married and has six children. Liisa, you know I love you. Only you! (Liisa and Kalle are no longer looking at pictures.)

perhe = isä, äiti ja lapset
suku = perhe + sukulaiset (isovanhemmat, sedät, tädit, serkut jne.)

vielä — enää
— Elääkö isoisänne vielä?
— Ei, hän ei elä enää.

vielä — jo
— Onko Matti jo kotona?
— Ei ole vielä.

En minä **halua** | Minä en halua — ostaa mitään.

Ei minulla **ole** | Minulla ei ole — rahaa.

minä **pidän** sinusta/minä **rakastan** sinua
minä **vihaan** sotaa

Kielioppia — Structural notes

1. Possessive suffixes

koti home			*veli* (gen. *velje/n*)		brother
(minun)	*koti/ni*	my home	*(minun)*	*velje/ni*	my brother
(sinun)	*koti/si*	your home	*(sinun)*	*velje/si*	your brother
hänen	*koti/nsa*	his/her home	*hänen*	*velje/nsä*	his/her brother
(meidän)	*koti/mme*	our home	*(meidän)*	*velje/mme*	our brother
(teidän)	*koti/nne*	your home	*(teidän)*	*velje/nne*	your brother
heidän	*koti/nsa*	their home	*heidän*	*velje/nsä*	their brother

Each person has a poss. suffix of its own, except the 3rd pers. sing. and pl., which have the same suffix (**-nsa**, **-nsä**).

The stem to which the poss. suffixes are added is obtained from the genitive: *veli, velje/n — velje/nne; rakas, rakkaa/n* dear, darling — *rakkaa/ni* my dear etc.

Note, however, that there is always a **strong grade** immediately before the poss. suffix, no matter what kind of syllable follows: *koti/nsa* (cp. gen. *kodi/n*); *kaupunki/mme* our town (gen. *kaupungi/n*); *lippu/nne* your ticket (gen. *lipu/n*); *lehte/nsä* their newspaper (*lehti*, gen. *lehde/n*).

When to omit the pers. pronouns:
minun, sinun, meidän, teidän are omitted in written language unless they carry a special emphasis:

Koti/ni on linna/ni. — My home is my castle.

Mutta:
Tämä on minun kotini, ei sinun. — This is my home, not yours.

minun, sinun, hänen, meidän, teidän, heidän are all omitted if they refer to the subject of the sentence:

Minä tapasin setä/ni. — I met my uncle.
Heikki tapasi setä/nsä. — Heikki met his (own) uncle.
Pojat tapasivat setä/nsä. — The boys met their (own) uncle.

Otherwise, *hänen* and *heidän* must not be left out:

Me tapasimme hänen/heidän setä/nsä. — We met his/their uncle.

Poss. suffixes are not added to adjectives:

Vanha talo/mme. — Our old house.
Hänen paras ystävä/nsä. — Her best friend.

2. Inflection of nouns with possessive suffixes

Sing.			*minun*	*hänen/heidän*	
Nom.	*pöytä*		*pöytä/ni*	*pöytä/nsä*	
Part.	*pöytää*		*pöytää/ni*	*pöytää/nsä*	
Gen.	*pöydän*	*(pöytä-)*	*pöytä/ni*	*pöytä/nsä*	
"on"	*pöydällä*		*pöydällä/ni*	*pöydällä/nsä*	= *pöydällä/än*
"from"	*pöydältä*		*pöydältä/ni*	*pöydältä/nsä*	= *pöydältä/än*
"onto"	*pöydälle*		*pöydälle/ni*	*pöydälle/nsä*	= *pöydälle/en*
"in"	*pöydässä*		*pöydässä/ni*	*pöydässä/nsä*	= *pöydässä/än*
"out of"	*pöydästä*		*pöydästä/ni*	*pöydästä/nsä*	= *pöydästä/än*
"into"	*pöytään*	*(pöytää-)*	*pöytää/ni*	*pöytää/nsä*	
Pl.					
Nom.	*pöydät*	*(pöytä-)*	*pöytä/ni*	*pöytä/nsä*	
Part.	*pöytiä*		*pöytiä/ni*	*pöytiä/nsä*	= *pöytiä/än*

Note the following points:

— The end cons. of a case ending is lost before a poss. suffix. As a result, the basic form sing. and pl. as well as the gen. sing. become identical in form; cp.

(veli)	*Velje/ni lähti Raumalle.*	My brother went to Rauma.
(veljet)	*Velje/ni lähtivät Raumalle.*	My brothers went to Rauma.
(veljen)	*Velje/ni perhe lähti Raumalle.*	My brother's family went to Rauma.

The "into" form also loses its **-n**: *kotii/ni, kotii/si, kotii/nsa, kotii/mme, kotii/nne, kotii/nsa.*

— In the 3rd pers., there is a parallel suffix, prolongation of vowel + **n**, which is preferred in modern Finnish. This parallel suffix cannot be used if there is already a long vowel (e.g. *pöytää*); it is never used in the basic form, genitive, or "into" case; cp.

Matti S. menee toimistoo/nsa.	Matti S. goes to his office.
Hän on nyt toimistossa/an.	He is now in his office.
Hän lähtee toimistosta/an.	He leaves his office.
Hänen toimisto/nsa on nyt kiinni.	His office is now closed.

(More about the pl. inflection with poss. suffixes in 40:1.)

Note: In casual every-day Finnish, particularly in the Helsinki area, poss. suffixes are frequently dropped altogether: *mun kirja = (minun) kirja/ni, sun ystävät = (sinun) ystävä/si, hänen uudessa asunnossa = hänen uudessa asunnossa/an* etc.

3. "Minä rakastan sinua" — verbs with partitive

A number of verbs (often ending in **-ella**), which express continuous action, have their direct object in the partitive. The group also includes most verbs of emotion. Among such verbs are:

ajatella to think of, think over	*Ajattele asia/a!*
auttaa to help	*Auttakaa hei/tä!*
häiritä to disturb	*Sinä häiritset minu/a.*
katsella / *katsoa* to look at, watch	*Katselemme* / *Katsomme televisio/ta.*
kuunnella to listen to	*Hän kuunteli radio/ta.*
odottaa to wait for, expect	*Odota minu/a!*
opiskella to study	*Tyttö opiskeli fysiikka/a.*
rakastaa to love	*Minä rakastan sinu/a.*
vihata to hate	*Kaikki vihaavat sota/a.*

Sanasto — Vocabulary

edessä (≠ *takana*)	in (the) front, before
elä/ä-n eli (cp. *elämä* life)	to live, be alive
eräs-tä erään eräitä	one, a (certain)
iso/isä-ä-n-isiä	grandfather
isä-ä-n isiä	father
keskellä	in the middle
kuol/la-en-i (cp. *kuolema* death)	to die
kuollut-ta kuolleen kuolleita	dead
maisteri-a-n maistereita	Master of Arts or Science (also used as a title)
naimisissa: olla n. jonkun kanssa	to be married to somebody
mennä naimisiin jonkun kanssa	to get married to somebody
-pa (-pä)	emphatic suffix: often used just to create a colloquial, intimate atmosphere
tule/pa(s) tänne!	come here, won't you?
minä/pä(s) olen oikeassa	I'm the one who's right!
olet/pa(s) sinä tarmokas!	why, you *are* energetic!

29

+rakas-ta rakkaan rakkaita	dear
rakasta/a-n rakasti (jotakin henkilöä) (cp. *rakkaus* love)	to love
+selittä/ä selitän selitti (cp. *selitys* explanation)	to explain
+serkku-a serkun serkkua serkkuja	cousin
pikku/serkku	second cousin
+setä-ä sedän setiä	uncle (paternal side)
eno-a-n-ja	maternal uncle
sisar-ta-en-ia	sister
sisko-a-n-ja	(colloq.) sister
sukulai/nen-sta-sen-sia	relative
+synty/ä synnyn syntyi (cp. *syntymä* birth)	to be born
olen syntynyt	I was born
takana (≠ *edessä*)	behind, beyond, at the back
tuossa (cp. *tässä*)	(right) there
veli veljeä veljen veljiä	brother
vuonna (abbr. *v.*)	in the year
-vuotias-ta-vuotiaan-vuotiaita	- years old
5-vuotias = 5 vuotta vanha	

☆

+sota-a sodan sotia	war
+tytär-tä tyttären tyttäriä	daughter
viha/ta-an-si (cp. *viha* hate)	to hate

Katsokaa tänne ja hymyilkää!

Kalle ottaa perhekuvan

1. Kalle. No niin, nyt se alkaa! Tulkaa kaikki tänne, minä otan sen kuvan nyt. Ottakaa pari tuolia mukaan. Ei, isoisä, älä sinä kanna tuolia itse! Olli, tuo tuoli isoisälle. Pane se tähän. Isoisä, ole hyvä ja istu siihen. Sinulla on syntymäpäivä, sinun täytyy istua keskellä. Isä ja äiti, istukaa isoisän vasemmalle ja oikealle puolelle.
2. Jaana. Sano missä minun paikkani on? Minä voisin seisoa tässä äidin vieressä, näin. Tai istua äidin ja isoisän välissä. Kumpi on parempi?
3. K. Odota nyt vähän, Jaana, älä häiritse taas! Sinä olet ihan mahdoton. Sinun vuorosi tulee kyllä.
4. J. Enhän minä häiritse yhtään! Minä halusin vain auttaa.
5. K. No, auta sitten, mene hakemaan Musti kuvaan. — Täti ja setä, voisitteko te seisoa tuolla äidin ja isoisän takana? Ei, älkää seisoko niin keskellä, menkää vähän enemmän vasemmalle. Hetkinen ... älkää olko liian kaukana äidistä, olkaa ihan hänen lähellään. Noin, nyt on hyvä. Ja Olli, seiso sinä isän luona.

6. Jaana (tulee Mustin kanssa). Tässä Musti on. Se nukkui kaikessa rauhassa sohvan alla. Hei Musti, älä juokse pois, Kalle ottaa meistä kuvan.

7. Äiti. Jaana ja Musti, älkää juosko siinä ja häiritkö. Istukaa ja olkaa hiljaa, jos mahdollista.
8. J. Hiljaa, Musti!
9. Olli. Hae sille makkaraa keittiöstä, se auttaa.

Look here and smile, please!

Kalle is taking the family picture

1. K. Well, here we go. Come here everybody, I'll take the picture now. Take a couple of chairs along. No, Grandpa, don't you carry the chair yourself! Olli, bring a chair for Grandpa. But it right here. Grandpa, please sit down there. It's your birthday, you must sit in the middle. Dad and Mom, please sit down to the left and right of Grandpa.
2. Jaana. Tell me where my place is? I could stand here, next to Mom, like this. Or I could sit between Mom and Grandpa. Which is better?
3. K. Wait a bit now, Jaana, don't disturb us again! You're quite impossible. You'll have your turn all right.
4. J. I'm not disturbing you at all! I just wanted to help.
5. K. Well, then help, go and fetch Musti for the picture. — Aunt and Uncle, could you stand over there, behind Mom and Grandpa? No, don't stand so much in the middle, go a little more to the left. One moment ... don't stay too far away from Mom, stay quite near her. Like that, now it's good. And Olli, stand by Dad, please.
6. Jaana (comes with Musti). Here's Musti. He was sleeping very peacefully under the sofa. Why, Musti, don't run away, Kalle is going to take a picture of us.
7. Mom. Jaana and Musti, don't run around, don't be a nuisance. Sit down and be quiet, if that's possible.
8. J. Quiet, Musti!
9. Olli. Go and get some sausage for him from the kitchen, that'll help.

10. Martta-täti. Kalle, lähetä sitten meillekin tämä kuva, kun se on valmis.	10. Aunt Martta. Kalle, send us this picture, too, won't you, when it's ready?
11. K. Tietysti minä lähetän. No niin, ovatko kaikki valmiit? Katsokaa tänne ja hymyilkää! Hymyilkää oikein kauniisti! Kiitos.	11. K. Of course I will. Well, is everybody ready? Look here and smile, please! A really good smile! Thank you.

tässä	**tuossa**	**siinä**
tästä	**tuosta**	**siitä**
tähän	**tuohon**	**siihen**

Kielioppia — Structural notes

1. Imperative (affirmative and negative)

a) **Imperative sing. (= informal imperative)**

Affirmative		Negative	
Tule tänne, Mikko!	Come here, Mikko!	*Älä tule tänne!*	Don't come here!
Kerro hänelle!	Tell her!	*Älä kerro hänelle!*	Don't tell her!
Tee se heti!	Do it at once!	*Älä tee sitä!*	Don't do it!

The affirmative imperative sing. was introduced in 5:2. The negative form uses the same stem, obtained from the 1st pers. present tense (*tule/n*, *kerro/n*, *tee/n*). The negation is *älä*.

The informal imperative is also used in orders or advice meant for everyone personally: *varo!* look out (for danger)! *käännä!* turn (the page), over; *katso* (abbr. *ks.*) *s. 170* see p. 170 etc.

b) **Imperative pl. (and formal)**

	Affirmative		Negative
Tul/kaa tänne, lapset!	Come here, children!	*Äl/kää tul/ko tänne!*	Don't come here!
Kerto/kaa hänelle!	Tell her!	*Äl/kää kerto/ko hänelle!*	Don't tell her!
Teh/kää se heti, nti Aho!	Do it at once, Miss Aho!	*Äl/kää teh/kö sitä!*	Don't do it!

The affirmative imperative pl. was introduced in 7:2. The negative form uses the same stem, obtained from the basic form of the verb (*tul/la*, *kerto/a*, *teh/dä*).

Structure of the negative form:

negation + inf. stem / **ko (kö)**

äl/kää *tul/ko*

haluta and *merkitä* verbs have **-t** before the imperative pl. ending:

levä/tä	to rest	*Levät/kää vähän!*	Rest a little!
häiri/tä	to disturb	*Äl/kää häirit/kö!*	Do not disturb!

c) **Direct object in imperative sentences**

Teen tämän työn.	I'll do this job.	*(En tee sitä.)*
Tee/tehkää tämä työ!	Do this job!	*(Älä tee/älkää tehkö sitä!)*

With the affirmative imperative, the direct object is in the basic form instead of the genitive.

However, a partitive object remains in the partitive: *Syö/syökää jäätelöä!* Have some icecream!

2. Postpositions with genitive

Päivällise/n jälkeen.	After dinner.
Rouva Salo/n kanssa.	With Mrs. Salo.
Tamperee/n kautta.	Via Tampere.
Asun Salon perhe/en luona.	I live with the Salos (at the Salo's).

The English language has a large number of prepositions (literally, ''words placed before another word'', e.g. ''after'', ''with''. The Finnish language also has a few, but it has far more **postpositions** (''words placed after another word''), e.g. *jälkeen, kanssa.*

The noun that precedes a postposition is most often in the **genitive** (sometimes in the **partitive**, see lesson 37:2).

Among postpositions with the genitive are:

aikana during
alla under
alapuolella below, underneath
edessä in front of
jälkeen after
kanssa (together) with
kautta through, via
keskellä in the middle of
luona at, by, near
lähellä near, close to
ohi(tse) past, by
poikki across
päällä on top of
sisällä (sisässä) in, inside
sisäpuolella inside
takana behind
ulkopuolella outside
vieressä by, next to
välillä (välissä) between
yli(tse) over, across
yläpuolella above
ympärillä around

Some of these postpositions may be used as prepositions as well, e.g. *ohi, poikki, yli: kadu/n poikki = poikki kadu/n* across the street etc.

When a postposition with the gen. is preceded by a pers. pronoun, a possessive suffix must be used:

(minun)	*kanssa/ni*	with me	*(meidän)*	*kanssa/mme*	with us
(sinun)	*kanssa/si*	with you	*(teidän)*	*kanssa/nne*	with you
hänen	*kanssa/an* *(kanssa/nsa)*	with him/her	*heidän*	*kanssa/an* *(kanssa/nsa)*	with them

(About postpositions with the gen. see also 35:2.)

Sanasto — Vocabulary

+alka/a alan alkoi	to begin, start, commence
enemmän (cp. *paljon*)	more
+hake/a haen haki	to fetch; to look for; to apply for
hiljaa	quiet(ly), softly; slowly
hiljai/nen-sta-sen-sia	quiet, silent
hymyil/lä hymyilen hymyili	to smile
ihan (= *aivan*)	quite, entirely, completely
juos/ta juoksen juoksi	to run
+kanta/a kannan kantoi	to carry, bear
+kumpi? kumpaa? kumman? kumpia?	which (of the two)?
mahdolli/nen-sta-sen-sia	possible, eventual
+mahdoton-ta mahdottoman mahdottomia	impossible
mukaan	along; with; according to
rauha-a-n (rauhoja) (≠ *sota*)	peace
tietysti (= *totta kai*)	of course, naturally
valmis-ta valmiin valmiita	ready; finished, complete

Kun bussi ei tullut

Olen ulkomaalainen, asun Helsingissä. Saanko kertoa, mitä minulle eilen tapahtui?

Seisoin bussipysäkillä. Odotin ja odotin. Bussi ei tullut.

En ollut yksin. Pysäkillä seisoi myös vanha herra, jota en tuntenut. En tiennyt, paljonko kello oli, koska minulla ei ollut kelloa. Lopulta en voinut enää odottaa. Päätin kysyä vanhalta herralta, paljonko kello oli.

Hän ei vastannut. Joko hän ei kuullut tai ei ymmärtänyt, tai ehkä hän vain ei halunnut vastata.

Toistin kysymykseni hyvin selvästi ja kovaa. Tällä kertaa herra katsoi minuun ja hymyili kohteliaasti, mutta ei sanonut mitään.

Miksi en huomannut sitä ennen? Ehkä hän oli suomenruotsalainen, joka ei osannut suomea.

Toistin kysymykseni ruotsiksi. Ei auttanut. Kohtelias hymy, mutta ei vastausta.

"Tik tak", sanoin. "Mitä? Tik tak."

Mitään ei tapahtunut.

En kestänyt enää. Huusin — englanniksi — jotain, jota en halua tässä toistaa.

Herra katsoi minuun taas. Hän ei enää hymyillyt. Hän sanoi vihaisesti:

"Tyypillinen amerikkalainen nuorimies!"

Englanniksi. Erittäin brittiläisesti.

When the bus did not come

I am a foreigner living in Helsinki. May I tell you what happened to me yesterday?

I was standing at a bus stop. I waited and waited. The bus did not come.

I was not alone. There was also an old gentleman, whom I did not know, standing at the stop. I did not know what the time was because I had no watch. Finally I could not wait any longer. I decided to ask the old gentleman what the time was.

He did not answer. Either he did not hear or did not understand, or perhaps he just did not want to answer.

I repeated my question very distinctly and loudly. This time the gentleman looked at me and smiled politely but didn't say anything.

Why didn't I notice it before? Perhaps he was a Swedish-speaking Finn, who did not speak Finnish.

I repeated my question in Swedish. It didn't help. A polite smile, but no answer.

"Tick-tock", I said. "*Mitä*? Tick-tock."

Nothing happened.

I couldn't stand it any longer. I shouted — in English — something that I don't want to repeat here.

The gentleman looked at me again. He wasn't smiling any longer. He said, angrily:

"A typical young American!"

In English. In a very British way.

31

Bussi tuli. Me kaksi anglosaksia nousimme siihen. Mutta emme istuneet samalla penkillä. Emmekä keskustelleet toistemme kanssa.

The bus came. We two Anglo-Saxons got on. But we did not sit on the same bench. Neither did we talk to each other.

enkä = **ja** en
etkä = ja et
eikä = ja ei
jne.

älkääkä = ja älkää
äläkä = ja älä

mihin?

Bussiin nousee ihmisiä. **Siihen** nousee 3 ihmistä.

missä?

Bussissa istuu ihmisiä. **Siinä** istuu monta henkeä.

mistä?

Bussista lähtee ihmisiä. **Siitä** nousee 2 miestä.

Kielioppia — Structural notes

1. Past tense negative

sano/a to say				*näh/dä* to see			
(minä) en		I	did not	*(minä) en*		I	did not
(sinä) et	*sano/nut*	you	say	*(sinä) et*	*näh/nyt*	you	see
hän ei		he/she		*hän ei*		he/she	
(me) emme		we	did not	*(me) emme*		we	did not
(te) ette	*sano/neet*	you	say	*(te) ette*	*näh/neet*	you	see
he eivät		they		*he eivät*		they	

Negative question:

enkö (minä) sano/nut?	did I not say?
emmekö (me) näh/neet?	did we not see?

Structure:

Negation		Past participle: inf. stem + **-nut (-nyt)** (sing.). **-neet** (pl.)
en, et, ei	+	*sano/nut, näh/nyt*
emme, ette, eivät	+	*sano/neet, näh/neet*

tulla verbs have **-ll-**, **-rr-**, **-ss-** in the past participle:

tul/la to come	*tul/lut, tul/leet*
sur/ra to mourn	*sur/rut, sur/reet*
nous/ta to rise	*nous/sut, nous/seet*

haluta and *merkitä* verbs have an extra **-n-** in the participle:

halu/ta to want	*halun/nut, halun/neet*
merki/tä to mean	*merkin/nyt, merkin/neet*

Note: *tietä/ä* has two past participles, *tietä/nyt* and *tien/nyt,* the latter being more commonly used.

Note also:
When *te* is used in formal speech to refer to one person, the past participle must appear in the sing. form:

(te) ette näh/nyt	you (one person) did not see
(te) ette näh/neet	you (many persons) did not see

2. Relative pronoun ''joka''

Tyttö, joka tulee tuolla, on serkkuni.	The girl who (that) is coming there is my cousin.
Poika, jo/n/ka nimi oli Martti, soitti sinulle.	A boy whose name was Martti called you.
Kirja, jo/sta pidän, on Hyryn Alakoulu.	A book which (that) I like is Hyry's ''Alakoulu''.
Tytöt, jo/t/ka tulevat tuolla, ovat serkkujani.	The girls who (that) are coming there are my cousins.
Kuvat, joi/ta katselitte, ovat Lapista.	The pictures you were looking at are from Lapland.

31

The relative pronoun in Finnish is *joka* (in English ''who'', ''which'', ''that'').
The pronoun *joka* agrees in number with the noun to which it refers: *tyttö, joka tulee — tytöt, jotka tulevat; kuva, jota katson — kuvat, joita katson.* Its form depends on its function in the sentence.
joka has a regular declension except that the second syllable **-ka** disappears in all cases but three (basic form sing. and pl. and gen. sing.): *joka, jo/n/ka, jo/ta, jo/ssa, jo/sta, jo/hon, jo/lla, jo/lta, jo/lle,* pl. *jo/t/ka, joi/ta.* (About complete declension see chart on p. 224.)

mikä is also used as a relative pronoun, mainly in three ways:

— to refer to superlatives

Tämä on paras puku, mi/n/kä omistan.	This is the best suit that I possess.

— to refer to an entire sentence

Virtaset saivat lapsen, mikä oli hauskaa.	The Virtanens got a baby, which was nice.
(cp. *Virtaset saivat lapsen, joka oli poika.)*	The Virtanens got a child that was a boy.)

— especially in speech, frequently to replace *joka*, except when referring to human beings

Kaupunki, mi/ssä asumme, on pieni.	The town in which (where) we live is small.

Note: *joka* ''every'' is an indeclinable indefinite pronoun: *joka maa/ssa* in every country etc.

Sanasto — Vocabulary

anglo/saksi-a-n-sakseja	Anglo-Saxon
ennen	before, earlier
erittäin	very, extremely
huoma/ta-an-si huomannut	to note, notice, become aware
+huuta/a huudan huusi huutanut	to shout, cry
hymy-ä-n-jä (cp. *hymyillä*)	smile
joko ... tai (cp. *ei ... eikä*)	either ... or

kohteli/as-ta-an-aita (≠ *epä/kohtelias*)	polite
kovaa (≠ *hiljaa*)	loudly; fast, at high speed
-kä (added to negation): en/kä, et/kä, ei/kä, emme/kä, ette/kä, eivät/kä	and not, neither, nor
lopulta (= *lopuksi*)	at last, in the end, finally
+penkki-ä penkin penkkejä	bench
+päättä/ä päätän päätti päättänyt	to decide, make up one's mind
+tapahtu/a (tapahdun) tapahtui tapahtunut	to take place, occur, happen
toistemme kanssa (toistenne k., toistensa k.)	with each other
tyypilli/nen-stä-sen-siä	typical

☆

+henki henkeä hengen henkiä (cp. *henkilö*)	spirit, soul, mind; life; person (only when telling how many people)

Kappale **32** Lesson

Vaatteita ostamassa (I)

Helsinkiläinen tavaratalo, naisten vaatetusosasto. Linda Hill tulee. Hän on hauskannäköinen, aika lyhyt, vaalea nainen. Hänellä on ruskea puku päällä.

1. Myyjä. Voinko minä auttaa?
2. L. Kiitos, minä katselen vain.

(Hän todellakin aikoo vain katsella. Hän katselee kauan aikaa erilaisia vaatteita: pukuja, puseroita, hameita, villatakkeja, villapuseroita jne. Mutta jokainen nainen tietää, mitä sitten tapahtuu.)

Shopping for clothes (I)

A department store in Helsinki, women's department. Enter Linda Hill. She is a nice-looking woman, fairly short, blonde. She is wearing a brown dress.

1. Salesgirl. May I help you, madam?
2. L. Thank you, I'm just looking.

(She really only intends to look. She looks for a long time at different kinds of clothes: dresses, blouses, skirts, cardigans, sweaters etc. But every woman knows what will happen next.)

3. L. Saisinko minä koettaa tätä punaista hametta? Ja tuota valkoista puseroa?
4. M. Tänne päin, olkaa hyvä, täällä on vapaa sovitushuone.
5. L. Hame on kiva. Mutta onkohan väri liian kirkas? Minä olen niin lihava.
6. M. Lihavako? Ei ollenkaan! Normaali nainen ei ole laiha kuin mannekiini. Minusta kirkkaan punainen sopii teille erittäin hyvin.
7. L. Minä tykkään tästä puserostakin. Mutta se on liian suuri.
8. M. Tässä on pienempi numero, koettakaapas tätä.
9. L. Minkä hintainen tämä on?
10. M. ... markkaa.
11. L. Onko se niin kallis? Eikö teillä ole halvempia?
12. M. Ei samaa mallia. Mutta tuossa on tuollainen malli, vain ... markkaa.
13. L. Mutta se ei ole yhtä kaunis kuin tämä. Niin se on: kauniimpi on usein myös kalliimpi. Mitäs minä nyt tekisin? Minä luulen, että minä otan vain tämän hameen.

3. L. Could I try on this red skirt? And that white blouse?
4. S. This way, please, here's a free fitting-room.
5. L. The skirt is nice. But I wonder if the color is too bright? I'm so fat.
6. S. Fat? Not a bit! A normal woman is not thin like a fashion model. I think bright red suits you very well.
7. L. I like this blouse, too. But it's too large.
8. S. Here's a smaller size, try this one on.
9. L. What price is this?
10. S. ... marks.
11. L. Is it so expensive? Don't you have cheaper ones?
12. S. Not in the same style. But there's that kind of style, at only ... marks.
13. L. But it isn't as pretty as this one. That's how it is: what's prettier is often also more expensive. What should I do now? I'll just take this skirt, I guess.

sama same	≠	**eri** different, not same
saman/lainen (kuin) same kind of, similar to	≠	**eri/lainen** (kuin) different (kind of), different from, not similar

Kielioppia — Structural notes

1. Comparative of adjectives

Vuori on korkea/mpi kuin mäki. — A mountain is higher than a hill.
Tämä talo on paljon iso/mpi kuin tuo. — This house is much bigger than that one.

Raketti on vielä nopea/mpi kuin suihkukone. — A rocket is faster still than a jet plane.

The comparative of adjectives is formed by adding the suffix **-mpi** to the stem. When the basic form and the gen. stem are different, the gen. stem is used. More examples:

nuori (nuore/n)	*nuore/mpi*	younger
uusi (uude/n)	*uude/mpi*	newer
kaunis (kaunii/n)	*kaunii/mpi*	prettier, more beautiful
valkoinen (valkoise/n)	*valkoise/mpi*	whiter
lämmin (lämpimä/n)	*lämpimä/mpi*	warmer
rakas (rakkaa/n)	*rakkaa/mpi*	dearer

The final short **-a** (**-ä**) in two-syllable adjectives changes into **-e**:

vanha	*vanhe/mpi*	older, elder
halpa (halva/n)	*halve/mpi*	cheaper
kylmä	*kylme/mpi*	colder

Note the following irregular comparatives:

hyvä	good	*pare/mpi*	better
pitkä	long, tall	*pite/mpi*	longer, taller

(Note here also the adverbs *paljon — enemmän* more, *vähän — vähemmän* less.)

The word used to tie together the two things compared with each other (Engl. ''than'', ''as'') is *kuin:*

Matti on vanhempi kuin Pekka.	Matti is older than Pekka.
Matti on yhtä vanha kuin Paavo.	Matti is as old as Paavo.
(Matti ja Paavo ovat yhtä vanhat.	Matti and Paavo are equally old.)
Pekka ei ole niin vanha kuin Matti.	Pekka is not so old as Matti.

With comparative, partitive can be used instead of *kuin:*

Matti on | *Pekka/a vanhempi* | *vanhempi Pekka/a.*	Matti is older than Pekka.
Tavallis/ta parempi.	Better than usual.
Normaali/a pienempi.	Smaller than normal.

The comparative is inflected like a normal adjective. Its principal parts are always of the type:

parempi — parempaa — paremman — parempia

(''into'' form *parempaan*). Examples:

Hiihto on hauskempaa kuin kävely.	Skiing is more fun than walking.
Tarvitsemme suuremman asunnon.	We need a larger apartment.
Perhe muuttaa uudempaan taloon.	The family is moving into a newer house.
Pidän vaaleammasta sinisestä.	I like a lighter blue.
Onko teillä halvempia hameita?	Have you got cheaper skirts?

2. Nouns and adjectives ending in -i

Look up the words ending in **-i** in the list on p. 99.
a) Review the **i→e** words and note the following points:

— All these words consist of two syllables. The group includes different word types (*ovi, pieni, uusi*) but they all share a similar partitive pl.
— The *ovi* words retain the **-e-** all through the sing.:

ovi	door	*ovea*	*oven*		*ovia*
+*lehti*	paper	*lehteä*	*lehden*	*(lehteen)*	*lehtiä*

— The *pieni* words drop the **-e-** in the part. sing.:

pieni	small	*pientä*	*pienen*	*pieniä*
saari	island	*saarta*	*saaren*	*saaria*
tuli	fire	*tulta*	*tulen*	*tulia*
lapsi	child	*lasta*	*lapsen*	*lapsia*
lumi	snow	*lunta*	*lumen*	*lumia*

— The *uusi* words form a special group of their own:

+*uusi*	new	*uutta*	*uuden*	*(uuteen)*	*uusia*
+*käsi*	hand	*kättä*	*käden*	*(käteen)*	*käsiä*

b) About *parempi* words (comparatives) see par. 1 above.

c) Review the **i — i** *(bussi, naapuri)* words and note the following points:

— These words retain the **-i-** all through the sing. The group comprises the majority of the words ending in **-i**, among them all those longer than two syllables.
— A large number of the **i — i** words are loanwords from other languages.

bussi	bus	*bussia*	*bussin*	*busseja*
+*paketti*	parcel	*pakettia*	*paketin*	*paketteja*
naapuri	neighbor	*naapuria*	*naapurin*	*naapureita*
lääkäri	doctor	*lääkäriä*	*lääkärin*	*lääkäreitä*

Sanasto — Vocabulary

eri/lai/nen-sta-sen-sia	different, various
hame-tta-en-ita	skirt
hintai/nen-sta-sen-sia:	
minkä hintainen?	what price?
jokai/nen-sta-sen	every; everybody, everyone

+kirkas-ta kirkkaan kirkkaita	bright, clear
+koetta/a koetan koetti koettanut (jotakin pukua)	to try, attempt; to try on
laiha-a-n laihoja	thin, lean, meager
lihava-a-n lihavia	fat, plump, corpulent
malli-a-n malleja	model; pattern; style
mannekiini-a-n mannekiineja	fashion model
näköi/nen-stä-sen-siä (jonkin n.)	looking like something
ollenkaan: ei o.	not at all
osasto-a-n-ja	section, department
+puku-a puvun pukuja	suit; dress; costume
pusero-a-n-ita	blouse
päällä: olla p. (= *yllä*)	to have on, wear
sovitus/huone-tta-en-ita (from *sovittaa* = *koettaa*)	fitting-room
tavara/talo-a-n-ja	department store
tuollai/nen-sta-sen-sia	that kind of, such
tällai/nen-sta-sen-sia	this kind of, such
vaalea-(t)a-n vaaleita	light(-colored); blond, fair
+vaate-tta vaatteen vaatteita (usu. pl)	garment; pl. clothes, clothing
vaatet/us-ta-uksen	clothing, apparel
villa/pusero-a-n-ita	lady's sweater
+villa/takki-a-takin-takkeja	cardigan
yhtä	equally; as (. . . as)

☆

saman/lai/nen-sta-sen-sia	similar
taivas-ta taivaan taivaita	sky; heaven

Vaatteita ostamassa (II)

Miesten vaatetusosasto. Herra Hill tulee. Hän on pitkä tumma mies, jolla on harmaa takki ja harmaat housut.

1. H. Haluaisin katsoa paitoja. Sellaisia, joita ei tarvitse silittää.
2. Myyjä. Mikä koko?
3. H. 41.
4. M. Entä väri?
5. H. Tumman- tai vaaleansininen.

Shopping for clothes (II)

Men's department. Enter Mr. Hill. He is a tall, dark man, who is wearing a grey jacket and grey trousers.

1. H. I'd like to see some shirts. Those which you don't have to iron.
2. Salesgirl. What size?
3. H. 41.
4. S. What about the color?
5. H. Dark or light blue.

6. M. Olkaa hyvä ja valitkaa tästä. Paitojen hinnat vaihtelevat ... markasta ... markkaan. Nämä ovat hienoja paitoja, kotimaista puuvillaa.

6. S. Please choose from here. The prices of the shirts vary from ... marks to ... marks. These are fine shirts, Finnish cotton.

7. H. Minä otan tämän vaaleansinisen. Saanko sitten nähdä sukkia?

7. H. I'll take this lightblue one. May I also see some socks?

8. M. Nailonia vai villaa?

8. S. Nylon or wool?

9. H. Villaa. Harmaat. Näiden sukkien väri on juuri sopiva. Saanko kaksi paria?

9. H. Wool. Grey. The color of these socks is just right. May I have two pairs, please.

10. M. Mitä muuta saa olla? Solmioita? Villapaita? Lämpimät käsineet? Hattu?

10. S. Do you want anything else? Ties? A sweater? Warm gloves? A hat?

11. H. Kiitos, tämä riittää tällä kertaa. Mutta meidän poika tarvitsee uudet farkut, haluaisin kysyä farkkujen hintoja.

11. H. Thank you, this is enough this time. But our son needs new jeans, I'd like to inquire about the prices of jeans.

12. M. Poikien housut ovat kolmannessa kerroksessa. Siellä on nyt juuri poikien vaatteiden ale, jossa on samettihousuja, farkkuja ja kenkiä.

12. S. Boys' trousers are on the third floor. Right now there's a sale of boys' clothes, with corduroy trousers, jeans, and shoes.

■■■

Kello kaksi herra Hill tapaa vaimonsa kahvion lähellä.

At two o'clock Mr. Hill meets his wife near the cafeteria.

13. Linda H. Hei! Minä olen hirveän väsynyt.

13. Linda H. Hi, Bob! I'm awfully tired.

14. Bob. Niin minäkin. Tule, mennään kahville!

14. Bob. So am I. Come on, let's have some coffee!

15. L. Mennään vain. Tässä on vapaa pöytä, istutaan siihen.

15. L. Yes, let's. Here's a free table, let's sit down there.

16. B. Minulla on kova jano.

16. B. I'm very thirsty.

17. L. Niin minullakin. Ihanaa kahvia! Otetaan vielä toinen kuppi.

17. L. So am I. Wonderful coffee! Let's have another cup.

18. B. Otetaan vain.

18. B. Okay, let's do that.

Mitä ainetta (**Mistä aineesta**)	pöytä on? Se on	**puuta.** (**puusta**).

Minä pidän sinisestä. — **Niin minäkin.**
Minusta tuo solmio on kaunis. — **Niin minustakin.**

10

Kielioppia — Structural notes

1. Genitive plural

Sing.			Pl.	
poja/n	the boy's	**(poiki/a)**	**poiki/en**	the boys'
äidi/n	the mother's	**(äitej/ä)**	**äiti/en**	the mothers'

When the part. pl. ends in **-i/a (-i/ä), -ej/a (-ej/ä),** the gen. pl. will end in **-i/en.**

tytö/n	the girl's	**(tyttöj/ä)**	**tyttöj/en**	the girls'

When the part. pl. ends in **-j/a (-j/ä),** the gen. pl. will end in **-j/en.**

tehtaa/n	of the factory	**(tehtai/ta)**	**tehtai/den** **tehtai/tten**	of the factories

When the part. pl. ends in **-ta (-tä),** the gen. pl. will end in **-den** (or **-tten;** this parallel ending is less commonly used).

Parallel forms in the part. pl. will result in parallel forms of the gen. pl.:

(omeni/a)	*omeni/en*	of the apples
(omenoi/ta)	*omenoi/den* *omenoi/tten*	

Why **lasten** ohjelma?

lapsi	child	part. pl.	*lapsi/a*	gen. pl.	*lapsi/en*	children's
		part. sing.	**las/ta**		**las/ten**	

Words which end in **consonant + ta** in their part. sing. may have a parallel form for the gen. pl.: **part. sing. stem + ten.** This kind of gen. pl. is particularly common with the words *lapsi* **(las/ten),** *mies* **(mies/ten),** and all words ending in *-nen,* for instance, *nainen* **(nais/ten),** *toinen* **(tois/ten),** *englantilainen* **(englantilais/ten).**

Old-type gen. plurals which do not follow the above rules are, for instance, *Yhdys/valtain (= Yhdys/valtojen)* and *vanhain(koti)* old people's (home).

Note: *(näi/tä kirjoj/a)* *näi/den (= näi/tten) kirjoj/en*
(noi/ta kirjoj/a) *noi/den (= noi/tten) kirjoj/en*
(nii/tä kirjoj/a) *nii/den (= nii/tten) kirjoj/en*
(mi/tä kirjoj/a?) *mi/n/kä kirjoj/en?*

Note also: The final **-n** will disappear before a poss. suffix: *vanhempien koti,* but *vanhempie/ni, -si, -nsa, -mme, -nne, -nsa koti.*

2. "Let us do" — tehdään!

mennä *Mennään kotiin!* Let's go home!
If the infinitive ends in one vowel, add **-an (-än).**

(lukea) lue/n *Luetaan jotakin!* Let's read something!
If the infinitive ends in two different vowels, add **-taan (-tään)** to the stem of the 1st pers. present tense.

e
(ottaa) ota/n otá- *Otetaan loma!* Let's take a vacation!
If the infinitive ends in **-aa (-ää)**, use the 1st pers. present stem but the **-a- (-ä-)** will change to **-e-**.

Negative form: *Ei mennä vielä!* Let's not go yet!
Ei lueta! Let's not read!
Ei oteta sitä! Let's not take it!

Direct object in connection with "let us do":

Kirjoitamme kortin. We'll write a card.
Kirjoitetaan kortti! Let's write a card!
(Cp. 30:1.)

Note. This form is widely used in colloquial Finnish to replace the standard form of the 1st pers. pl.:

Me menemme kotiin. (colloq.) *Me mennään kotiin.*
Me emme ota sitä. *Me ei oteta sitä.*

(About the use of "tehdään" to express the passive see Finnish for Foreigners 2.)

Sanasto — Vocabulary

+farkut (pl.) farkkuja	jeans
+hattu-a hatun hattuja	hat
hieno-a-n-ja	fine, elegant
housut (pl.) housuja	trousers, pants, slacks
kahvio-ta-n-ita (= *kahvila*)	cafeteria
+kenkä-ä kengän kenkiä	shoe
+koko-a koon kokoja (cp. *koko* indecl. whole, entire, all)	size
koti/mai/nen-sta-sen-sia (≠ *ulko/mainen*)	domestic, made in one's own country
käsine-ttä-en-itä	glove
nailon-ia-in-eja	nylon
+paita-a paidan paitoja	shirt
puu/villa-a-n	cotton
+riittä/ä riitän riitti riittänyt	to be enough, suffice
+sametti-a sametin sametteja	velvet, corduroy
sellai/nen-sta-sen-sia	such
+silittä/ä silitän silitti silittänyt	to iron
solmio-ta-n-ita	tie
sopiva-a-n sopivia	suitable, convenient, all right
+sukka-a sukan sukkia	sock; stocking
+takki-a takin takkeja	coat, jacket
tumma-a-n tummia	dark (-colored)
+vaihdel/la vaihtelen vaihteli vaihdellut	to vary, keep changing, alternate
vali/ta-tsen-tsi-nnut	to choose, pick, select, elect
+villa/paita	men's sweater
väsynyt-tä väsyneen väsyneitä	tired

☆

aine-tta-en-ita	matter, substance; material; essay, theme

Mäkiset ovat kutsuneet vieraita

The Mäkinens have invited some guests

1. Hra Mäkinen. Kuinka kauan sinä olet ollut Suomessa, Tom?

1. Mr. Mäkinen. How long have you been in Finland, Tom?

2. T. Kohta kuukauden. Minä tulin tänne elokuun alussa.

2. T. It'll soon be a month. I came here at the beginning of August.

3. Rva M. No, kuinka sinä täällä viihdyt?

3. Mrs. M. Well, how do you like it here?

4. T. Ainakin tähän saakka minä olen viihtynyt oikein hyvin. On ollut vielä kaunista ja lämmintä, ja kaikki on ollut uutta ja mielenkiintoista.

4. T. At least so far I've liked it very much. It has still been fine and warm, and everything has been new and interesting.

5. Rva M. Eikö sinulla ole ollut koti-ikävä?

5. Mrs. M. Haven't you been homesick?

6. T. Ei ollenkaan. Kaikki ovat olleet kovin ystävällisiä. Minulla on ollut seuraa, minun ei ole tarvinnut olla yksin.

6. T. Not at all. Everybody has been very kind. I've had company, I haven't had to be alone.

7. Hra M. Sehän on hyvä. Toivottavasti sinä olet saanut mukavan asunnon.

7. Mr. M. That's good. I hope you've got a nice apartment.

8. T. En vielä. Minä olen etsinyt koko ajan, mutta en ole löytänyt sopivaa asuntoa.

8. T. Not yet. I've been looking for one all the time, but I haven't found a suitable apartment.

9. Rva M. Sinun on siis täytynyt asua hotellissa. Hotellihuoneet ovat aika kalliita opiskelijalle.

9. Mrs. M. So you've had to stay at a hotel. Hotel rooms are quite expensive for a student.

10. T. Minä olen samaa mieltä. En minä voi jäädä hotelliin. Kai minä pian löydän jonkinlaisen asunnon.

10. T. I agree. I can't remain at the hotel. I suppose I'll soon find some kind of apartment.

11. Hra M. Muuten, missä sinä olet oppinut noin hyvin suomea?

11. Mr. M. By the way, where did you learn Finnish so well?

12. T. Kotona Yhdysvalloissa. Minä olen aina harrastanut kieliä. Ja opiskeluaikana eräs huonetoverini oli suomalainen vaihto-opiskelija. Me olemme olleet kirjeenvaihdossa siitä lähtien.

12. T. At home in the States. I've always been interested in languages. And in college, a room-mate of mine was a Finnish exchange student. We've been corresponding ever since.

13. Rva M. No, mitä mieltä sinä olet: onko suomen kieli mahdotonta oppia?
14. T. Ei tietystikään. Mutta kyllä minä olen sitä mieltä, että se vaatii ahkeraa työtä ja hyvää muistia. Muuten, oletteko te käyneet Amerikassa?
15. Rva M. Emme vielä.
16. Hra M. Mutta me olemme suunnitelleet matkaa Yhdysvaltoihin tänä vuonna.

Muut vieraat saapuvat.

17. Hra M. Päivää päivää, tervetuloa! Esko ja Tarja Vuori ovat vanhoja ystäviämme. Tom Lake on Yhdysvalloista. Me olemme kertoneet teille hänestä.
18. T.V. Päivää. Kauanko sinä olet ollut meidän maassamme?
19. E.V. Ja miten sinä täällä viihdyt?

13. Mrs. M. Well, what's your opinion: is Finnish impossible to learn?
14. T. Of course not. But I'm definitely of the opinion that it takes hard work and a good memory. By the way, have you been to America?
15. Mrs. M. Not yet.
16. Mr. M. But we've been planning a trip to the U.S. this year.

The other guests arrive.

17. Mr. M. Hello, nice to have you here! Esko and Tarja Vuori are old friends of ours. Tom Lake is from the United States. We've told you about him.
18. T.V. Hello, Tom. How long have you been in our country?
19. E.V. And how do you like it here?

Mihin bussilippusi jäi? — Koti**in**.
Pöydä**lle**.

mieli (= **mielipide**) opinion
Mitä mieltä olette asiasta?
Olen **sitä mieltä,** että ...
Olen **samaa mieltä** kanssanne "I agree with you" ≠ olen **eri mieltä**

Minä viihdyn täällä. — Niin minäkin.
Minusta täällä on kivaa.
— Niin minustakin.
Ruokakin on hyvää.

Minä en viihdy täällä. — **En minäkään.**
Minusta täällä ei ole kivaa.
— **Ei minustakaan.**
Ruokakaan (= **myöskään** ruoka) ei ole hyvää.

Kielioppia — Structural notes

1. Perfect tense

näh/dä to see

Affirmative				Negative			
olen	*näh/nyt*	I have	seen	*en*	*ole näh/nyt*	I have	not
olet		you have		*et*		you have	seen
on		he/she has		*ei*		he/she has	
olemme	*näh/neet*	we have		*emme*	*ole näh/neet*	we have	
olette		you have		*ette*		you have	
ovat		they have		*eivät*		they have	

Question:
olenko (minä) näh/nyt? etc. — have I seen? etc.

Negative question:
enkö (minä) ole näh/nyt? etc. — haven't I seen? etc.

Structure:
— The auxiliary, which is always *olla,* is in the present tense;
— The main verb is in the past participle (see 31:1): sing. *näh/nyt*, pl. *näh/neet.*

Note: *te* (one person) *olette näh/nyt*
te (many persons) *olette näh/neet*

The perfect tense is used very much in the same way in Finnish as in English. Sometimes, however, Finnish (feeling that the action of the verb continues to influence the present) uses the perfect where English would prefer the past tense. Examples:

En ole koskaan käynyt Skotlannissa.	I never went to Scotland.
Huomenta, Raili, oletko nukkunut hyvin?	Good morning, Raili, did you sleep well?
Mistä olet ostanut tuon huivin?	Where did you buy that scarf (which you go on wearing)?
Missä te olette oppineet suomea?	Where did you learn Finnish (which you still speak)?
Seitsemän veljestä on kirjoittanut Aleksis Kivi.	*Seven Brothers* was written by Aleksis Kivi (the book is still with us).
Tuomas on syntynyt v. 1950.	T. (living person) was born in 1950.

See also Tenses of verbs in Finnish, p. 227, about the difference of the past tense and perfect tense.

2. Complement of the verb olla (predikatiivi)

The complement of the verb *olla* tells
— what the subject is **(noun complement)**, or
— what the subject is like **(adjective complement)** (see also lessons 15:1 and 22:1).

A. Noun complement

Sing.

Uncountables, indefinite amount: **partitive**		Countables, definite amount: **basic form**	
Mitä tämä on?	What is this?	*Mikä tämä on?*	What is this?
Se on tee/tä,	It is tea,	*Se on kissa,*	It's a cat,
jalkapallo/a,	football,	*jalkapallo,*	a football,
jäätelö/ä.	icecream.	*Liisan jäätelö.*	Liisa's icecream.
		Neg. *Se ei ole kissa* etc.	It is not a cat.

Pl.

Indefinite number: **partitive**		Entity, pair, or series; definite number: **basic form**	
Mitä nämä ovat?	What are these?	*Mitkä nämä ovat?*	What are these?
Ne ovat lasej/a.	They are glasses.	*Ne ovat silmälasi/t,*	They are (a pair of) glasses,
		Marin viini-lasi/t.	Mari's wine glasses.
		Neg. *Ne eivät ole silmälasi/t.*	They are not (a pair of) glasses.

B. Adjective complement

The use of the partitive or basic form depends on the quality of the subject. (In the following examples, the subject appears in italics.)

a) Sing. subject

Uncountable subject: **partitive**		Countable subject: **basic form**	
Kahvi on kuuma/a.	(The) coffee is hot.	*Pannu* on/ei ole kuuma.	The pot is (not) hot.
Hiihtäminen on helppo/a.	Skiing is easy.	*Kysymys* on/ei ole helppo.	The question is (not) easy.
Kaikki oli uutta.	Everything was new.	*Asia* oli/ei ollut uusi.	The matter was (not) new.

Common mistake:
Tämä ei ole kissaa. Pannu ei ole kuumaa.

Note: If the subject is not a noun (or a word used as a noun) or if there is no subject, use the **partitive** complement:

On mahdoton/ta *ymmärtää sinua.*	It is impossible to understand you.
On hirveä/ä, *että sellaista voi tapahtua.*	It is terrible that such things can happen.
Lapissa on kaunis/ta.	It is beautiful in Lapland.

Some very common adjectives may appear in such sentences either in the **part.** or the **basic form** (*helppo, vaikea, hauska, mukava, kiva, ikävä, selvä, kylmä, lämmin* etc.):

On helppo(a) *oppia tätä kieltä.*	It is easy to learn this language.
Täällä on lämmin(tä).	It is warm here.

The adjectives *hyvä* and *paha* are always used in the **basic form** in such sentences:

(Oli) hyvä, *että kerroit meille tästä.*	It was good that you told us about this.

b) Pl. subject

"Normal" plural: **partitive**		Entity, pair, series: **basic form**	
Taulut ovat kallii/ta.	Pictures are expensive.	*Silmälasit* ovat/eivät ole kallii/t.	The glasses (= a pair) are (not) expensive.
Viime päivät ovat olleet kylmi/ä.	The past few days have been cold.	*Tytön kädet* ovat /eivät ole kylmä/t.	The girl's hands are (not) cold.
Kirjat ovat hauskoj/a.	Books are fun.	*Häät* olivat/eivät olleet hauska/t.	The wedding was (not) nice.
Nuo talot ovat korkei/ta.	Those houses are high.	*Huoneen seinät* ovat/eivät ole korkea/t.	The walls of the room are (not) high.

Note:
Common mistake: *Maitoa on valkoista.* Milk is white.
Koiria ovat kotieläimiä. Dogs are domestic animals.

When the sentence includes a complement of the verb *olla*, the subject cannot appear in the partitive.

Sanasto Vocabulary

ahkera-a-n ahkeria (≠ *laiska*)	hard-working, diligent
+alku-a alun alkuja (≠ *loppu*)	beginning, start
etsi/ä-n etsi-nyt (jotakin)	to look for, search
harrasta/a-n harrasti harrastanut (jotakin)	to take an (active) interest in, go in for
ikävä-ä-n ikäviä	tedium, longing, yearning; dull, boring, unpleasant
jonkin/lai/nen-sta-sen-sia	some kind of
jää/dä-n jäi jäänyt (johonkin)	to stay, remain, be left
-kaan (-kään) (in negative sentences)	not . . . either; often just an emphatic suffix
+kirjeen/vaihto-a-vaihdon	correspondence
kohta (= *pian*)	soon, presently
koti-ikävä-ä-n	home-sickness
lähtien (= *asti, saakka*)	from, since, ever since
kesästä lähtien	ever since the summer
mielen/kiintoi/nen-sta-sen-sia (cp. *mielen/kiinto* interest)	interesting
mieli mieltä mielen mieliä	mind, soul, spirit; mood; opinion
muisti-a-n muisteja	memory (= ability to remember)
muuten	otherwise; by the way
opiskelu-a-n	study, studying, studies
seura-a-n seuroja	company; society
+suunnitel/la suunnittelen suunnitteli suunnitellut (cp. *suunnitelma* plan)	to plan
toivottavasti	I hope, we hope, let's hope that, hopefully
+vaati/a vaadin vaati-nut	to require, call for, demand
+viihty/ä viihdyn viihtyi viihtynyt	to feel at home, like living somewhere
+Yhdys/vallat (sing. *valta*) -valtoja-valtojen	United States
Yhdys/valloissa, -valloista -valtoihin	in, from, to the U.S.

☆

haastattelu-a-n-ja	interview
+mieli/pide-ttä-piteen-piteitä	opinion

Millerit vuokraavat huoneiston

Herra ja rouva Miller, talonmies.

1. T. Tämä on hyvä huoneisto. Kolme huonetta ja keittiö. Mennään ensin olohuoneeseen.
2. H. Onpa hauska iso ikkuna! Minä pidän isoista ikkunoista, on tarpeeksi valoa. Ja kiva, että on parveke.
3. R. Miksi he ovat panneet kirjoituspöydän parvekkeen oven lähelle? Ovista tulee aina kylmää. Minä saan reumatismin.
4. H. No, muutetaan pöytä pois oven luota. Pannaan se television luokse.
5. R. Ja tämä nojatuoli kirjahyllyn eteen.
6. H. Ja tuo korkea lamppu sohvan takaa nojatuolin viereen.

The Millers rent an apartment

Mr. and Mrs. Miller, the janitor.

1. J. This is a good apartment. Three rooms and a kitchen. Let's go first into the living-room.
2. Mr. M. What a nice large window! I like large windows, there's enough light. And how nice that there's a balcony.
3. Mrs. M. Why did they place the writing-desk so near the balcony door? There's always cold air coming in through the doors. I'll get rheumatism.
4. Mr. M. Well, let's move the desk away from the door. Let's put it near the TV.
5. Mrs. M. And this armchair to the front of the book-shelf.
6. Mr. M. And that high lamp from behind the sofa next to the armchair.

7. R. Minä en tykkää näistä moderneista huonekaluista.
8. H. Mutta näissä tuoleissa on mukava istua, ja se on pääasia. Mehän olemme täällä vain vuoden.
9. T. Sitten tullaan keittiöön.
10. R. No, se on siisti ja valoisa. Sähköhella ... Jääkaappi voisi olla suurempi.

11. T. Kylpyhuone on täällä keittiön ja makuuhuoneiden välissä. Ja WC.

12. R. Suomalaisilla on aina niin pieni kylpyhuone.
13. H. Hehän käyttävät niin paljon saunaa. Katsotaan sitten makuuhuoneisiin. Ensin vanhempien makuuhuone.

14. R. Onpa epämukava sänky, kova kuin kivi. Osaammekohan me nukkua näissä?
15. H. Täytyy yrittää. Tuo pienempi makuuhuone sopisi hyvin meidän lapsille. No, mitäs sanot?
16. R. Ajatellaan asiaa vielä, Jack. Käydään muissakin huoneistoissa.
17. H. Mutta jos toiset vievät tämän, joka on niin hyvällä paikalla?
18. R. No, sama se, otetaan sitten tämä. (Talonmiehelle.) Kiitoksia näyttämisestä!

7. Mrs. M. I don't like this modern furniture.
8. Mr. M. But these chairs are comfortable to sit, and that's the main thing. We'll only stay here for a year.
9. J. Then we come to the kitchen.
10. Mrs. M. Well, it's clean and light. An electric stove ... The refrigerator might be bigger.
11. J. The bathroom is here, between the kitchen and the bedrooms. And the toilet.
12. Mrs. M. Finns always have such small bathrooms.
13. Mr. M. They use their saunas so much, don't they? Let's then look into the bedrooms. First the parents' bedroom.
14. Mrs. M. What an uncomfortable bed, as hard as a stone. I wonder if we can sleep in these beds?
15. Mr. M. We must try. That smaller bedroom would be all right for our children. Well, what do you say?
16. Mrs. M. Let's think it over, Jack. Let's go and see some more apartments.
17. Mr. M. But if somebody else takes this one, which is so well located?
18. Mrs. M. Well, all right, let's take this one, then. (To the janitor.) Thanks for showing us the apartment, Mr. Nieminen!

yksiö = 1 huoneen huoneisto
kaksio = 2 huoneen huoneisto

me **makaamme** sängyssä (= vuoteessa); sänky (vuode) on **makuu**huoneessa

huone — huonei**sto**
kirja — kirj**asto**
huonekalu — (huone)kalu**sto**

mukava ≠ **epä**mukava
varmasti ≠ **epä**varmasti

35

VUOKRATAAN
kal. huoneisto
valoisa, 3 h., k., kh., 70 m².
Pitkäk. 10 B 6. Talonmies
näyttää, puh. 987 654.

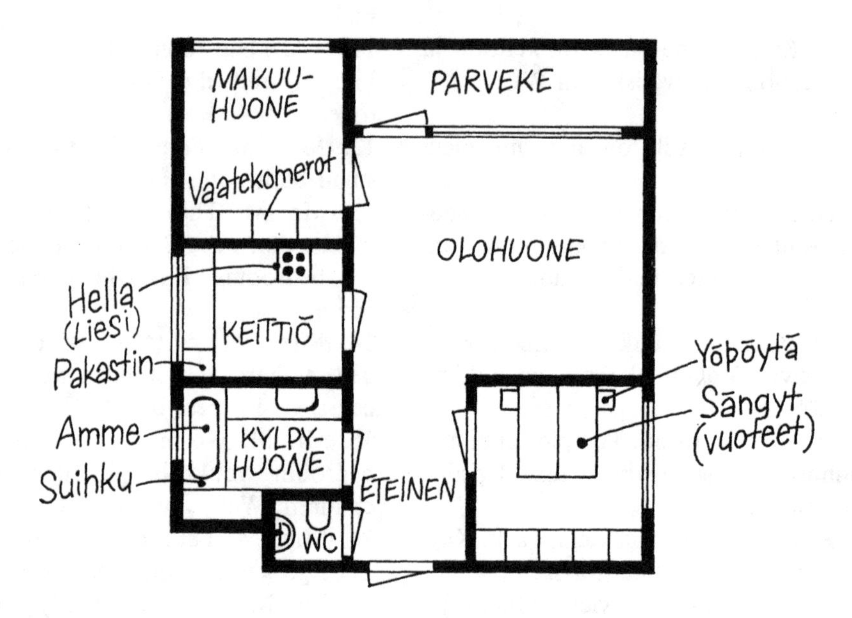

asunto voi olla

kerrostalo-huoneisto (tämä talo on 5-kerroksinen)	rivitalo-huoneisto	omakotitalo	maalaistalo

Kielioppia — Structural notes

1. Plural of nouns: local cases (I)

The **endings** are, in general, the same as in the sing. (About the ''into'' case see below.)

The **stem** is obtained from the partitive pl. It always ends in the plural marker **-i-** (between vowels **-j-**).

This paragraph will deal with the large number of nouns which use the part. pl. stem unchanged all through their local cases. Such nouns are

— words with no **k p t** changes, or

— words with **strong grade** in the genitive sing.

Examples of words with no **k p t** changes:

	Sing.				Pl.			
	tuoli		*järvi* (*järven*)		*tuolej/a* (*tuolei-*)		*järvi/ä* (*järvi-*)	
''on''	*tuoli*	*lla*	*järve*	*llä*	*tuolei*	*lla*	*järvi*	*llä*
''from''		*lta*		*ltä*		*lta*		*ltä*
''onto''		*lle*		*lle*		*lle*		*lle*
''in''		*ssa*		*ssä*		*ssa*		*ssä*
''out of''		*sta*		*stä*		*sta*		*stä*

For these five local cases, the endings are identical with those of the sing. forms (see 8:1, 10:1, 13:1—2, 20:1).

The ''into'' case has the same endings as in the sing. (see 19:1), except that the pl. for **-seen** is **-siin** (sometimes also **-hin**):

''into''	*tuoli/in*	*(tuolej/a)*	*tuolei/hin*
	järve/en	*(järvi/ä)*	*järvi/in*
	huonee/seen	*(huonei/ta)*	*huonei/siin*

Note that the sing. and pl. form of the same word do not always have the same type of ending. By far the most common ''into'' ending in the pl. is **-hin**.

Examples of words with **strong grade** in the genitive sing.

	Sing.				Pl.			
	+tehdas (tehtaan)		*+liike (liikkeen)*		*tehtai/ta*		*liikkei/tä*	
''on''	*tehtaa*	*lla*	*liikkee*	*llä*	*tehtai*	*lla*	*liikkei*	*llä*
''from''		*lta*		*ltä*		*lta*		*ltä*
''onto''		*lle*		*lle*		*lle*		*lle*
''in''		*ssa*		*ssä*		*ssa*		*ssä*
''out of''		*sta*		*stä*		*sta*		*stä*
''into''		*seen*		*seen*		*siin*		*siin*

Note: Remember that the ''into'' form loses its final **-n** before poss. suffixes: *tuoleihi/ni, tuoleihi/si, tuoleihi/nsa, tuoleihi/mme, tuoleihi/nne, tuoleihi/nsa.*

Note also: The local cases of *mikä* are identical in the sing. and pl.:

mi/llä tuoli/lla? *(mi/tä)* *mi/llä tuolei/lla?*
mi/hin tehtaa/seen? *mi/hin tehtai/siin?*

(For the plural of local cases part II, see 37:3.)

2. alla — alta — alle: inflected forms of postpositions

(Before studying this paragraph, review lesson 30:2.)

Many local postpositions have three different forms, often resembling the local cases and answering the questions

missä? *mistä?* *mihin?*

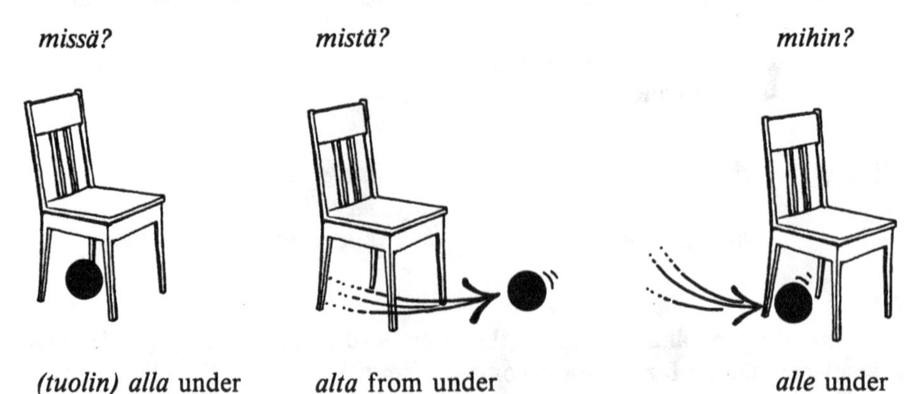

(tuolin) alla under *alta* from under *alle* under

Used similarly are *keskellä* in the middle, *lähellä* near, *päällä* on top of, *sisällä* inside, *välillä* between, *ympärillä* around, *alapuolella* underneath, *yläpuolella* above, *sisäpuolella* inside, *ulkopuolella* outside.

(talon) edessä
in front of

edestä
from the front of

eteen
to the front of

Used similarly are *sisässä* inside, *vieressä* by, next to, *välissä* between.

(ikkunan) luona
near, by

luota
from

luo(kse) to

(puun) takana
behind

takaa
from behind

taa(kse)
behind

Note: *luo/luokse* and *taa/taakse* are interchangeable, except that the longer form must be used in connection with poss. suffixes: *Menen Liisan luo(kse). Menen hänen luokse/en (luokse/nsa).*

Sanasto — Vocabulary

epä-	un-, in-, dis-, non-
hella-a-n helloja (= *liesi*)	stove
huoneisto-a-n-ja	apartment, flat
huone/kalu-a-n-ja	piece of furniture; pl. furniture
+jää/kaappi-a-kaapin-kaappeja (*kaappi* cupboard)	refrigerator
korkea-(t)a-n korkeita	high
kylpy/huone-tta-en-ita (*kylpe/ä* to take a bath)	bathroom
+käyttä/ä käytän käytti käyttänyt (jotakin)	to use; to run, operate
makuu/huone (*maa/ta makaan* to lie down)	bedroom
moderni-a-n moderneja	modern
+muutta/a muutan muutti muuttanut	to change; to move
noja/tuoli-a-n-tuoleja	armchair, easy chair
olo/huone	livingroom
pakast/in-ta-imen-imia	freezer
+parveke-tta parvekkeen parvekkeita	balcony
suihku-a-n-ja	shower
sähkö-ä-n-jä	electricity
talon/mies-tä-miehen-miehiä	janitor, caretaker (of a house)
valo-a-n-ja	light
valoisa-a-n valoisia (≠ *pimeä*)	light, bright, well-lighted
WC WC:tä WC:n (colloq. *vessa*)	toilet, restroom
vuokra/ta-an-si-nnut (cp. *vuokra* rent)	to rent, hire, let, lease
+yrittä/ä yritän yritti yrittänyt (cp. *koettaa*)	to attempt, try, undertake

☆

+kalustettu-a kalustetun kalustettuja (≠ *kalustamaton*)	furnished
kirjasto-a-n-ja	library
neliö/metri-ä-n-metrejä (abbr. m^2)	square meter

Vuodenajat ja sää

Annikki Miettinen ja Linda Hill keskustelevat. On ensimmäinen (päivä) helmikuuta.

1. L. Aika kova pakkanen tänään!
2. A. Niin, viisitoista astetta pakkasta. Celsiusta, tarkoitan.
3. L. Ja vielä tällainen kova tuuli.
4. A. Meren rannalla tuulee paljon. Muuten, harvoin Helsingissä on näin paljon pakkasta. Huomenna voi taas sataa vettä, Helsingin ilmasto on sellainen. Mutta sisämaassa on oikea talvi ja sataa paljon lunta.
5. L. On kai paras lähteä Lappiin, jos haluaa todella hiihtää.
6. A. Mutta ei vielä. Lapissa on paras hiihtokausi maalis- ja huhtikuussa. Aurinko paistaa eivätkä päivät ole enää niin lyhyitä.
7. L. Kuinka pitkä talvi on täällä Helsingissä?
8. A. Yleensä marras- tai joulukuusta maaliskuuhun. Huhtikuussa lumi sulaa, tulee kevät.
9. L. Kukat alkavat kukkia ja tulee lämmin?
10. A. Vähitellen.
11. L. Minkälainen ilma on kesällä? Onko milloinkaan todella kuuma?
12. A. Joskus voi olla vähän yli 30° (kolmekymmentä astetta) lämmintä.
13. L. Joku on sanonut, että te suomalaiset olette aivan erilaisia kesällä ja talvella. Onkohan se totta?
14. A. Millä tavalla erilaisia?
15. L. Iloisia kesällä, surullisia talvella.
16. A. No, onhan se mahdollista. Talvi on pimeä ja kylmä, kesä ihana, vaikka

Seasons and weather

Annikki Miettinen and Linda Hill are having a talk. It's the first of February.

1. L. Pretty cold today!
2. A. Yes, minus fifteen (degrees). Centigrade, I mean.
3. L. And such a wind, too.
4. A. It is very windy by the sea. By the way, it's seldom that we have so many degrees of frost in Helsinki. Tomorrow it may rain again, the Helsinki climate is like that. But inland, they have real winter, and it snows a lot.
5. L. I suppose you'd better go to Lapland if you really want to ski.
6. A. But not yet. The best skiing season in Lapland is in March and April. The sun shines and the days are no longer so short.
7. L. How long is winter here, in Helsinki?
8. A. From November or December to March, in general. The snow melts in April; spring arrives.
9. L. The flowers start coming out and it gets warm?
10. A. By and by.
11. L. What's the weather like in summer? Is it ever really hot?
12. A. It can sometimes be a little over thirty plus.
13. L. Somebody told me that you Finns are quite different in summer and in winter. I wonder if it's true?
14. A. Different in what way?
15. L. Happy in summer, sad in winter.
16. A. Well, it's possible, of course. The winter is dark and cold, the summer love-

lyhyt. Silloin kaikki ovat lomalla, uivat ja ottavat aurinkoa — ja ovat hyvällä tuulella.

ly, although it is short. Everybody is on vacation then, swimming and sunbathing — and they are in a good mood.

17. L. Kuinka pitkä kesäloma täällä on?

17. L. How long are summer holidays in Finland?

18. A. Työntekijöiden vuosiloma on kuukausi tai enemmän. Koulut loppuvat toukokuun lopussa ja alkavat elokuussa, yliopistot syyskuussa.

18. A. The annual vacation for employees is a month or more. Schools break up at the end of May and start in August; universities in September.

■■■

■■■

Lappi on kevättalvella hiihtäjän paratiisi

+100° Celsiusta = +212° Fahrenheitia

Hiihtäjällä on **sukset** ja **sauvat**.
Hiihtäjän tie on **latu**.

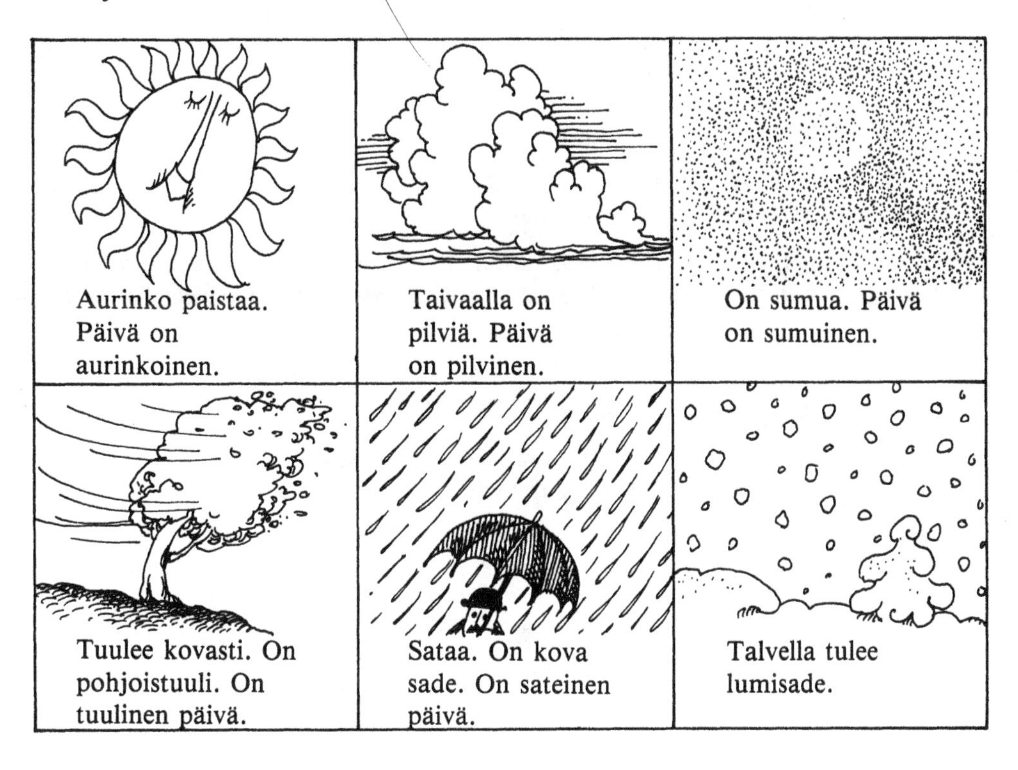

Aurinko paistaa. Päivä on aurinkoinen.

Taivaalla on pilviä. Päivä on pilvinen.

On sumua. Päivä on sumuinen.

Tuulee kovasti. On pohjoistuuli. On tuulinen päivä.

Sataa. On kova sade. On sateinen päivä.

Talvella tulee lumisade.

Kielioppia — Structural notes

1. "huone" words

(Review the **huone** words in the list on p. 102. Also look up this type in the list on p. 215.)

Finnish	English
Tämä on suuri huone.	This is a large room.
Tämä on suuri liike.	This is a big shop.
Talossa on viisi huonet/ta.	The house has five rooms.
Talossa on viisi liiket/tä.	There are five shops in the building.
Huonee/n asukas.	The inhabitant of the room.
Liikkee/n omistaja.	The owner of the shop.
Kuinka paljon huonei/ta?	How many rooms?
Kuinka paljon liikkei/tä?	How many shops?
Tule tähän huonee/seen!	Come into this room!
Tule tähän liikkee/seen!	Come into this shop!

Note these points about **huone** words, a very common word type:

— The principal parts are
huone huonetta huoneen huoneita
liike liikettä liikkeen liikkeitä
— The "into" case ends in **-seen** (pl. **-siin**)
— Only two forms have weak grade: **liike, liikettä**

Words ending in **-e** used to end in a consonant. This is why they still closely resemble words ending in a consonant.

Note: Among the very few **-e** words inflected differently from **huone** are *nukke (nukkea nuken nukkeja)* doll, *itse* (*-ä-n*) self, *kolme* (*-a-n*) three, *ale (-a-n-ja)* sale, and first names like *Kalle, Ville, Anne* etc.

2. Date and other expressions of time

15.9.1986 = *viidestoista (päivä) syyskuu/ta* | *(vuonna) 1986*
syyskuun viidestoista (päivä)

(The ordinals are listed in lesson 19:2.)

vuodenaika		*milloin?*
kevät (kevää/n)	spring	*kevää/llä* in spring
kesä	summer	*kesä/llä* in summer
syksy	autumn, fall	*syksy/llä* in autumn, fall
talvi (talve/n)	winter	*talve/lla* in winter
kuukausi		
tammikuu	January	*tammikuu/ssa* in January
joulukuu	December	*joulukuu/ssa* in December

(If needed, review other expressions of time, lessons 20:2 and 23:1.)

3. Third person singular of the verb used impersonally

Koiria ei saa tuoda myymälään.	It is not allowed to ("One must not") bring dogs into the store.
Lapissa voi hiihtää.	One can ski in Lapland.
Kun on väsynyt, unohtaa helposti asiat.	When one is (we, you, people are) tired, one easily forgets things.

The 3rd pers. sing. of the verb can be used impersonally, and does not refer to any specific person. The verb is, then, used without any subject-word in Finnish, whereas the corresponding English expression has a subject like "one", "we", "you", "they", "people" (French "on", German "man").

The use of a formal subject-word is, in general, unknown in Finnish, as shown in the examples below where English uses the subject ”it”:

Sataa. On kuuma.	It is raining. It is hot.
On helppo sanoa niin.	It's easy to say so.

(Cp. also Lesson 17:1 on the word ”there”.)

4. ”haluta” and ”merkitä” verbs

a) **haluta** verbs (see the lists on p. 132 and 218)

Basic form		Present	Past	Past participle	Imperative
halu/ta	to want	*halua/n*	*halu/si*	*halun/nut*	*halut/kaa!*
vasta/ta	to answer	*vastaa/n*	*vasta/si*	*vastan/nut*	*vastat/kaa!*

Most verbs ending in **vowel + ta** belong to the *haluta* type. They show the following characteristics in their conjugation:

— The present tense has an ”extra” **-a- (-ä-)**
— The past tense has an ”extra” **-s-**
— The past participle has an ”extra” **-n-**
— The imperative pl. has an ”extra” **-t-**
— The entire present and all forms using its stem have strong grade while the rest of the forms are weak:

tava/ta	to meet	*tapaa/n*	*tapasi/n*	*tavan/nut*	*älkää*
		tapaa/t	*tapasi/t*		*tavat/ko!*
		tapaa	*tapasi*		
		etc.	etc.		

b) **merkitä** verbs (see the lists on p. 132 and p. 218)

merki/tä	to mean	*merkitse/n*	*merkits/i*	*merkin/nyt*	*merkit/kää!*

Most verbs ending in **i + ta (tä)** belong to the *merkitä* type. They show the following characteristics in their conjugation:
— The present and past tense have an ”extra” element **-ts-**
— The other forms have the same ”extra” elements as *haluta* verbs.
— no **k p t** changes occur

Sanasto — Vocabulary

aste-tta-en-ita	degree, grade
harvoin (≠ *usein*)	seldom, rarely
+hiihtä/ä hiihdän hiihti hiihtänyt (cp. *hiihto* skiing)	to ski
ilmasto-a-n-ja	climate
iloi/nen-sta-sen-sia (cp. *ilo* joy)	glad, joyful, merry, jolly, happy, gay
+kausi kautta kauden kausia	period, term, season
+kukki/a kukin kukki kukkinut	to flower, bloom, blossom
lumi lunta lumen lumia	snow
sataa lunta	to snow
meri merta meren meriä	sea
pakka/nen-sta-sen-sia	frost, temperature below freezing-point
pimeä-(t)ä-n pimeitä (≠ *valoisa*)	dark, obscure
+sata/a (sadan) satoi satanut	to rain
sula/a-n suli sulanut	to melt, thaw
surulli/nen-sta-sen-sia (cp. *suru* sorrow, grief)	sad, melancholy, dreary
sää-tä-n säitä (cp. *ilma*)	weather
+tarkoitta/a tarkoitan tarkoitti tarkoittanut (cp. *tarkoitus* meaning, purpose)	to mean, refer to, purport
+tosi totta toden tosia	true
se on totta; puhua totta	it's true; tell the truth
tuuli tuulta tuulen tuulia	wind; mood, humor, temper
tuul/la (tuulen) tuuli tuullut	to be windy, to blow
työn/tekijä-ä-n-tekijöitä (cp. *työn/antaja* employer)	employee
vähitellen	gradually, by and by
yleensä (cp. *yleinen* general, common)	in general

Kuu/kaudet:

tammi/kuu-ta-n-kuita	January
helmi/kuu (*helmi* pearl)	February
maalis/kuu	March
huhti/kuu	April
touko/kuu (*touko* sowing; crop)	May
kesä/kuu (*kesä* summer)	June
heinä/kuu (*heinä* hay)	July
elo/kuu (*elo* harvest; life)	August

syys/kuu (*syys* = *syksy*)	September
loka/kuu (*loka* mud, dirt)	October
marras/kuu (*marras* obsol. dead)	November
joulu/kuu (*joulu* Yule, Christmas)	December

Vuoden/ajat:

kevät-tä kevään keväitä	spring
kesä-ä-n kesiä	summer
syksy-ä-n-jä	autumn, fall
talvi talvea talven talvia	winter

☆

pilvi pilveä pilven pilviä	cloud
+sade-tta sateen sateita	rain
sateen/varjo-a-n-ja	umbrella
suksi suksea suksen suksia	ski (one of a pair of skis)

Valkovuokko on tyypillinen Etelä-Suomen kevätkukka

37

HELSINGIN KESKUSTA

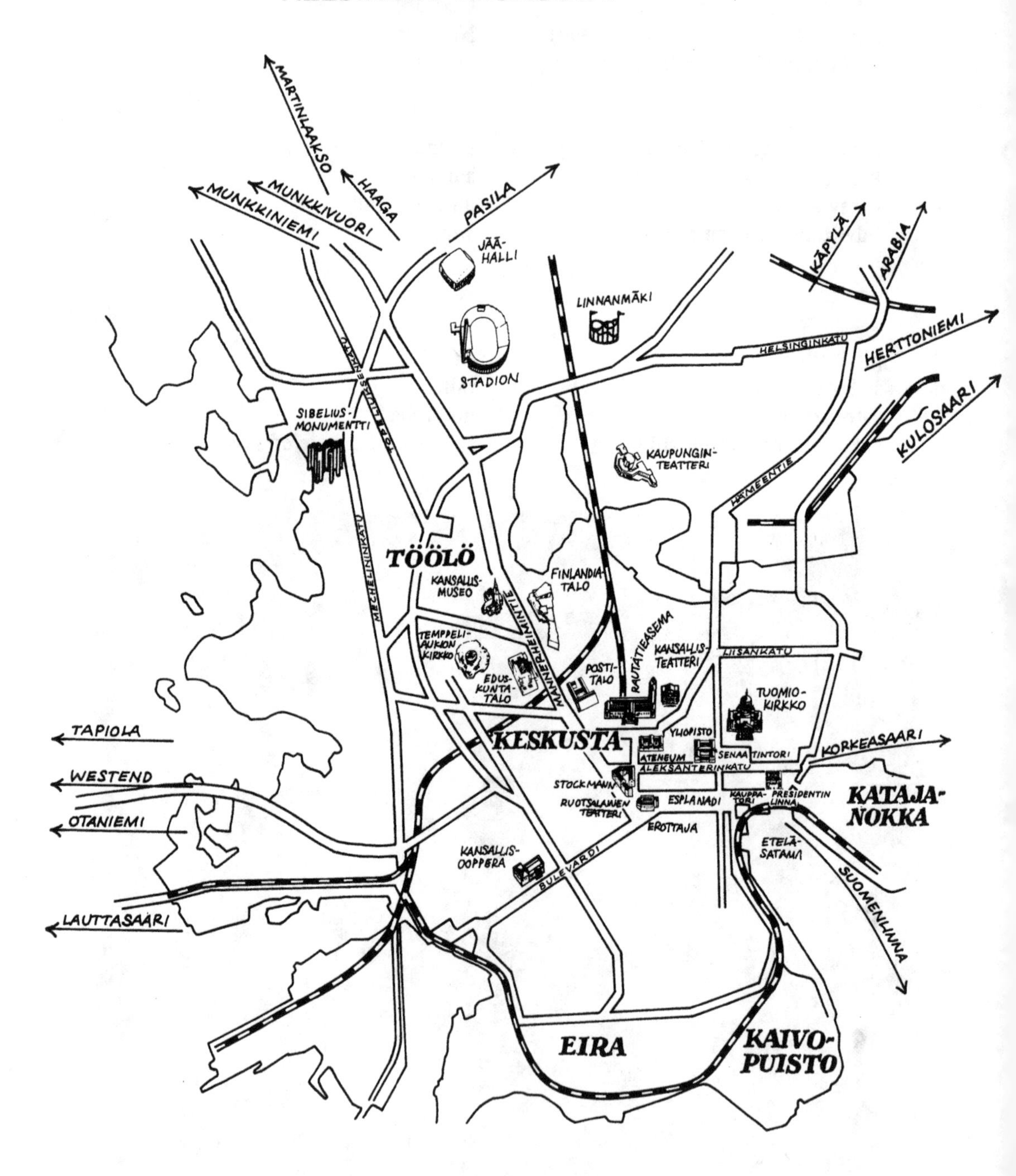

Katsellaanpa Helsinkiä

Kalle Oksanen ja James Brown ovat nousseet Stadionin torniin katselemaan Helsinkiä.

1. K. No niin, täällä ollaan! Täällä ovat maan suurimmat urheilukilpailut. Ja tästä tornista on paras näköala yli koko kaupungin.
2. J. Missä päin on etelä?
3. K. Tuolla. Etelässä on meri, Suomenlahti, joka on osa Itämerta. Tuolla on siis pohjoinen, tuolla itä ja tuolla länsi.

Let's take a look at Helsinki

Kalle Oksanen and James Brown have gone up to the Stadium Tower to take a look at H.

1. K. Well, here we are! The biggest sports events in Finland take place here. And from this tower we have the best view of the whole city.
2. J. Which direction is south?
3. K. Over there. In the south is the sea, the Gulf of Finland, which is part of the Baltic Sea. So there is north, there is east, and there is west.

Paavo Nurmen patsas Stadionin edessä

4. J. Katso tuonne alas, lähelle Stadionia. Mikä tuo matala, harmaa rakennus on?

4. J. Look down there, near the Stadium. What's that low grey building?

5. K. Se on Jäähalli.

5. K. It's the Ice Hall.

6. J. Silloin tuo katu on Mannerheimintie.

6. J. Then that street is Mannerheim Road.

7. K. Niin on, Helsingin pisin katu. Jos kuljetaan sitä pitkin Töölöstä keskustaa kohti, on vasemmalla puolella Finlandia-talo, pääkaupungin konsertti- ja kongressitalo.

7. K. Yes, the longest street in Helsinki. If we go along it from Töölö towards the Center, Finlandia Hall, the capital's concert and congress hall, is on the left.

8. J. Anna minun jatkaa. Finlandia-taloa vastapäätä on Kansallismuseo.

8. J. Let me go on. Across the street from Finlandia Hall is the National Museum.

Helsingin keskustaa. Edessä Kauppatori ja presidentin linna, takana Senaatintori, tuomiokirkko ja yliopisto.

9. K. Sen takana oikealla on Temppeliaukion kirkko.
10. J. Kaunein kaikista moderneista kirkoista, mitä olen nähnyt.
11. K. Takaisin Mannerheimintielle. Näethän tuolla Eduskuntatalon?

12. J. Kyllä, ja sitten ollaankin aivan keskustassa. Ahaa, rautatieasema! Tunnen sen tornin.
13. K. Mannerheimintieltä vasemmalle lähtee Aleksanterinkatu.
14. J. Helsingin tärkein liikekatu, eikö niin?
15. K. Kyllä, mutta tärkeä on myös Esplanadi, jonka toisessa päässä, meren rannalla, on Kauppatori.
16. J. Tiedän. Siellä on myös Eteläsatama ja tulli. Sinne tulevat matkustajalaivat ulkomailta.

17. K. Tuo suuri vihreä alue on Kaivopuisto, jossa on useita ulkomaiden lähetystöjä.
18. J. Ja presidentin linna.
19. K. Ei, presidentin linna on tuolla, Eteläsataman ja tuomiokirkon välillä. Tuomiokirkon ympärillä sijaitsevat yliopisto, yliopiston kirjasto ja Suomen pankki. Se on kaupungin vanha keskusta.
20. J. Minä pidän siitä enemmän kuin uusista kaupunginosista.
21. K. Idässä ja pohjoisessa on Helsingin suurin teollisuusalue. Tunnetuin sen tehtaista on Arabian posliinitehdas.

22. J. Onko Helsingissä eläintarhaa?
23. K. On, Korkeasaari, tuolla. Sen lähellä ovat Suomenlinnan saaret.

24. J. Helsinki on kauniilla paikalla. Se on minusta miellyttävä kaupunki.
25. K. Niin minustakin. Mutta tietysti elämä on vähemmän vilkasta kuin suurkaupungeissa.

9. K. Beyond the Museum, to the right, is the Temple Square Church.
10. J. The most beautiful of all modern churches that I have seen.
11. K. Back to Mannerheim Road. Can you see the Parliament Building over there?
12. J. Yes, I can, and then we are right in the Center. Ah, the Railroad Station! I recognize its tower.
13. K. To the left of Mannerheim Road runs Alexander Street.
14. J. The most important business street in Helsinki, isn't it?
15. K. Yes, but the Esplanade is important, too. At its other end, by the sea, is the Market Square.
16. J. I know. That's where the South Harbor is, too, and the Customs Office. That's where passenger boats arrive from abroad.
17. K. That large green area is Kaivopuisto Park where there are several foreign embassies.
18. J. And the President's Castle.
19. K. No, the President's Castle is over there, between the South Harbor and the Cathedral. The University, the University Library, and the Bank of Finland are located around the Cathedral. It's the old center of the city.
20. J. I like it better than the new districts.
21. K. In the east and north is Helsinki's largest industrial area. The best known of its factories is the Arabia porcelain factory.
22. J. Does Helsinki have a Zoo?
23. K. Yes, Korkeasaari, there. In the neighborhood are the islands of Suomenlinna.
24. J. Helsinki is beautifully situated. I think it's a pleasant city.
25. K. I think so, too. But life in Helsinki is naturally less busy than in big cities.

37

26. J. Minä olen väsynyt suurkaupunkeihin ja niiden saasteisiin. — Paljonko asukkaita Helsingissä on?

27. K. 501 700 henkeä[1]. Helsingissä ja sen ympäristössä asuu nykyisin noin 17 prosenttia Suomen kansasta.

26. J. I'm tired of big cities and their pollution. — How many inhabitants does Helsinki have?

27. K. 501 700 people. Today about 17 per cent of the Finnish people live in Helsinki and its vicinity.

Saamelaiset (= lappalaiset) asuvat **Pohjois**-Suomessa (''in the north of Finland''). Kemi on Oulu**sta** **pohjoiseen** (päin) tai Oulu**n** **pohjoispuolella** (''to the north of'').

ylhäällä	**ylhäältä**	**ylös**
alhaalla	**alhaalta**	**alas**

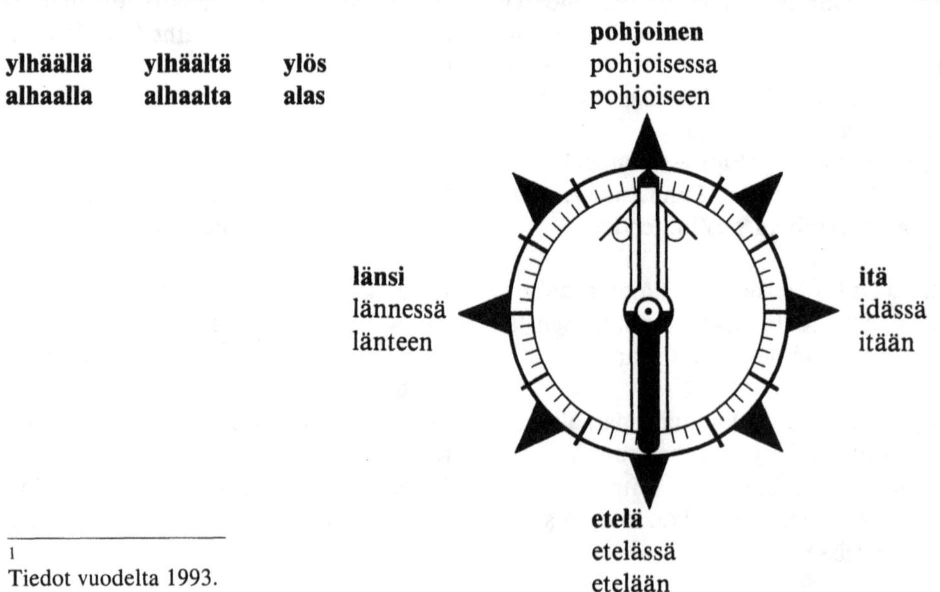

[1] Tiedot vuodelta 1993.

Kielioppia — Structural notes

1. Superlative of adjectives

Tämä on hieno/in pukuni.	This is my finest dress/suit.
Maailman korke/in rakennus.	The highest building in the world.
Kaikkein suur/in.	The biggest of all, the very biggest.

The superlative of adjectives is formed with the suffix **-in**.

As in the comparative (see lesson 32:1), the stem for forming the superlative is obtained from the genitive. The final vowel of the stem may undergo some changes:

The final **-a, -ä, -e** is dropped:

+*halpa*	*halva/n*	cheap	(comp. *halvempi)*	*halv/in*	cheapest
+*rakas*	*rakkaa/n*	dear	*(rakkaampi)*	*rakka/in*	dearest
vihreä		green	*(vihreämpi)*	*vihre/in*	greenest
pieni	*piene/n*	small	*(pienempi)*	*pien/in*	smallest
vihainen	*vihaise/n*	angry	*(vihaisempi)*	*vihais/in*	angriest
terve	*tervee/n*	healthy	*(terveempi)*	*terve/in*	healthiest

The final **-i(i)** of the stem changes into **-e-**:

siisti	*siisti/n*	clean	(comp. *siistimpi*)	*siiste/in*	cleanest
kaunis	*kaunii/n*	beautiful	*(kauniimpi)*	*kaune/in*	most beautiful

The following superlatives do not follow these rules:

hyvä		good	(comp. *parempi*)	*paras (parhain)*	best
pitkä		long	*(pitempi)*	*pisin*	longest
+*uusi* (and other *uusi* words)	*uude/n*	new	*(uudempi)*	*uusin*	newest
lyhyt	*lyhye/n*	short	*(lyhyempi, lyhempi)*	*lyhyin, lyhin*	shortest
monet		many	*(useammat)*	*useimmat*	most
useat		several			

Note here also the adverbs *paljon (enemmän) eniten* most, *vähän (vähemmän) vähiten* least.

The superlative is inflected like a normal adjective. The principal parts are always of the type

+*lähin — lähintä — lähimmän — lähimpiä*

(''into'' case *lähimpään*).

Examples:

Haluan hienointa kiinalaista teetä.	I want some of the finest Chinese tea.
Oletko nähnyt Saabin uusimman automallin?	Have you seen the newest car model of the Saab?
Helsingin lähimmät naapurit ovat Espoo, Vantaa ja Kauniainen.	The nearest neighbors of Helsinki are Espoo, Vantaa, and Kauniainen.
Savonlinna on Suomen kauneimpia kaupunkeja.	S. is one of the most beautiful cities in Finland.
Tulemme nyt Suomen pohjoisimpaan kaupunkiin.	We are now coming to the northernmost city in F.

2. Post and prepositions with the partitive

(Before studying this paragraph, review the postpositions with the gen. in lessons 30:2 and 35:2.)

There are also post and prepositions with the partitive.

Postpositions:
kohtaan to, toward(s)
varten for (the purpose of)
vastaan against
    mennä vastaan to go and meet somebody

Prepositions:
ilman without
paitsi except; besides

Post or prepositions:
ennen before, prior to
kohti toward(s), in the direction of
pitkin along
vailla without, lacking
vasta/päätä opposite, on the opposite side, across ... from

Examples:

Olet aina niin ystävällinen mei/tä kohtaan (= meille).	You are always so kind towards us.
Mi/tä varten (= miksi) teit sen?	What did you do it for?
Olemme tä/tä päätös/tä vastaan.	We are against this decision.
Perhe meni isä/ä vastaan asemalle.	The family went to meet Father at the station.
Laiva kulkee satama/a kohti.	The ship is going towards a harbor.
Tulkaa kotiin ennen kuut/ta!	Come home before six!
En voi elää ilman sinu/a.	I cannot live without you.
Paitsi tei/tä tunnemme täällä vain pari ihmistä.	Besides you, we know only two or three people here.
Mies on | *työ/tä vailla.* / *vailla työ/tä.*	The man is without a job.
Posti on | *pankki/a vastapäätä.* / *vastapäätä pankki/a.*	The post office is across the street from the bank.

Note: *keskellä* and *lähellä* are used either as postpositions with the gen. or prepositions with the part.:

piha/n keskellä = *keskellä piha/a* in the middle of the yard
Helsingi/n lähellä = *lähellä Helsinki/ä* near Helsinki

3. Plural of nouns: local cases (II)

(Review part I in lesson 35:1.)
To finish with the plural of nouns, words with **weak grade** in the genitive sing. must still be examined.

Note in the examples below that the pl. cases have the same **k p t** grade as the corresponding sing. cases. In other words:
– use the part. pl. stem unchanged only for the ''into'' case;
– ''weaken'' the stem for the other local cases.

Examples:

	Sing.			Pl.		
	+koti	*kodin*		*kotej/a* (*kotei-*, weak *kodei-*)		
''into''	*kotiin*			*kotei/hin*		
''on''		*kodi*	*lla*		*kodei*	*lla*
''from''			*lta*			*lta*
''onto''			*lle*			*lle*
''in''			*ssa*			*ssa*
''out of''			*sta*			*sta*
	+tyttö	*tytön*		*tyttöj/ä* (*tyttöi-*, weak *tytöi-*)		
''into''	*tyttöön*			*tyttöi/hin*		
''on''		*tytö*	*llä*		*tytöi*	*llä*
''from''			*ltä*			*ltä*
''onto''			*lle*			*lle*
''in''			*ssä*			*ssä*
''out of''			*stä*			*stä*

37

	+poika	*pojan*	*poiki/a* (*poiki-*, weak *poji-*)	
"into"	*poikaan*		*poiki/in*	
"on"		*poja* | *lla*		*poji* | *lla*
"from"		*lta*		*lta*
"onto"		*lle*		*lle*
"in"		*ssa*		*ssa*
"out of"		*sta*		*sta*

	+halpa	*halvan*	*halpoj/a* *halpoi-*, weak *halvoi-*)	
"into"	*halpaan*		*halpoi/hin*	
"on"		*halva* | *lla*		*halvoi* | *lla*
"from"		*lta*		*lta*
"onto"		*lle*		*lle*
"in"		*ssa*		*ssa*
"out of"		*sta*		*sta*

Sanasto — Vocabulary

alas (≠ *ylös*)	down, downward
alue-tta-en-ita	area, region
+anta/a annan antoi antanut	(also:) to allow, let
Anna minu/n mennä!	Let me go!
+asukas-ta asukkaan asukkaita	inhabitant
aukio-ta-n-ita	open space: square
+edus/kunta-a-kunnan-kuntia	Diet, (Finnish) parliament
elämä-ä-n	life
etelä-ä-n	south
+itä-ä-idän	east
jatka/a jatkan jatkoi jatkanut	to continue, go on
kansa-a-n kansoja	people, nation

kaupungin/osa-a-n-osia	city district
kilpailu-a-n-ja (cp. *kilpailla*)	competition, contest; race
+kulke/a kuljen kulki kulkenut	to go, travel, move
linna-a-n linnoja	castle
+länsi länttä lännen	west
matala-a-n matalia	low; shallow
miellyttävä-ä-n miellyttäviä (from *miellyttää* to please)	pleasant, agreeable
nykyisin	today, nowadays
näkö/ala-a-n-aloja	view
osa-a-n osia	part
puisto-a-n-ja	park, public garden
rakennus-ta rakennuksen rakennuksia (from *rakentaa* to build)	building
rauta/tie-tä-n-teitä	railway, railroad
saaste-tta-en-ita	pollution
satama-a-n satamia	harbor, port
sijai/ta-tsen-tsi-nnut	to lie, be located, be situated
suur/lähetystö-ä-n-jä	embassy
+teollisuus teollisuutta teollisuuden teollisuuksia	industry, manufacturing
torni-a-n torneja	tower
tulli-a-n tulleja	custom(s); custom-house; duty
+tunnettu-a tunnetun tunnettuja	well-known
+tuomio/kirkko-a-kirkon-kirkkoja	cathedral
ulko/maa-ta-n-maita (usu. pl.)	foreign country
ulko/mailla	abroad
urheilu-a-n-ja (cp. *urheilla*)	athletics, sport(s)
usea-a-n useita (usu. pl.)	several
+vilkas-ta vilkkaan vilkkaita	lively, vivid, vivacious; (of traffic) busy
ympäristö-ä-n-jä	surroundings, neighborhood; environment

☆

alhaalla (≠ *ylhäällä*)	down
+porras-ta portaan portaita	step, stair; pl. stairs, stairway
ylhäällä (≠ *alhaalla*)	up
ylös (≠ *alas*)	up, upward

Mikko Laakso on sairaana

Mikko tulee koulusta kotiin

1. M. Hei, äiti.
2. Ä. Hei Mikko. Oletko sinä saanut nuhan? Sinä näytät sairaalta. Miten sinä voit?
3. M. Ihan hyvin. Minä olen vain väsynyt, siinä kaikki.
4. Ä. Ainakin sinussa on kova nuha. Voi, älä käytä enää tuota nenäliinaa, sehän on ihan likainen. Tässä on paketti paperinenäliinoja. Minun pitää antaa sinulle heti lääkettä.
5. M. Mutta yskänlääke maistuu niin pahalta. Sitä paitsi se on lopussa.
6. Ä. Onneksi minä ostin juuri apteekista uuden pullon. Sinun pitäisi ottaa myös pari C-vitamiinitablettia. Haenko kuumemittarin?
7. M. En minä usko, että minussa on kuumetta.
8. Ä. Mene kuitenkin heti sänkyyn, ole kiltti. On hyvä olla varovainen, nyt on kaikilla ihmisillä flunssaa.

Seuraavana aamuna rouva Laakson täytyy soittaa terveyskeskuksen lääkärille.

9. Rva L. Onko tohtori Kuusi? Täällä on rouva Laakso. Meidän Mikko-poika on sairaana. — On, hänellä on korkea kuume, melkein 40 astetta. — Eilenkö? Ei muuta kuin paha nuha. Nyt hänellä on kova päänsärky ja kurkku on kipeä. — Tyypillinen influenssa? Lepoa, aspiriinia ja paljon juotavaa ... Entä tuo korkea kuume? — Pitäisi laskea parissa päiväs-

Mikko Laakso is ill

Mikko comes home from school

1. M. Hi, Mommy.
2. Mother. Hi, Mikko. Have you caught a cold? You look ill. How do you feel?
3. M. Just fine. I'm just tired, that's all.
4. Mother. You have at least a bad cold. Oh dear, don't use that handkerchief any more, it's quite dirty. Here's a packet of paper handkerchiefs. I must give you some medicine at once.
5. M. But the cough medicine tastes so bad. Besides, there isn't any left.
6. Mother. Fortunately I just bought a new bottle at the pharmacy. You ought to take a couple of vitamin C pills, too. Shall I go and get the thermometer?
7. M. I don't believe I'm running any temperature.
8. Mother. Anyway, go to bed at once, please. It's good to be careful, everybody has got the flu now.

On the following morning Mrs. Laakso has to call the doctor at the Health Center.

9. Mrs. L. Dr. Kuusi? This is Mrs. Laakso calling. Our son Mikko is ill. — Yes, he's got a high temperature, nearly 40 degrees. — Yesterday? Nothing but a bad cold. Now he's got a bad headache and a sore throat. — A typical influenza? Rest, aspirin, and a lot to drink ... How about that high temperature? — Ought to go down in a couple of days. — Yes,

38

sä. — Kyllä, minä soitan, jos se ei ala laskea. Kiitos neuvoista, tohtori, minä olen jo paljon rauhallisempi. Kuulemiin!

I'll call you if it doesn't start going down. Thank you for your advice, doctor, I'm much calmer already. Goodbye, Dr. Kuusi!

Mitä (sinu**lle**) **kuuluu?** Kiitos hyv**ää**, entä(s) sinulle? Mitä koti**in** kuuluu? Mitä Rovaniemel**le** kuuluu?	asking about one's general news
Kuinka voit? **Miten(kä) jaksat?** Kiitos **hyvin.**	asking about one's health

Mikä sinulla on?

Pääni on kipeä.

Kurkkuni on kipeä.

Vatsani on kipeä.

Jalkani on kipeä.

38

pitää

Hän pitää kynää vasemmassa kädessä.

Me pidämme ruokatavaraa jääkaapissa.

He pitävät kokouksen.

Hän pitää puheen.

He pitävät hauskaa.

Minna pitää Anna**sta**.

Minu**n** pitää mennä nukkumaan.

Kielioppia — Structural notes

1. täytyy, pitää, tarvitsee, on pakko

Täytyykö sinun lähteä jo?	Must you go already?
Ei minun tarvitse lähteä vielä.	I don't have to go yet.

Ihmisten pitää syödä paljon hedelmiä. (He eivät saa syödä niin paljon sokeria.)	People must eat a lot of fruit. (They must not eat so much sugar.)
Pekan täytyi mennä työhön, vaikka hän oli sairaana.	Pekka had to go to work although he was ill.
Sinun pitäisi polttaa vähemmän.	You ought to smoke less.
Kaikkien pitää tehdä velvollisuutensa.	Everybody must do his duty.
Meidän piti tavata neljältä.	We were supposed to meet at four.
Onko meidän pakko hyväksyä nämä ehdot?	Do we have to accept these terms?

With verbs denoting obligation to do something (*täytyä* must, have to; *pitää* shall, must, ought to, be supposed to; *tarvita* need to, be necessary to; *olla pakko* must, be compelled to):
— the person who has to do something appears in the genitive
— the verb denoting obligation appears in the 3rd pers. sing.
— as with other auxiliaries, the other verb which completes their meaning appears in the basic form.

No genitive in impersonal sentences:

Nyt täytyy lähteä.	We must go now.
Auto pitää pestä.	The car must be washed.

Note also the ''have'' structure:

Opettajalla täytyy olla kärsivällisyyttä.	A teacher must have patience.
Vanhemmilla pitäisi olla aikaa lapsilleen.	Parents should have time for their children.

The direct object in ''täytyy'' sentences: basic form instead of the genitive.

Hän tekee työn (työtä).	He'll do the job (some work).
But:	
Hänen pitää tehdä työ (työtä).	He must do the job (some work).
Note: *En tarvitse rahaa.*	I don't need money.

tarvita in the meaning ''to need something'' is a normal verb conjugated in different persons.

2. The essive case

Mikko on sairaa/na (sairas).	Mikko is ill.
Tulimme kotiin väsynei/nä.	We came home tired.
Juotko kahvisi musta/na?	Do you drink your coffee black?

The essive case expresses a state, condition, or capacity which can be thought of as temporary, subject to change.

Esp. with nouns, the essive often corresponds to the English expression ''as something'':

Liisa on oppaa/na (nom. *opas*) *Oulussa.*	L. works as a guide in Oulu.
Lapse/na olin kovin ujo.	As a child I was very shy.

The essive is also used in time expressions, esp. of the days of the week and month and annual festivals:

maanantai/na on Monday
toise/na (kolmante/na) elokuuta (on) August 2nd (3rd)
joulu/na at Christmas

Structure:

Sing. *sairas*	*(sairaa/n)*	*sairaa/na*
Pl.	*(sairai/ta)*	*sairai/na*

However, the essive always has strong grade:

Sing. *parempi*	*(paremma/n)*	*parempa/na*
Pl.	*(parempi/a)*	*parempi/na*

Note:

tämä joulu	*tä/nä joulu/na*
se joulu	*si/nä joulu/na*
mikä joulu?	*mi/nä joulu/na?*

(More about the essive case in Book 2.)

3. About colloquial Finnish

Standard Finnish, as taught in textbooks, is mainly used in the written language, in educated speech, and in rather formal situations. In informal every-day situations, however, Finnish speech differs a great deal from the standard. There are local dialects which are still widely used. A strong influence today is the colloquial Finnish spoken in the Helsinki area. As most foreigners coming to Finland stay in or near Helsinki, they might profit from learning about the most characteristic aspects of the ''Helsinki dialect''. (There have been earlier references to some of them in certain structural notes as well as in the readers.)

Note the following points:
a) Final vowels, esp. **-i**, are frequently dropped: *yks(i), anteeks(i), jos Pekka lähtis(i), mul(la) on, mut(ta)*

b) The vowel **-i-** is commonly dropped in unstressed diphthongs: *puna(i)nen, sella(i)nen* or *semmo(i)nen* such, *kirjo(i)ttaa, sano(i), otta(i)s(i)*

c) Unstressed vowel combinations with **-a (-ä)** become long vowels: *hirveen nopee (= hirveän nopea), en haluu maitoo (= en halua maitoa), paljon poikii (= poikia)*

d) The final **-t** is dropped in participles: *posti on tullu(t), bussi ei lähteny(t)*

e) **-ma (-mä)** is dropped in *tekemään* etc.: *mennä nukkuun (= nukkumaan), lähtee hiihtään (= lähteä hiihtämään)*

f) Poss. suffixes are commonly dropped: *m(in)un kirja(ni), s(in)un koti(si), teidän nimi*

g) short quick-speech forms or dialect variants of certain words abound: *onk(o)s tä(m)ä, eik(ö)s nii(n), kat(s)o, oon (= olen), tuut (= tulet), mee (= mene), tiiän (= tiedän), m(in)ä, m(in)usta, s(in)ulle, t(u)on, noi (= nuo), mei(d)än, kah(d)eksan*

h) *se* and *ne* frequently replace *hän* and *he*: *se sano(i), anna niille (= heille), sen kanssa (= hänen kanssaan)*

i) The verb is used in the sing. also in the 3rd pers. pl.: *tytöt nauraa (= nauravat), ne lähti (= he lähtivät), lapset on syöny (= ovat syöneet)*

j) ''me tehdään'' largely replaces ''me teemme'': *me lähdetään pois, me ei jäädä tänne*

The colloquial present tense of the verb *olla* is conjugated as follows:

mä oon	*me ollaan*
sä oot	*te ootte*
se on	*ne on*

Sanasto — Vocabulary

+apteekki-a apteekin apteekkeja	chemist's, pharmacy, drugstore
+kiltti-ä kiltin kilttejä	well-behaved, good, nice
kipeä-(t)ä-n kipeitä	ill, sick; sore
kuitenkin (neg. *ei kuitenkaan*)	however, still, yet, nevertheless
+kurkku-a kurkun kurkkuja	throat; cucumber
kuume-tta-en-ita	fever, temperature

kuume/mittari-a-n-mittareita	(clinical) thermometer
lämpö/mittari	thermometer
laske/a-n laski laskenut	go down; put down; count; reckon, calculate
+lepo-a levon lepoja (cf. *levätä*)	rest
likai/nen-sta-sen-sia (≠ *puhdas*)	dirty, soiled
+lääke-ttä lääkkeen lääkkeitä	medicine, drug
maistu/a-n-i-nut (joltakin)	to taste (like something)
nenä/liina-a-n-liinoja	handkerchief (''nose-cloth'')
nuha-a-n nuhia	cold (in the nose)
+näyttä/ä näytän näytti näyttänyt (joltakin)	(also:) to look, seem (like something)
onneksi (≠ *valitettavasti*)	fortunately
+pitä/ä pidän piti pitänyt	(also): to hold; to keep
minun pitää (cp. *minun täytyy*)	I shall, I have to; I am supposed to
+pään/särky-ä-säryn-särkyjä	headache
rauhalli/nen-sta-sen-sia	peaceful, quiet
sitä paitsi	besides, furthermore
+tabletti-a tabletin tabletteja	pill
+terve/ys-yttä-yden	health
terveys/keskus	health center
usko/a-n-i-nut (cp. *usko* belief, faith)	to believe
Cp. Luulen, että hän on täällä.	I think he's here.
En usko, että hän on täällä	I don't think (believe) he's here.
+valitta/a valitan valitti valittanut	to complain, regret
varovai/nen-sta-sen-sia (≠ *varomaton*)	careful, cautious
voi/da-n voi voinut	(also:) to feel (well, ill)
Kuinka sinä voit? (cp. *mitä sinulle kuuluu?*)	how are you, how do you feel?
yskä-ä-n (cp. *yski/ä*)	cough

☆

jaksa/a-n jaksoi jaksanut (= *voida*)	to have the strength; to feel (well, ill)
+pitä/ä hauskaa	to have a good time, enjoy oneself
+täyttä/ä täytän täytti täyttänyt	to fill, fulfil; complete
hän täyttää 6 vuotta	he'll be 6 years old, turn six
vatsa-a-n vatsoja	stomach

Heikki ja Betty menevät illalla ulos

1. H. Kuule Betty, mennäänkö ulos tänä iltana?
2. B. Minä lähtisin kyllä hirveän mielelläni, mutta tänään minulla on niin paljon töitä ...
3. H. Betty, sinä tulet ihan hulluksi, kun aina vain luet ja luet. Nythän on viikonloppu.
4. B. No, mennään sitten. Mutta mihin?
5. H. Katsotaan millaisia ilmoituksia on tämän päivän lehdessä.

Tutkivat yhdessä sanomalehteä.

6. H. Lähtisitkö sinä mieluummin teatteriin vai elokuviin?
7. B. Riippuu ohjelmasta. Mistä sinä itse olet kiinnostunut?
8. H. Minä olen kiinnostunut kaikesta. Teatterit ... Kansallisteatterissa menee Kesäyön unelma.
9. B. Minä en välittäisi nähdä Shakespearea suomeksi. Minä haluaisin nähdä suomalaisen näytelmän, vaikka en ymmärtäisikään siitä kaikkea.
10. H. Kaupunginteatterin suurella näyttämöllä on Kiven Seitsemän veljestä. Mutta se on ensi-ilta ja loppuunmyyty!
11. B. Onpa meillä huono onni!
12. H. Se on minun syyni. Miksi minä en ajatellut tätä asiaa aikaisemmin!
13. B. No, ei se mitään tee. Tehdään jotain muuta. Minä olen kuullut, että ooppera on Suomessa hyvin suosittua. Olisi kiva nähdä jokin suomalainen ooppera, esimerkiksi Aulis Sallisen Punainen viiva. Minä en ole ollut oopperassa pitkään aikaan.

Heikki and Betty are going out for the evening

1. H. Look here, Betty, shall we go out this evening?
2. B. I'd really love to go, but I have such a lot of work to do today ...
3. H. Betty, you'll go completely crazy if you just study and study all the time. It's weekend now, isn't it?
4. B. Well, let's go then. But where?
5. H. Let's see what sort of ads there are in today's paper.

They study the newspaper together.

6. H. Would you rather go to the theater or to the cinema?
7. B. Depends on the program. What are you interested in yourself?
8. H. I'm interested in everything. The theaters ... "A Midsummer Night's Dream" is on at the National Theater.
9. B. I wouldn't care to see Shakespeare in Finnish. I'd like to see a Finnish play, even if I wouldn't understand all of it.
10. H. The big stage of the City Theater has Kivi's "Seven Brothers". But it's a première, and it's sold out.
11. B. We do have bad luck!
12. H. It's my fault. Why didn't I think of this earlier!
13. B. Well, never mind. Let's do something else (instead). I've heard that the opera is very popular in Finland. It would be nice to see some Finnish opera, for instance Aulis Sallinen's "Red Line". I haven't been to the opera for a long time.

39

Kohtaus oopperasta Punainen viiva

14. H. Minä ihailen kovasti Jorma Hynnistä, joka laulaa Punaisessa viivassa. Hänellä on erittäin kaunis ääni. Hetkinen ... ei mene tällä viikolla!

15. B. Mitäs tämä on? Kansanlauluja ja -tansseja eri maista Finlandia-talossa. Mitä sinä ajattelet siitä?

16. H. Jos sinä olet kiinnostunut kansanlauluista, niin minulla ei ole mitään sitä vastaan. Mennäänkö konsertin jälkeen diskoon tanssimaan?

17. B. Ei kiitos diskoon, minä pelkään kovia ääniä.

18. H. No, sitten johonkin ravintolaan. Kumpaan haluaisit mieluummin, Majesteettiin vai Kultalintuun?

14. H. I greatly admire Jorma Hynninen, who sings in the ''Red Line''. He has a very beautiful voice. One moment ... it's not on this week!

15. B. Now what's this? Folksongs and dances from different countries at Finlandia Hall. What do you think of that?

16. H. If you are interested in folksongs, I've got nothing against it. Shall we go dancing at a disco afterwards?

17. B. No thanks, not a disco, I'm afraid of loud noises.

18. H. Well, some restaurant, then. Which would you prefer, the ''Majesty'' or the ''Golden Bird''?

19. B. Minulle sopii kumpi vain.	19. B. Either is all right with me.
20. H. Ainakin Kultalinnussa on aina hauska ohjelma ja tanssia. Ja paljon ihmisiä, varsinkin lauantaisin. Minun pitää tilata pöytä heti.	20. H. At least the "Golden Bird" always has a nice show and dancing. And lots of people, especially on Saturdays. I must reserve the table at once.

matkustan mielelläni = minusta on hauska matkustaa
hän matkustaa mielellä**än**
matkustatteko te mielellä**nne**?
en, minä olen **mieluummin** kotona

sunnuntai**sin** (= aina sunnuntaina), keskiviikkoi**sin**; arki**sin** (arkipäivi**sin**), pyhäi**sin**; aamui**sin**, iltai**sin**, öi**sin**; keväi**sin**, kesäi**sin**

missä?	koto**na**	ulko**na**	kauka**na**
mistä?	koto**a**	ulko**a**	kauka**a**
mihin?	kotiin	ulos	kauas

Kielioppia — Structural notes

1. Direct object

The basic rules for the direct object were learned in lessons 25:1, 26:1 and 29:3; some additional information on the matter has been accumulated later. This lesson will offer a survey of the direct object, including a couple of new details.

A. Negative sentences

Rule 1. In negative sentences, the direct object is always in the **partitive**.

B. Affirmative sentences

Rule 2. If the direct object expresses indefinite amount or number, it is always in the **partitive**:

Ostan liha/a ja omeni/a.	I'll buy (some) meat and (some) apples.

Rule 3. If the direct object expresses definite number, it is in the **basic form pl.**:

Söimme omena/t.	We ate the apples.

Rule 4. If the direct object is one countable thing or a definite amount, it is in the **genitive**:

Syön omena/n.	I'll eat an/the apple.
Paistamme liha/n.	We'll roast the meat.

Exceptions:

a) **Basic form sing.** must be used instead of the **gen.**

— in imperative sentences

Syö omena!	Eat an/the apple!

— in "täytyy" sentences

Sinun täytyy syödä omena.	You must eat an/the apple.

— in "tehdään" sentences

Syödään omena!	Let's eat an/the apple!
Me syödään omena.	We'll eat an/the apple.
(*Omena syödään.*	The apple will be eaten.)

— in impersonal phrases of the type *on aika tehdä se; on hauska tehdä se* (impers. verb, usu. *olla* + noun/adj. + inf. + its obj.)

On aika syödä omena.	It's time to eat an apple.
On hauska syödä omena.	It's nice to eat an apple.

b) The accusative in **-t** of personal pronouns and *kuka* corresponds to both the **gen.** and the **basic form** of nouns:

Tuon | *lapse/n tänne.* | *häne/t*	I'll bring | the child here. | him
Tuokaa | *lapsi tänne!* | *häne/t*	Bring | the child here! | him

c) Numbers, except for *yksi*, never appear in the **gen.** in the direct object:

Syön yhde/n (omena/n).	I'll eat one (apple).
Syön kaksi (omenaa).	I'll eat two (apples).
Syö yksi (omena)!	Eat one (apple)!
Syö kaksi (omenaa)!	Eat two (apples)!

Rule 5. The **partitive** may also be used to express that the action of the verb in the sentence is continuous, incomplete, irresultative (= not leading to a final result):

Syön omena/a.	I'm eating an/the apple.
Luetko sinä tä/tä romaani/a illalla?	Will you read this novel (but not finish it) in the evening?
Cp. *Syön omena/n.*	I'll eat an (entire) apple.
Luetko tämä/n romaani/n?	Will you read this novel (and finish it)?

Note that some verbs inherently express continuous or irresultative action and therefore always or mostly appear with the part. Among them are most verbs denoting emotion, e.g. *rakastaa* to love, *vihata* to hate, *ihailla* to admire, *pelätä* to fear; many verbs in **-ella**, e.g. *ajatella* to think, *onnitella* to congratulate, *opiskella* to study, *totella* to obey; and a large number of others, e.g. *auttaa* to help, *etsiä* to look for, *harrastaa* to take an interest in, *häiritä* to disturb, *odottaa* to wait for, expect.

Important to remember: **Any reason for using the partitive in the direct object will overrule all other considerations.**

2. The translative case

Mikko tuli sairaa/ksi.	Mikko became ill.
Onko hän tullut paremma/ksi?	Has he become any better?
Virtaset maalasivat talonsa punaise/ksi.	The Virtanens painted their house red.
Syksyllä lehdet muuttuvat keltaisi/ksi.	In fall, leaves become (change) yellow.
Kaija lukee lääkäri/ksi.	K. studies to become a doctor.

The translative case expresses change in a state, condition, or capacity (cp. the essive case, lesson 38:2). It is used with the verb *tulla* to become and other verbs indicating change.

In time expressions, the translative denotes the point or period of time for which something is planned.

Tämä läksy on huomise/ksi (ensi maanantai/ksi).	This assignment is for tomorrow (for next Monday).
Perhe lähti maalle viikonlopu/ksi.	The family went to the country for the weekend.

The translative has an extensive idiomatic usage. Examples:

Onne/ksi ei alkanut sataa.	Fortunately, it did not start raining.
Mitä ostaisimme lahja/ksi isälle?	What could we buy as a present for father?
Mitä sisu on englanni/ksi?	What is ''sisu'' in English?

Structure:

Sing. *sairas*	*(sairaa/n)*	*sairaa/ksi*
Pl.	*(sairai/ta)*	*sairai/ksi*
Sing. *parempi*	*(paremma/n)*	*paremma/ksi*
Pl.	*(parempi/a)*	*paremmi/ksi*

Note:

tämä | *päivä*	*tä/ksi* | *päivä/ksi*
se |	*si/ksi* |
mikä päivä?	*mi/ksi päivä/ksi?*

(More about the translative in Finnish for Foreigners 2.)

Sanasto — Vocabulary

aikaisemmin (≠ *myöhemmin*)	earlier
+ensi-ilta-a-illan-iltoja	opening night, première
hullu-a-n-ja	crazy, mad
ihail/la ihailen ihaili ihaillut (jotakin henkilöä tai asiaa)	to admire (somebody or something)
ilmoitus-ta ilmoituksen ilmoituksia (cp. *ilmoittaa*)	announcement; advertisement
kiinnostunut:	
olla k. jostakin	to be interested (in something)
+kulta-a kullan kultia	gold; darling, dear
laulu-a-n-ja	song; singing
+loppuun/myyty-ä-myydyn-myytyjä	sold out
mielellä/ni-si-än-mme-nne-än	with pleasure, willingly
tehdä mielellään	to like to do, like doing
luen mielelläni	I like to read
mieluummin (comp. of *mielellään*)	rather, more willingly, preferably
tehdä mieluummin (kuin)	rather do, prefer doing
näytelmä-ä-n näytelmiä	(theater) play
näyttämö-ä-n-itä	stage
+pelä/tä pelkään pelkäsi pelännyt (jotakin henkilöä t. asiaa)	to fear, be afraid (of somebody or something)
+riippu/a riipun riippui riippunut (jostakin)	to hang; to depend on, be up to (something)
+suosittu-a suositun suosittuja	popular, well-liked
syy-tä-n syitä	reason, cause; fault
tila/ta-an-si-nnut (cp. *tilaus*)	to order, reserve; subscribe to
tutki/a-n tutki tutkinut (cp. *tutkimus*)	to study, examine, investigate, do research
unelma-a-n unelmia	dream
viiva-a-n viivoja	line, stroke
ääni ääntä äänen ääniä	voice, sound; noise

☆

+arki arkea arjen arkia *(= arki/päivä)*	weekday, working day
pyhä-ä-n pyhiä	holy, sacred, saint
pyhä/päivä	holiday, Sunday

How to use the partitive: A review

Basic meaning:

Part. sing.	Part. pl.
Indefinite amount	Indefinite number

The partitive is used in this meaning

— as the subject of ''there is'' type of sentences (17:1) and ''have'' sentences (17:2):

Kupissa on kahvia. *Pöydällä on kuppeja.*
Onko sinulla rahaa? *Onko sinulla postimerkkejä?*

— as the direct object (26:1):

Ostan syötävää. *Ostan omenoita.*

— as the complement of the verb *olla* (34:2):

Tuo on maitoa. *Nämä ovat ruusuja.*

The partitive is also used

— to express the thing that is not there, the thing not possessed (17:1, 2), and the negative direct object (25:1, 26:1):

Kuvassa ei ole taloa. *Talossa ei ole portaita.*
Meillä ei ole puhelinta. *Miehellä ei ole silmälaseja.*
He eivät osta autoa. *En löydä silmälasejani.*

— as the direct object to show that the action of the verb is continuous, incomplete, or irresultative (39:1):

Isä lukee lehteä. *Etsin silmälasejani.*
Minä rakastan häntä. *Kaikki odottavat Liisan häitä.*

— as the complement of the verb *olla,* to tell what an uncountable is like (34:2):

Vesi on kylmää.

— as the complement of the verb *olla,* to tell what people or things are like (34:2):

Ruusut ovat kauniita.

— with words indicating measure or amount (14:2, 21:2):

Osta kilo sokeria! *Osta kilo banaaneja!*
Erkki juo paljon olutta. *Syön paljon hedelmiä.*

— with *monta* and with cardinal numbers other than *yksi* (16:1):

Heillä on kaksi koiraa.
Montako lasta teillä on?

— in greetings, wishes, and exclamations (14:2, 21:2):

Hyvää huomenta!
Hauskaa matkaa! *Kauniita unia!*

— with a number of post and prepositions (37:2):

Tulkaa kotiin ennen kuutta! *Hän on kiltti meitä kohtaan.*
Mitä varten hän teki niin? *Älä mene ulos ilman käsineitä!*

— in comparisons, to replace *kuin* (32:1):

Hän on sinua vanhempi. *Tupakoivatko naiset miehiä vähemmän?*

Jane tutustuu Lehtisen perheeseen

1. Ritva L. (puhelimessa). Niin, Jane, voisitko sinä tulla meille iltapäiväkahville sunnuntaina neljältä? Voisimme tutustua paremmin toisiimme, ja sinähän olet kiinnostunut suomalaisista kodeista.

2. J. Kiitos kutsusta, tulen oikein mielelläni.

3. R. Näkemiin sitten sunnuntaina ja tervetuloa!

■■■

4. R. Hei, Jane, tervetuloa!

5. J. Hei! Tässä on sinulle vähän kukkia, ole hyvä.

6. R. Ahaa, sinä tunnet jo suomalaisia tapoja. Kiitos kauniista kukista!

7. J. Minä toin myös pienen lahjan lapsille, vähän suklaata. Sinullahan on suuri perhe.

8. R. Niin, meitä on kahdeksan, kolme aikuista ja viisi lasta. Minun äitini asuu meillä. Kiitos vain, lapsista on aina kiva saada suklaata.

9. J. Vaikka se onkin paha hampaille.

10. R. Tulehan nyt tervehtimään muita. Tässä on Jane Nelson. Äitini. Mieheni Arto. Lapsilla ei ole paljon aikaa olla kotona sunnuntaisin, heillä on niin paljon harrastuksia. Tytöillä urheilu ja pojilla musiikki. Ja nuorin on leikkimässä pihalla.

11. Arto. Ritva on kertonut, että sinä olet lehtinainen. Mihin lehteen sinä kirjoitat?

Jane gets acquainted with the Lehtinen family

1. Ritva L. (on the phone). Yes, Jane, could you come and have afternoon coffee with us at four on Sunday? We could get to know each other better, and you're interested to see a Finnish home, aren't you?

2. J. Thank you for the invitation, I'll be very glad to come.

3. R. I'm looking forward to seeing you on Sunday.

■■■

4. R. Hello, Jane, nice to have you here!

5. J. Hello! I've got some flowers for you here.

6. R. Ah, you're familiar with some Finnish customs, already. Thank you for the beautiful flowers!

7. J. I also brought a little present for the children, a little chocolate. You have a large family, I understand.

8. R. Yes, we are eight, three grown-ups and five children. My mother lives with us. Thanks, children always love to get chocolate.

9. J. Although it's bad for the teeth.

10. R. Come along now and meet the others. This is Jane Nelson. My mother. My husband Arto. The children don't have much time to stay home on Sundays, they have so many interests. Sports for the girls and music for the boys. And the youngest is playing in the yard.

11. Arto. Ritva told us that you are a journalist. Which paper do you write for?

12. J. Minä kirjoitan eri lehtiin. Eniten minä teen juttuja amerikkalaisille naistenlehdille.
13. Isoäiti. Minkälaisista aiheista?
14. J. Melkein mistä vain. Eri maiden ihmisistä, heidän ongelmistaan, tavoistaan ja kodeistaan. Minä kirjoitan paljon naisista ja lapsista, vähemmän miehistä.
15. Arto. Oletko sinä feministi?
16. J. En radikaali feministi, mutta minä olen kyllä hyvin kiinnostunut naisten asemasta eri maissa.
17. R. Otetaanpas nyt kahvia. Ottakaa kahvileipää, se on kotona leivottua. Muuten, Jane, onko sinusta jo tullut hyvä hiihtäjä?
18. J. Ei ihan vielä. Kun aloittaa aikuisena, oppii luonnollisesti paljon hitaammin. Minä pelkään aina kaatumista. Mutta hauskaa se on.
19. Arto. Olitko sinä hiihtänyt koskaan, ennen kuin tulit Suomeen?
20. J. Olin minä kerran yrittänyt slalomia. Mutta se oli ihan mahdotonta. Minun mielestäni tämä suomalainen hiihto sopii minulle paremmin.
21. Isoäiti. Muuten, missä te tutustuitte toisiinne?
22. R. Jane ja minäkö? Me olimme samoilla kutsuilla. Minulla oli ollut siellä hirveän ikävää, mutta sitten minä tapasin Janen. Meistä tuli heti ystävät.
23. J. Minusta tuntui, että me olimme tunteneet toisemme jo kauan aikaa. Ja minusta on todella hauskaa tutustua myös Ritvan perheeseen.
24. R. Voi, minä unohdan tarjota lisää kahvia. Saako olla toinen kuppi?
25. J. Kyllä kiitos, sinun kahvisi on erinomaista. Samoin tämä mustikkapiirakka. Se ihan sulaa suussa.
26. R. Ota sitten lisää piirakkaa! Arto, sinä kai otat mieluummin pullaa?
27. Arto. Niin otan. Minä pidän enemmän pullasta kuin makeista kahvileivistä.

12. J. I write for different papers. Most of my stories are for American women's magazines.
13. Grandmother. About what sort of topics?
14. J. Almost anything. About people in different countries, their problems, customs, and homes. I write a lot about women and children, less about men.
15. Arto. Are you a feminist?
16. J. Not a radical feminist, but I really am very much interested in the position of women in different countries.
17. R. Well, let's have some coffee now. Take some cakes, they're home baked. By the way, Jane, have you become a good skier already?
18. J. Not quite yet. When you start as a grown-up, you learn much more slowly, of course. I'm always afraid of falling. But it's fun.
19. Arto. Had you ever done any skiing before you came to Finland?
20. J. Yes, I had once tried slalom. But that was quite impossible. I think the Finnish way of skiing suits me better.
21. Grandmother. By the way, where did you meet each other?
22. R. Jane and me? We were at the same party. I had been terribly bored there, but then I met Jane. We became friends right away.
23. J. I had the feeling that we had known each other for a long time. And it's really a pleasure for me to meet Ritva's family, too.
24. R. Oh dear, I've forgotten to give you some more coffee. How about another cup?
25. J. Yes, please, your coffee is excellent. So is this blueberry pie. It really melts in the mouth.
26. R. Then do have some more pie, please! Arto, you probably prefer *pulla*?
27. Arto. Yes, I do. I prefer *pulla* with coffee to sweet things.

28. R. Oletteko te kaikki maistaneet tätä kakkua? Se ei ole liian makeaa. Ole hyvä, äiti. Saako olla kolmas kuppi?

28. R. Have you tasted this cake, all of you? It isn't too sweet. Have some, mother. What about a third cup?

Millainen tuo kuva on?
Se on **parempi** kuin tämä.
Kuinka Timo piirtää?
Hän piirtää **paremmin** kuin me muut.

Montako **teitä** on?
— **Meitä on neljä.**

"play"
Lapsi **leikkii.**
Leikki on lapsen työtä.

Näyttelijä **näyttelee** Romeota.
Romeo ja Julia on **näytelmä.**

Poika **soittaa** viulua.
Viulun**soitto** on vaikeaa.

Miehet **pelaavat** jalkapalloa.

Kielioppia — Structural notes

1. Declension of nouns with possessive suffixes: a survey

The inflection of nouns with poss. suffixes has been explained in connection with each new case. A survey of the possessive declension in the sing. was presented in lesson 29:2, which should be reviewed.

The chart below lists both the sing. and pl. cases of the word *(heidän) pöytänsä.*

	Sing.	Pl.
	+pöytä-ä pöydä/n	*pöyti/ä* (weak stem *pöydi-*)
Nom.	*pöytä/nsä*	*pöytä/nsä*
Gen.	*pöytä/nsä*	*pöytie/nsä*
Part.	*pöytää/nsä*	*pöytiä/än (-nsä)*
"into"	*pöytää/nsä*	*pöytii/nsä*
"on"	*pöydällä/än (-nsä)*	*pöydillä/än (-nsä)*
"from"	*pöydältä/än (-nsä)*	*pöydiltä/än (-nsä)*
"(on)to"	*pöydälle/en (-nsä)*	*pöydille/en (-nsä)*
"in"	*pöydässä/än (-nsä)*	*pöydissä/än (-nsä)*
"out of"	*pöydästä/än (-nsä)*	*pöydistä/än (-nsä)*

2. "He pitävät toisistaan" (each other)

(Minä rakastan sinua ja sinä rakastat minua.)	*Me rakastamme toisia/mme.*	We love each other.
	Te rakastatte toisia/nne.	You love each other.
	He rakastavat toisia/an (-nsa).	They love each other.

As a reciprocal pronoun (''each other'') Finnish uses the pl. forms of *toinen* provided with a poss. suffix.

Further examples:

Me tunnemme toise/mme (*toiset* + **mme**)	We know each other.
He keskustelevat usein toiste/nsa kanssa. (*toisten* + **nsa**)	They often talk to each other.
He pitävät toisista/an.	They are fond of each other.
Missä te tutustuitte toisii/nne. (*toisiin* + **nne**)	Where did you meet each other?
Kirjoitimme ennen toisille/mme.	We used to write to each other.

3. Pluperfect tense

näh/dä to see

Affirmative				Negative			
olin	*nähnyt*	I had	seen	*en*	*ollut nähnyt*	I had	not seen
olit		you had		*et*		you had	
oli		he/she had		*ei*		he/she	
olimme	*nähneet*	we had		*emme*	*olleet nähneet*	we had	
olitte		you had		*ette*		you had	
olivat		they had		*eivät*		they had	

Question:		Negative question:	
Olitko (sinä) nähnyt? etc.	had you seen? etc.	*etkö (sinä) ollut nähnyt?* etc.	hadn't you seen? etc.

Structure:

— The auxiliary *olla* is inflected in the past tense;
— The main verb is in the past participle (lesson 31:1): sing. *näh/nyt,* pl. *näh/neet.*

Sanasto — Vocabulary

Sanasto	Vocabulary
aihe-tta-en- ita	topic, theme, subject matter
aikui/nen-sta-sen-sia	grown-up, adult
erin/omai/nen-sta-sen-sia	excellent
+hammas-ta hampaan hampaita	tooth
harrast/us-ta-uksen-uksia	interest, hobby
+juttu-a jutun juttuja	story, anecdote; affair, thing
+kaatu/a kaadun kaatui kaatunut	to fall (from a standing position); to be killed in the war
+kahvi/leipä-ä-leivän-leipiä	collectively for cakes, scones etc. taken with coffee
+kakku-a kakun kakkuja	cake
kutsu-a-n-ja	invitation; pl. party
lahja-a-n lahjoja	present, gift; talent
+leikki/ä leikin leikki leikkinyt (cp. *leikki* play)	to play (like children)
+leipo/a leivon leipoi leiponut (cp. *leipuri* baker)	to bake
+leivottu-a leivotun leivottuja	baked
lisää	some more
luonnolli/nen-sta-sen-sia	natural
luonnollisesti	naturally, of course
maista/a-n maistoi maistanut	to taste (some food)
makea-(t)a-n makeita	sweet
mielestä: minun mielestäni (= *minusta*)	in my opinion, I think that
+mustikka-a mustikan mustikoita	blueberry
ongelma-a-n ongelmia	problem
piha-a-n pihoja	yard
+piirakka-a piirakan piirakoita	pie, pasty
pulla-a-n pullia	scone, roll, bun; sweet wheat bread taken with coffee
tarjo/ta-an-si-nnut	to offer, serve; to treat
+tervehti/ä tervehdin tervehti tervehtinyt (cp. *tervehdys*)	to greet
+tuntu/a tunnun tuntui tuntunut	to seem, feel like something
minusta tuntuu, että ...	it seems to me that, I feel that, I have the feeling that
tutustu/a-n-i-nut (johonkin henkilöön t. asiaan)	to learn to know, get acquainted (with someone or something), meet
+unohta/a unohdan unohti unohtanut (≠ *muistaa*)	to forget

☆

+aatto-a aaton aattoja	eve, day before a holiday
enti/nen-stä-sen-siä	former, ex-
häät (pl.) häitä häiden	wedding
juhann/us-ta-uksen-uksia	Midsummer
juhla-a-n juhlia (cp. *juhli/a* to celebrate)	feast, festival; celebration; entertainment, party
+kinkku-a kinkun kinkkuja	ham
+kokko-a kokon kokkoja	bonfire
kummalli/nen-sta-sen-sia	strange, odd, peculiar
kynttilä-ä-n kynttilöitä	candle
+muoto-a muodon muotoja	form, shape
+näytel/lä näyttelen näytteli näytellyt	to play, act (in the theater)
pela/ta -an-si-nnut (korttia, tennistä)	to play (games)
+piirtä/ä piirrän piirsi piirtänyt (= *piirustaa*)	to draw, design
+puukko-a puukon puukkoja	*puukko* knife
puuro-a-n-ja	porridge
pääsiäi/nen-stä-sen-siä	Easter
+tuotta/a tuotan tuotti tuottanut (cp. *tuote* product)	to cause, bring about; to produce
+vappu-a vapun vappuja (= *vapun/päivä*)	1st of May

Nouns in lessons 22—40 by inflection types

(Nouns in lessons 1—21 on p. 99)

1. Words ending in a long vowel or a diphthong

maa words
(maa-ta-n maita)
harmaa 22
kuu 28
paluu 26
syy 39
sää 36
häät (pl.) 40

2. 2-syllable words ending in a vowel

auto words
(auto-a-n-ja)
+aatto-a aaton aattoja 40
+alku-a alun alkuja 34
eno 29
+farkku-a farkun farkkuja 33
+hattu-a hatun hattuja 33
hieno 33
housu 33
hullu 39
huone/kalu 35
hymy 31
+juttu-a jutun juttuja 40
+kakku-a kakun kakkuja 40
+kinkku-a kinkun kinkkuja 40
+koko-a koon kokoja 33
+kurkku-a kurkun kurkkuja 38
kutsu 40
laulu 39

+lepo-a levon lepoja 38
+lintu-a linnun lintuja 28
+loppuun/myyty-ä -myydyn -myytyjä 39
matka/muisto 27
+muoto-a muodon muotoja 40
puisto 37
+puku-a puvun pukuja 32
puuro 40
sateen/varjo 36
+serkku-a serkun serkkuja 29
sisko 29
syksy 36
sähkö 35
+särky-ä säryn särkyjä 38
taulu 26
+vaihto-a vaihdon vaihtoja 34
valo 35

päivä words
(päivä-ä-n päiviä)
isä 29
+kenkä-ä kengän kenkiä 33
kesä 36
kylä 24
lehmä 22
polku/pyörä 27
pyhä 39
selvä 26
+setä-ä sedän setiä 29
yskä 38

kuva words
(kuva-a-n kuvia)
+edus/kunta-a -kunnan -kuntia 37
juhla 40
juna 26
+kulta-a kullan kultia 39
+luokka-a luokan luokkia 25
nuha 38
osa 37
pulla 40
+sota-a sodan sotia 29
+sukka-a sukan sukkia 33
tumma 33

kirja words
(kirja-a-n kirjoja)
+aika-a ajan aikoja 23
eläin/tarha 22
hella 35
kana 22
kansa 37
lahja 40
laiha 32
laiva 27
linna 37
nenä/liina 38
näkö/ala 37
+paita-a paidan paitoja 33
rauha 30
seura 34
+sika-a sian sikoja 22
+tapa-a tavan tapoja 24
varma 25
vatsa 38
viiva 39
villa 22
+valta-a vallan valtoja (Yhdys/vallat) 34

bussi words
(bussi-a-n busseja)
anglo/saksi 31
+esi/merkki-ä-merkin -merkkejä 28
+jää/kaappi-a-kaapin -kaappeja 35
+kiltti-ä kiltin kilttejä 38
+kortti-a kortin kortteja 25
malli 32
metri 35
muisti 34
+penkki-ä penkin penkkejä 31
poni 22
+posti/merkki-ä-merkin -merkkejä 26
siisti 27
+takki-a takin takkeja 33
tanssi 24
torni 37
tulli 37
+tunti-a tunnin tunteja 23
+täti-ä tädin tätejä 22
väri 22

i→e:
ovi words
(ovi ovea oven ovia)
+arki arkea arjen arkia 39
+henki henkeä hengen henkiä 31
+joki jokea joen jokia 27
+lehti lehteä lehden lehtiä 23
+mäki mäkeä mäen mäkiä 27
pilvi 36
suksi 36
talvi 36
veli veljeä veljen veljiä 29

pieni words
(pieni pientä pienen pieniä)
lumi lunta lumen lumia 36
meri merta meren meriä 36
mieli mieltä mielen mieliä 34
saari saarta saaren saaria 27
tuuli tuulta tuulen tuulia 36
ääni ääntä äänen ääniä 39

uusi words
(uusi uutta uuden uusia)
+kausi kautta kauden kausia 36
+länsi länttä lännen

(länsiä) 37
+tosi totta toden tosia 36

3. Longer words ending in a vowel

toimisto words
(toimisto-a-n-ja)
haastattelu 34
huoneisto 35
ilmasto 36
+kalustettu-a kalustetun kalustettuja 35
keskustelu 28
kilpailu 37
kirjasto 35
+leivottu-a leivotun leivottuja 40
opiskelu 34
osasto 32
+posti/laatikko-a -laatikon -laatikkoja 26
+suosittu-a suositun suosittuja 39
+tunnettu-a tunnetun tunnettuja 37
urheilu 37
+varattu-a varatun varattuja 28
ympäristö 37

radio words
(radio-ta-n-ita)
aukio 37
kahvio 33
solmio 33
osake/yhtiö 28
näyttämö-ä-n näyttämöitä 39
pusero-a-n puseroita 32

ostaja words
(ostaja-a-n ostajia)
valoisa 35
matala 37
asema 26
elämä 36
näytelmä 39
ohjelma 23
ongelma 40
satama 37
unelma 39
ahkera 34
ikävä 34
lihava 32
miellyttävä 37
nähtävä 27
sopiva 33
tuttava 27

opiskelija words
(opiskelija-a-n opiskelijoita)
työn/tekijä 36
asia 26
+mustikka-a mustikan mustikoita 40
+piirakka-a piirakan piirakoita 40
+tupakka-a tupakan tupakoita 26
kynttilä 40
tavara 26

vaikea words
(vaikea-(t)a-n vaikeita)
hirveä 22
kipeä 38
korkea 35
makea 40
pimeä 36
ruskea 22
tärkeä 27
usea 37
vaalea 32
vihreä 22

hotelli words
(hotelli-a-n hotelleja)
+apteekki-a apteekin apteekkeja 38
+automaatti-a automaatin automaatteja 26
mannekiini 32
moderni 35
normaali 27
+sametti-a sametin sametteja 33
+tabletti-a tabletin tabletteja 38

naapuri words
(naapuri-a-n naapureita)
kaveri 27
laituri 26
maisteri 29
mittari 38
tiikeri 22
toveri 25

parempi words
(parempi parempaa paremman parempia)
+kumpi kumpaa kumman kumpia 30
+molemmat (pl.) molempia 25
+vanhemmat (pl.) vanhempia 23

4. Words ending in a short -e or a consonant

huone words
(huone-tta-en-ita)
aihe 40
aine 33
alue 37
aste 36
hame 32
kirje 23
kone 27
kuume 38
käsine 33
+liikenne-ttä liikenteen 27
+lääke-ttä lääkkeen lääkkeitä 38
+mieli/pide-ttä -piteen -piteitä 34
+parveke-tta parvekkeen

parvekkeita 35
saaste 37
+sade-tta sateen sateita 36
+vaate-tta vaatteen vaatteita 32

nainen words
(nainen naista naisen naisia)
hevonen 22
likainen 38
(and all other **-nen** words)

puhelin words
(puhelin-ta puhelimen puhelimia)
eläin 22
+levy/soitin-ta -soittimen -soittimia 24

mahdoton words
+mahdoton-ta mahdottoman mahdottomia 30 (and all other **-ton** words)

sairas words
(sairas-ta sairaan sairaita)
+asukas-ta asukkaan asukkaita 37
eräs 29
+hammas-ta hampaan hampaita 40
+kirkas-ta kirkkaan kirkkaita 32
kohtelias 31
+lammas-ta lampaan lampaita 22
lounas 23
+porras-ta portaan portaita 37
+rakas-ta rakkaan rakkaita 29
taivas 32
+tehdas-ta tehtaan tehtaita 27
vieras 24
+vilkas-ta vilkkaan vilkkaita 37
-vuotias 29

kaunis words
(kaunis-ta kauniin kauniita)
valmis 30

vastaus words
(vastaus-ta vastauksen vastauksia)
harrastus 40
ilmoitus 39
juhannus 40
kokous 27
rakennus 37
vaatetus 32
kerros 33

väsynyt words
väsynyt-tä väsyneen väsyneitä 33
kiinnostunut 39
kuollut 29
(and all other past participles)

sisar words
sisar-ta sisaren sisaria 29
+tytär-tä tyttären tyttäriä 29

5. Exceptional or rare paradigms

salaisuus words
(salaisuus salaisuutta salaisuuden salaisuuksia)
+teollisuus 37
+terveys terveyttä terveyden 38

kevät-tä kevään keväitä 36

nailon words (foreign words ending in a consonant)
nailon-ia-in-eja 33

Pronouns:
kukaan ketään kenenkään keitään 25
kumpi kumpaa kumman kumpia 30
molemmat (pl.) molempia 25

A list of the verbs in lessons 27—40 by verb types

(Verbs in lessons 1—26 on p. 132)

1.
voida verbs
jää/dä-n jäi jäänyt 34
soi/da-n soi soinut 28

2.
puhua verbs
+kaatu/a kaadun kaatui kaatunut 40
+leipo/a leivon leipoi leiponut 40
maistu/a-n-i-nut 38
+riippu/a riipun riippui riippunut 39
+synty/ä synnyn syntyi syntynyt 29
+tahto/a tahdon tahtoi tahtonut 28
+tapahtu/a (tapahdun) tapahtui tapahtunut 31
+tuntu/a (tunnun) tuntui tuntunut 40
tutustu/a-n-i-nut 38
usko/a-n-i-nut 38
+viihty/ä viihdyn viihtyi viihtynyt 34

+**hake/a** haen haki hakenut 30
+kulke/a kuljen kulki kulkenut 34
laske/a-n laski laskenut 38

etsi/ä-n etsi etsinyt 34
+kukki/a (kukin) kukki kukkinut 36
+leikki/ä leikin leikki leikkinyt 40
+sopi/a sovin sopi sopinut 28
tutki/a-n tutki tutkinut 39
+tervehti/ä tervehdin tervehti tervehtinyt 40
+vaati/a vaadin vaati vaatinut 34

elä/ä-n eli elänyt 29
+hiihtä/ä hiihdän hiihti hiihtänyt 36
kestä/ä-n kesti kestänyt 27
+käyttä/ä käytän käytti käyttänyt 35
+näyttä/ä näytän näytti näyttänyt 38
+päättä/ä päätän päätti päättänyt 31
+riittä/ä riitän riitti riittänyt 33
+selittä/ä selitän selitti selittänyt 29
+silittä/ä silitän silitti silittänyt 33
+yrittä/ä yritän yritti yrittänyt 35

+**aloitta/a** aloitan aloitti aloittanut 28
harrasta/a-n harrasti harrastanut 34
+koetta/a koetan koetti koettanut 32
+muutta/a muutan muutti muuttanut 35
+odotta/a odotan odotti odottanut 28
rakasta/a-n rakasti rakastanut 29
sula/a-n suli sulanut 36
toista/a-n toisti toistanut 28
+tarkoitta/a tarkoitan tarkoitti tarkoittanut 36
+tuotta/a tuotan tuotti tuottanut 40
+unohta/a unohdan unohti unohtanut 40
+valitta/a valitan valitti valittanut 38

aja/a-n ajoi ajanut 27
+alka/a alan alkoi alkanut 30
jaksa/a-n jaksoi jaksanut 38
jatka/a-n jatkoi jatkanut 37
+kanta/a kannan kantoi kantanut 30
maista/a-n maistoi maistanut 40
+sata/a (sadan) satoi satanut 36

+**huuta/a** huudan huusi huutanut 31
+piirtä/ä piirrän piirsi piirtänyt 40

3.
tulla verbs
hymyil/lä-en-i-lyt 30
ihail/la-en-i-lut 39
keskustel/la-en-i-lut 28
kuol/la-en-i-lut 29
+näytel/lä näyttelen näytteli näytellyt 40
+suunnitel/la suunnittelen suunnitteli suunnitellut 34
tuul/la (tuulen) tuuli tuullut 36
+vaihdel/la vaihtelen vaihteli vaihdellut 33

4.

haluta verbs
huoma/ta-an-si-nnut 31
osa/ta-an-si-nnut 28
pela/ta-an-si-nnut 40
+pelä/tä pelkään pelkäsi pelännyt 39
tila/ta-an-si-nnut 39
tarjo/ta-an-si-nnut 40
viha/ta-an-si-nnut 29
vuokra/ta-an-si-nnut 35

merkitä verbs
häiri/tä-tsen-tsi-nnyt 28
sijai/ta-tsen-tsi-nnut 37
vali/ta-tsen-tsi-nnut 33

5.

Irregular verbs
juos/ta juoksen juoksi juossut 30
käy/dä käyn kävi käynyt 27

APPENDICES

1. INFLECTION OF NOUNS: DIFFERENT TYPES

(V = vowel, C = consonant)

I. Words ending in a vowel other than a short -e

1. Words ending in -VV or a diphthong

	Basic form	Part. sing.	Gen.sing.	(Illat.sing.)	Part.pl.
—VV	**maa**	-ta	-n	(-han)	maita
—Vi	**tiistai**	-ta	-n	(-hin)	tiistaita
-ie,	**tie***	-tä	-n	(-hen)	teitä
-uo,	suo	-ta	-n	(-hon)	soita
-yö	työ	-tä	-n	(-hön)	töitä

2. 2-syllable words ending in a vowel

-o,-ö,	**auto**	-a	-n	(-on)	-ja
-u, -y	koulu	-a	-n	(-un)	-ja
-ä	**päivä**	-ä	-n	(-än)	päiviä
-a	**kuva**	-a	-n	(-an)	kuvia
	kirja	-a	-n	(-an)	kirjoja
-i	**bussi**	-a	-n	(-in)	busseja
	ovi	ovea	oven	(oveen)	ovia
	pieni	pientä	pienen	(pieneen)	pieniä
	uusi	uutta	uuden	(uuteen)	uusia
	Exceptional or rare paradigms:				
-e	nukke	-a	nuken	(nukkeen)	nukkeja
-i	meri	merta	meren	(mereen)	meriä (type
	lumi	lunta	lumen	(lumeen)	lumia **pieni**)
	lapsi	lasta	lapsen	(lapseen)	lapsia
	länsi	länttä	lännen	(länteen)	länsiä (type **uusi**)

3. Longer words ending in a vowel

-o, -ö,	**toimisto**	-a	-n	(-on)	-ja
-u, -y	kilpailu	-a	-n	(-un)	-ja
	radio	-ta	-n	(-on)	-ita
	henkilö	-ä	-n	(-ön)	-itä
	numero	-a	-n	(-on)	-ita
	näyttämö	-ä	-n	(-ön)	-itä
-a, -ä	**ostaja**	-a	-n	(-an)	ostajia
	ongelma	-a	-n	(-an)	ongelmia
	ystävä	-ä	-n	(-än)	ystäviä
	opiskelija	-a	-n	(-an)	opiskelijoita
	asia	-a	-n	(-an)	asioita
	mustikka	-a	mustikan	(mustikkaan)	mustikoita
	vaikea	-(t)a	-n	(-an)	vaikeita

-i	**hotelli**	-a	-n	(-in)	hotelleja
	naapuri	-a	-n	(-in)	naapureita
	parempi	parempaa	paremman	(parempaan)	parempia

II. Words ending in a short -e or -C

-e	**huone**	-tta	-en	(huoneeseen)	huoneita
-n	**nainen**	naista	naisen	(naiseen)	naisia
	puhelin	-ta	puhelimen	(puhelimeen)	puhelimia
	mahdoton	-ta	mahdottoman	(mahdottomaan)	mahdottomia
-s	**sairas**	-ta	sairaan	(sairaaseen)	sairaita
	kaunis	-ta	kauniin	(kauniiseen)	kauniita
	vastaus	-ta	vastauksen	(vastaukseen)	vastauksia
-t	**lyhyt**	-tä	lyhyen	(lyhyeen)	lyhyitä
	väsynyt	-tä	väsyneen	(väsyneeseen)	väsyneitä
-l, -r	**sisar**	-ta	sisaren	(sisareen)	sisaria
	Exceptional or rare paradigms:				
-n	**lämmin***	-tä	lämpimän	(lämpimään)	lämpimiä
	lähin	-tä	lähimmän	(lähimpään)	lähimpiä (cp. *parempi*)
-s	**mies***	-tä	miehen	(mieheen)	miehiä
	paras*	-ta	parhaan	(parhaaseen)	parhaita
	salaisuus	salaisuutta	salaisuuden	(salaisuuteen)	salai-suuksia (cp. **uusi**)
	terveys	terveyttä	terveyden	(terveyteen)	terveyk-siä
	kolmas	kolmatta	kolmannen	(kolmanteen)	kolmansia (cp. **länsi**)
-t	**tuhat***	-ta	tuhannen	(tuhanteen)	tuhansia
	kevät*	-tä	kevään	(kevääseen)	keväitä
foreign words ending in -C	**nailon**	-ia	-in	(-iin)	-eja
	Smith	-iä	-in	(-iin)	-ejä

Nouns and adjectives which appear in Finnish for Foreigners 1 are listed according to these types on p. 99 (lessons 1—21) and p. 213 (lessons 22—40).

*The only word of its kind

2. INFLECTION OF VERBS: DIFFERENT TYPES

1.
voida verbs (basic form ends in **-da, -dä**)

voi/da	-n	voi	voinut	voidaan
saa/da	-n	sai	saanut	saadaan
vie/dä	-n	vei	vienyt	viedään
juo/da	-n	joi	juonut	juodaan
syö/dä	-n	söi	syönyt	syödään

Note:

käy/dä	-n	kä**v**i	käynyt	käydään

2.
puhua verbs (basic form ends in two vowels)

puhu/a	-n	-i	-nut	-taan
luke/a	luen	luki	lukenut	luetaan
oppi/a	opin	oppi	oppinut	opitaan
näyttä/ä	näytän	näytti	näyttänyt	näytetään
osta/a	-n	osti	ostanut	ostetaan
anta/a	annan	antoi	antanut	annetaan
lentä/ä	lennän	lensi	lentänyt	lennetään

Note:

tietä/ä	tiedän	tiesi	tie**n**/**n**yt tietä/nyt	tiedetään

3.
tulla verbs (basic form ends in two consonants + **a, ä**)

tul/la	-en	-i	-lut	-laan
men/nä	-en	-i	-nyt	-nään
sur/ra	-en	-i	-rut	-raan
nous/ta	-en	-i	-sut	-taan

Note:

ol/la	olen	oli	ollut	ollaan
3rd pers.	**on, ovat**			
juos/ta	juo**k**sen	juo**k**si	juossut	juostaan

4.
a) **haluta** verbs (basic forms ends in a vowel + **ta, tä**)

halu/ta	-an	-si	-nnut	-taan	halutkaa!

b) **merkitä** verbs (most verbs in **-ita, -itä**)

merki/tä	-tsen	-tsi	-nnyt	-tään	merkitkää!

c) **paeta** verbs (generally ending in **-eta, -etä**)

pae/ta	pakenen	pakeni	paennut	paetaan	paetkaa!

5.
Irregular verbs:

näh/dä	näen	näki	nähnyt	nähdään
teh/dä	teen	teki	tehnyt	tehdään

3. INFLECTION CHARTS

I. k p t changes in the inflection of nouns

1. Nouns with weak grade in the genitive sing.

	Singular			Plural				
Nominative *+pöytä*								pöydät
Partitive	*ä*			*pöyti*	*ä*	(pöydi-)		
Genitive		pöydä	n		*en*			
Adessive			llä			pöydi	llä	
Ablative			ltä				ltä	
Allative			lle				lle	
Inessive			ssä				ssä	
Elative			stä				stä	
Illative	*än*				*in*			
Essive	*nä*				*nä*			
Translative			ksi				ksi	

2. Nouns with strong grade in the genitive sing.

	Singular				Plural	
Nominative			+tehdas		*tehtaat*	
Partitive				ta	*tehtai*	*ta*
Genitive	*tehtaa*	*n*				*den (-tten)*
Adessive		*lla*				*lla*
Ablative		*lta*				*lta*
Allative		*lle*				*lle*
Inessive		*ssa*				*ssa*
Elative		*sta*				*sta*
Illative		*seen*				*siin*
Essive		*na*				*na*
Translative		*ksi*				*ksi*

The forms with **strong grade** are in italics.

Note. Word types **kolmas** (kolmansia), **tuhat** (tuhansia) and **salaisuus** (salaisuuksia) are not subject to **k p t** changes in the pl.

II. A few important pronouns

Nom.	**minä**		**sinä**		**hän**		**me**		**te**		**he**	
Part.	minua		sinua		häntä		meitä		teitä		heitä	
Gen.	minu	n	sinu	n	häne	n	mei	dän	tei	dän	hei	dän
Acc.		t		t		t		dät		dät		dät
Adess.		lla		lla		llä		llä		llä		llä
Abl.		lta		lta		ltä		ltä		ltä		ltä
All.		lle		lle		lle		lle		lle		lle
Iness.		ssa		ssa		ssä		ssä		ssä		ssä
Elat.		sta		sta		stä		stä		stä		stä
Illat.		un		un		en		hin		hin		hin
Ess.		na		na		nä		nä		nä		nä
Transl.		ksi		ksi		ksi		ksi		ksi		ksi

Nom.	**tämä**		**tuo**		**se**	**nämä**		**nuo**		**ne**	
Part.	tätä			ta	sitä	näi	tä	noi	ta	nii	tä
Gen.	tämän			n	sen		den		den		den
Adess.	tä	llä		lla	sillä		llä		lla		llä
Abl.		ltä		lta	siltä		ltä		lta		ltä
All.		lle		lle	sille		lle		lle		lle
Iness.		ssä		ssa	siinä		ssä		ssa		ssä
Elat.		stä		sta	siitä		stä		sta		stä
Illat.		hän		hon	siihen		hin		hin		hin
Ess.		nä		na	sinä		nä		na		nä
Transl.		ksi		ksi	siksi		ksi		ksi		ksi

	Sing.		Pl.		Sing.		Pl.	Sing.		Pl.	
Nom.	**joka**		jotka		**mikä**		mitkä	**kuka**		ketkä (kutka)	
Part.	jota		joi	ta	mitä			ketä		kei	tä
Gen.	jonka			den	minkä			kene	n		den
Acc.									t		
Adess.	jo	lla		lla	mi	llä			llä		llä
Abl.		lta		lta		ltä			ltä		ltä
All.		lle		lle		lle			lle		lle
Iness.		ssa		ssa		ssä			ssä		ssä
Elat.		sta		sta		stä			stä		stä
Illat.		hon		hin		hin			en		hin
Ess.		na		na		nä			nä		nä
Transl.		ksi		ksi		ksi			ksi		ksi

	Sing.	Pl.	Sing.	Pl.
Nom.	**jokin**	jotkin	**jo/ku**	jot/kut
Part.	jotakin	joitakin	jota/kuta	joita/kuita
Gen.	jonkin	joidenkin	jon/kun	joiden/kuiden
Adess.	jollakin	joillakin	jolla/kulla	joilla/kuilla
Illat.	johonkin	joihinkin	johon/kuhun	joihin/kuihin
etc.				

Note: The 4-syllable forms of **joku** are rare, esp. in speech.

Nom.	+**kumpi**				+**molemmat**			
Part.	kumpa	a			(molemmi	-)	molempi	a
Gen.			kumma	n				en
Adess.				lla		lla		
Iness.				ssa		ssa		
Illat.		an						in
Ess.		na						na

III. k p t changes in the inflection of verbs

+**ottaa** to take (representing **puhua** verbs)
+**mitata** to measure (representing **tulla**, **haluta**, and **paeta** verbs)

The *strong grade* is in italics.
(Only the forms of **ottaa** are translated below.)

	Affirmative			Negative	
Active Indicative					
Present					
Sing.	1. otan *(mittaan)*	I take	en	ota *(mittaa)*	I do not take
	2. otat *(mittaat)*	you take	et		you do not take
	3. *ottaa (mittaa)*	he takes	ei		he does not take
Pl.	1. otamme *(mittaamme)*	we take	emme		we do not take
	2. otatte *(mittaatte)*	you take	ette		you do not take
	3. *ottavat (mittaavat)*	they take	eivät		they do not take
Past					
Sing.	1. otin *(mittasin)*	I took	en	*ottanut* (mitannut)	I did not take
	2. otit *(mittasit)*	you took	et		you did not take
	3. *otti (mittasi)*	he took	ei		he did not take
Pl.	1. otimme *(mittasimme)*	we took	emme	*ottaneet*	we did not take
	2. otitte *(mittasitte)*	you took	ette	(mitanneet)	you did not take
	3. *ottivat (mittasivat)*	they took	eivät		they did not take

Perfect

Sing.	1. olen	*ottanut*	I have taken	en ole	*ottanut*	I have not taken
	2. olet	(mitannut)	you have taken	et ole	(mitannut)	you have not taken
	3. on		he has taken	ei ole		he has not taken
Pl.	1. olemme		we have taken	emme ole		we have not taken
	2. olette	*ottaneet* (mitanneet)	you have taken	ette ole	*ottaneet* (mitanneet)	you have not taken
	3. ovat		they have taken	eivät ole		they have not taken

Pluperfect

Sing.	1. olin	*ottanut*	I had taken	en ollut	*ottanut*	I had not taken
	2. olit	(mitannut)	you had taken	et ollut	(mitannut)	you had not taken
	3. oli		he had taken	ei ollut		he had not taken
Pl.	1. olimme	*ottaneet*	we had taken	emme olleet	*ottaneet*	we had not taken
	2. olitte	(mitanneet)	you had taken	ette olleet	(mitanneet)	you had not taken
	3. olivat		they had taken	eivät olleet		they had not taken

Conditional
Present

Sing.	1.	*ottaisin (mittaisin)*	I should take	en	*ottaisi*	I should not take
	2.	*ottaisit (mittaisit)*	you would take	et	*(mittaisi)*	you would not take
	3.	*ottaisi (mittaisi)*	he would take	ei		he would not take
Pl.	1.	*ottaisimme (mittaisimme)*	we should take	emme		we should not take
	2.	*ottaisitte (mittaisitte)*	you would take	ette		you would not take
	3.	*ottaisivat (mittaisivat)*	they would take	eivät		they would not take

Imperative

Sing.	2. ota *(mittaa)*	take!	älä ota *(mittaa)*	do not take!
Pl.	2. *ottakaa* (mitatkaa)	take!	älkää *ottako* (mitatko)	do not take!
	otetaan (mitataan) (= Passive Present)	let us take!	ei oteta (ei mitata)	let us not take!

Infinitives

1st infinitive
(= basic form) *ottaa* (mitata) to take
3rd infinitive *ottamassa (mittaamassa)* (in the process of) taking
ottamaan (mittaamaan) taking, to take

Verbal noun in
-minen *ottaminen (mittaaminen)* (the act of) taking

Participles

Past Active *ottanut* (mitannut) (one who has) taken

4. TENSES OF VERBS IN FINNISH

PLUPERFECT
(entirely in the past)

PAST
(entirely in the past)

PRESENT

(FUTURE = PRESENT)

time
→ **Olin opiskellut** suomea, ennen kuin **tulin** Suomeen.
(eilen
viime viikolla
viime kuussa
viime vuonna)

Nyt **opiskelen** sitä täällä ja **opiskelen** ensi vuonnakin.

PERFECT
(action started in the past but is still going on or affecting the present)

Olen opiskellut sitä vuoden.

(Tänään	
tällä viikolla	olen opis-
tässä kuussa	kellut hyvin
tänä vuonna	ahkerasti.)
viime aikoina	

5. ALPHABETICAL WORD LIST

A

aamiainen 23
aamu 19
aamupäivä 23
aatto 40☆
ahkera 34
ai 7
aihe 40
aika (adv.) 11; (noun) 23
aikaisemmin 39
aikaisin 24
aikana 30☆
aikataulu 26
aikoa 13
aikuinen 40
aina 9
ainakin 25
aine 33☆
aivan 15
aivan niin 15
ajaa 27
ajatella 19
alapuolella 30☆
alas 37
ale 20
alhaalla 37☆
alhaalta 37☆
alkaa 30
alku 34
alla 30☆
alle 35☆
aloittaa 28
alta 35☆
alue 37
amerikkalainen 3
anglosaksi 31
antaa 13☆; 37
anteeksi 5
appelsiini 21
apteekki 38
arki 39☆
arkipäivä 39☆
asema 26
asia 26
asiakas 15
aste 36
asua 10
asukas 37
asunto 10
auki 20
aukio 37
aurinko 21
auto 1
automaatti 26
auttaa 23

B

baari 10☆
banaani 21
bussi 1

E

edelleen 24
edessä 29
edestä 35☆
eduskunta 37
ehkä 9
ei 2
ei . . . eikä 17
eikö niin 28
eilen 3☆
ei ole 2
elokuu 36
elokuva 24
eläin 22
eläintarha 22
elämä 37
elää 29
en 3
enemmän 30
englanniksi 6☆
Englanti 3
englantilainen 3
ennen 31
ennen kuin 24
ensi 20
ensi-ilta 39
ensimmäinen 19 ☆
ensin 14
entinen 40☆
entä 4
enää 12
epä- 35
eri 24
erikoinen 27
erilainen 32
erinomainen 40
erittäin 31
eräs 29
esimerkki 28
esitellä 8
eteen 35☆
eteenpäin 25
etelä 37
etsiä 34
että 9
etunimi 5

F

farkut 33
firma 12

G

gramma 16

H

haastattelu 34☆
hakea 30
halpa 7
haluaisin 25
haluta 7☆
hame 32
hammas 40
-han (-hän) 28
harmaa 22
harrastaa 34
harrastus 40
harvoin 36
hattu 33
hauska 10☆; 27
he 9☆
hei 3
heinäkuu 36
hella 35
helmikuu 36
helppo 11
henki 31☆
henkilö 11
herra 4☆
heti 15
hetkinen 9
hevonen 22
hieno 33
hiihtää 36
hiljaa 30
hiljainen 30
hinta 7
-hintainen 32
hirveä 22
hissi 19☆
hitaasti 7
hotelli 8☆
housut 33
huhtikuu 36
hullu 39
huomata 31
huomenna 5☆
huomenta 8
huone 9
huoneisto 35
huonekalu 35
huono 2
huonosti 4
huutaa 31
hylly 17
hymy 31
hymyillä 30
hyvin 3
hyvä 2
hyvästi 15
hyvää päivää 4
häiritä 28
hän 2
häät 40☆

I

ihailla 39
ihan 30
ihana 14☆
ihminen 10
ikkuna 13
ikävä 34
ilma 8
ilman 37☆
ilmasto 36
ilmoitus 39
iloinen 36
ilta 13
iltapäivä 23
insinööri 12
Irlanti 3☆
iso 2
isoisä 29
istua 5
isä 29
itse 18
itä 37
Itävalta 3☆

J

ja 2
jaksaa 38☆
jalan 27☆
jalka 18
jano 17☆
jatkaa 37
jo 11
johtaja 28☆
joka 12; 13
jokainen 32
joki 27☆
jokin 27

K

L

6. INDEX

7. BOOKS YOU MIGHT NEED

Aaltio, Maija-Hellikki, *Finnish for Foreigners 2.* 2nd ed. Otava. Keuruu 1990.
Branch, Michael – Niemikorpi, Antero – Saukkonen, Pauli, A *Student's Glossary of Finnish.* WSOY. Helsinki 1980. A frequency word-list with translations into English (and a few other languages).
Karlsson, Fred, *Finnish Grammar.* 2nd ed. WSOY. Helsinki-Juva 1987.
Aaltio, Maija-Hellikki (ed.), *Helppoa lukemista suomeksi*
1. Eino Leino, *Musti.* Otava. Keuruu 1979.
2. Mika Waltari, *Kuka murhasi rouva Skrofin?* 2nd ed. Otava. Keuruu 1983.
3. Johannes Linnankoski, *Laulu tulipunaisesta kukasta.* Otava. Keuruu 1979.

Photographs:
Lehtikuva Oy,
Ulkoasiainministeriö, Kuva-arkisto

CPSIA information can be obtained
at www.ICGtesting.com
Printed in the USA
BVHW071921291020
592034BV00008B/310